T0244488

A GENTLEMAN
from JAPAN

A GENTLEMAN *from* JAPAN

THE UNTOLD STORY OF AN INCREDIBLE JOURNEY FROM ASIA TO QUEEN ELIZABETH'S COURT

THOMAS LOCKLEY

HANOVER
SQUARE
PRESS

HANOVER
SQUARE
PRESS™

Recycling programs
for this product may
not exist in your area.

ISBN-13: 978-1-335-01671-3

A Gentleman from Japan

Hanover Square Press
22 Adelaide St. West, 41st Floor
Toronto, Ontario M5H 4E3, Canada
HanoverSqPress.com
BookClubbish.com

Printed in U.S.A.

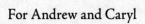

For Andrew and Caryl

A GENTLEMAN *from* JAPAN

Prologue

American Dreaming

Thomas Cavendish, High Marshal of the Roanoke expedition, courtier to Elizabeth I of England, Squire of Grimston Hall in the county of Suffolk, and sometime member of parliament for the Dorset constituency of Shaftesbury, stood on a narrow beach at Roanoke in the North American land of Wyngandacoia.

It was August 25, 1585.

Waves brushed softly upon the gently sloping, golden beach before a rushing retreat back to sea, and a soft breeze ruffled the Englishman's curly blond locks.

His small ship of fifty tuns, *Elizabeth*, bobbed in the narrow channel before him. She was in good repair and ready to depart, the tuns were full of sweet local water and there was ample food for the voyage home.

But her hold, where plundered booty should have lain, was bare. Only a few rough English ballast stones would make an unplanned return journey back across the Atlantic.

The stones should have been staying in Wyngandacoia.

New World riches should have been there in their stead.

He would lose money on this voyage, his first, but it wasn't a complete failure. The twenty-four-year-old Cavendish had gained valuable experience in the veritable Garden of Eden that was the New World. Perhaps most important for the action-seeking young nobleman was his first taste of blood during the capture of two Spanish vessels, and the destruction of a Native American village.

The adrenaline and fire of battle had awakened in him a lust for adventure.

Cavendish's compatriots believed that Wyngandacoia was "the godliest soil under the cope of Heaven, so abounding with sweet trees, that bring sundry rich gums, grapes of such greatness," and "so fruitful and good, that England is not to be compared to it." The inhabitants wanted for nothing; their lands were wealthy in resources. So different to Cavendish's homeland, which, as Queen Elizabeth bemoaned, lacked "merchandise and fruit."

As wonderful as this land was, Cavendish craved not juicy meat and sweet fruit, but gold, silks, and spices for his monarch.

Such wealth for the Queen would mean honor for him, and a place among the immortals of the age. Mere money could not buy such status unless it were accompanied by glorious deeds and death-defying spectacle. Elizabeth demanded such lengths of her subjects. She barely raised an eyebrow if it was not forthcoming.

Cavendish's first step had been to name his ship for her.

Now he gazed at the sleek wooden vessel preparing to traverse the treacherous channels, sand banks, and low-lying islands that lay before the open sea. Boat crews stood to, oars and towlines ready to tug *Elizabeth* until she could unfurl her sails in safety. They needed no repeat of the near wreck which their companion *Tiger* had suffered on arrival two months previously.

Cavendish turned and looked up contemplatively to the scrubby tree line at the top of the beach. The inhabitants were few, but the distances vast in this New World. One day, perhaps in the near future, if it could be planted with people, their sweat and blood would provide wealth for England.

But that path was not for him; he craved instant gratification and the thrill of heroic deeds. Wyngandacoia, soon to be named "Virginia" for the unmarried English Queen by another fawning courtier, Sir Walter Raleigh, could not provide that.

Glamour would have to be sought elsewhere. Somewhere no other Englishman had been. That place would also need ready access to riches and someone, preferably Spanish, to plunder them from. England did not possess goods of ample value to trade for the expensive luxuries that London consumers demanded.

They had to be stolen.

The English were in North America as Cavendish's contemporary Sir Humphrey Gilbert put it, to "annoy the king of Spain" by planting a government-licensed pirate base from which they could attack Spanish shipping returning from the colonies to the south. The gigantic galleons were filled with silver and gold, the fruit of a genocidal exploitation of enslaved Indigenous and African people. A system of greed, blood, profiteering, and indifference to human suffering, which would only blossom further in the coming centuries.

Thanks to its conquests in the New World, Spain controlled the majority of the world's silver supply. This plundered wealth funded ever-increasing slave wars in Western Africa and unending religious conflict in Western Europe.

Spain itself had been united with Portugal in the Iberian Union since 1580, after King Henry of Portugal died without an heir, leaving King Philip, by the Grace of God, King of the Spains and the Indies, an easy path to seize his neighbor, adding it to the vast European tracts of what is now the Netherlands, Belgium, Italy, and France that he already claimed.

Henry VIII, Queen Elizabeth's father, had broken from the Roman Church in 1533 and proclaimed himself Supreme Head of the Church of England because the Pope refused to grant him a divorce from his Spanish queen, Catherine of Aragon.

Although he had not seen this as an anti-Catholic move, simply an anti-Roman one, and he himself remained a devout Catholic, in the rapidly swelling wake of the Reformation, his country became more and more Protestant.

The Spanish and their Habsburg monarchs deplored the insult to one of Spain's most noble ladies and, furthermore, were determined to use American colonial riches to perpetuate their holy war against anyone who did not adhere to Roman Catholic orthodoxy.

England was the prime candidate for Philip's ire.

He and Elizabeth endured an ephemeral-seeming peace, pockmarked by diplomatic rows, trade embargos, unofficial piratical warfare, and support for the enemy's enemy, hostile insurgents such as Dom António, rival claimant to the Portuguese crown, and the Earl of Desmond in Ireland.

Spanish invasion of England had been threatened for decades.

Roanoke, as the settlement was known, in what is now the state of North Carolina, was the perfect place to plant a military colony to support state-legitimized piracy against Spain. It was abundant in food, water, and timber. Well hidden from passing ships and relatively distant from any hostile outpost. The climate was healthy, and, until the recent conflict, the local people had been friendly. Two Natives, Manteo and Wanchese, had even visited London, been feted by the great and good, and returned home to lend support to English designs.

As he stood on the low Roanoke beach, Thomas Cavendish conceived of the deeds that would propel him to glory and riches beyond other Englishmen's wildest dreams.

He would circumnavigate the globe by fitting out a fleet to sail through the atrociously dangerous Strait of Magellan at the very foot of South America, terrorize the Spanish settlements on the mysterious western coast of the New World and from there hit out to lands untrodden by Englishmen.

The only other place on earth that came close to Spain in the extraction of precious metals was Japan, which was said to abound in gold and silver mines.

COURTESY OF THE INTERNATIONAL RESEARCH CENTER FOR JAPANESE STUDIES (NICHIBUNKEN).

Nova et Accurata Iaponiae Insulae *(Valk & Schenk, late seventeenth century) shows Japan and the surrounding islands (including Korea, which is portrayed incorrectly as an island). The great silver mines of Iwami* (argenti fodince) *are clearly shown accurately at the far western end of Honshu Island. Japan produced around one third of the world's silver at the turn of the seventeenth century.*

That is where he would go, to access the fabled, and long dreamed of riches of the East Indies, then he would return home in triumph via the Spice Islands, the southern tip of Africa, and the Atlantic Ocean.

The young courtier would bring home treasure, intelligence, and if possible, people like Manteo and Wanchese to teach the English the mysteries of the East.

There was good precedent for this. Europe had only recently gone wild for the very first Japanese nobles to visit the continent.

The four young lords had been the sensation of the decade, and even a big hit in parts of the Continent they did not travel through, such as England. The fascinated Queen Elizabeth was rumored to have ordered regular reports on their activities in Spain and the Italian peninsula.

Perhaps he could replicate that success.

Fame, prestige, honor, and a knighthood would follow, and

the nation would celebrate him. Cavendish's name would be immortal!

The would-be hero had been born into landed money in 1560 at Grimston Hall, Trimley, on the southeastern coast of England. His father died when he was twelve, leaving him the family fortune. At fifteen he went to Cambridge, but as was common among his sort, left two years later without a degree.

At age twenty, he started to attend Elizabeth's court and his sister Anne became a maid in waiting to the Queen.

Cavendish appears to have impressed, because he was elected member of parliament twice, in 1584 and 1586, and Sir Walter Raleigh appointed the young man second-in-command of the 1585 Roanoke mission, for which Cavendish built and furnished his own ship, *Elizabeth*, nearly exhausting his fortune in the process.

He was a flamboyant, rich daredevil who thought big, perhaps bigger than any other courtier, and it was while in Roanoke that he conceived of the deeds which would make his name.

The audacious plan to be the first English explorer to reach the Far East received eager encouragement at court. Not only for the prestige of the actions, but because Spain was tightening the thumbscrews on England, cutting trade and even imprisoning captured English merchants. Any attack on Spanish assets was fair game, and the coup of taking the fight to the Pacific, where Spanish pride would be hurt most, would be immense.

Less than a year later Thomas Cavendish sat in the solar of his manor at Trimley and pondered the path that his life had taken. He was about to set sail with a small fleet of new ships, *Desire*, *Content*, and *Hugh Gallant*, and had mortgaged his inheritance, his life in effect, to do it.

Was it worth it? Only God knew, and he would reveal his plans for the circumnavigation soon enough.

For the last time, Cavendish listened to the barely discernible sound of water trickling slowly through to the marshy banks of the River Orwell in the valley below, wondering whether he would ever see the magnificent long, low, green valley and the tall oaks of Grimston Hall again.

The candles fluttered. Cavendish drained the dregs of his wine, carefully avoiding the bitty deposit at the bottom of the tankard, and retired to the bedroom next door.

The next day, June 27, 1586, Thomas Cavendish and his three crews set out to circumnavigate the globe. It was the contemporary equivalent of setting foot on Mars—virtually inconceivable, the stuff of dreams.

He was the first person to actually plan this undertaking; the previous voyagers had done it by mistake. Magellan's few surviving men in 1522 had been the first, and just under a decade ago Sir Francis Drake had been the second.

Cavendish's small fleet, led by his flagship *Desire*, followed loosely in Drake's footsteps, sojourning briefly and violently in what is now Sierra Leone, Africa, and then crossing the Atlantic to Brazil. They sailed down the South American seaboard to the freezing seas off Patagonia, and upon landing at a place which Cavendish named Port Desire after his ship, gave chase to the famous giant archers of those parts. The huge men, however, were too fleet of foot, and escaped into the wilderness of the hinterland. From there, they entered and passed through the treacherous Strait of Magellan in a relatively speedy seven weeks, to the Pacific Ocean.

Rejoicing at their feat of navigation, they slowly and violently made their way northward toward California, and as Cavendish reported,

I navigated alongst the coast of Chili, Peru, and [Mexico,] where I made great spoiles: I burnt and sunke 19 sailes of ships small and great. All the villages and townes that ever I landed at, I burnt and spoiled.

While Cavendish himself found renown to echo down the ages, on his journey he would meet a man whose story is in many ways far more astonishing for its sheer improbability. A man who, like the English commander, was sojourning far from the land of his birth in virtually uncharted seas.

Christopher. A young Japanese traveler whose birth name is lost to the mists of time.

This man was to be feted by Queen Elizabeth, celebrated by English nobles, lauded by European scholars, and feared by global foes.

During his epic odyssey he would see action on five continents and be the first recorded Asian person to set foot in the Americas and the British Isles.

This is his story.

1

Christopher

November 14, 1587.

Christopher, a slight but strong twenty-year-old Japanese man, had been at sea for a long and tedious five months since Manila.

He had not seen a single sail since clearing the northern Philippine island of Babuyan. Nor had *Santa Ana*, the ship on which he served, sighted land since Mount Fuji's haloed peak had bid them farewell as they navigated north on the warm ocean currents that led past his homeland.

And now they were tacking slowly off the coast of a place called California, a peninsula, some said it was an island, just off New Spain (modern-day Mexico), with an endless continental landmass behind it. From time to time a protruding spit of rock or low, scrubby, brown desert hills, and rocky cliffs would come into view, but for the most part, California seemed bound in an unwelcoming, slow-moving, impenetrable fog, very different from the tropical, verdant brilliance of the islands *Santa Ana* had left behind.

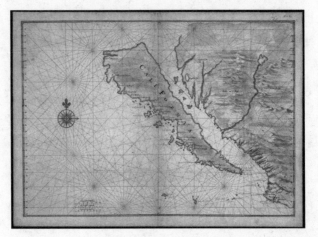

Joan Vinckeboon's map (ca 1650) was one of many maps to show California as an island instead of a peninsula. Others showed it as part of continental North America. In an age when so much cartography was uncertain, and subject to revision, no one was quite sure which version was correct.

Christopher shivered. What was this place?

By the sun, it was around eight in the morning and *Santa Ana*'s people had been busy for several hours. Christopher was preparing a simple breakfast of wine, stale biscuit, hard cheese, and olives for his master, a Spanish merchant who had made his fortune in the colonies and was now making the long voyage home. They were only weeks away from their destination, Acapulco. At least the end seemed in sight.

Suddenly there was a ripple of excited commotion among the crew and passengers; two ships had been sighted by a lookout high in the rigging. They were assumed to be friendly in these seas where the Spanish sailed unchallenged, probably carrying dispatches from Acapulco, or possibly the survey and discovery ship recently sent from Manila.

The officers, merchants, and priests chatted excitedly about fresh food, and contemplated what messages the newcomers might bring. News and letters from home?

Acapulco, the terminus for galleons from Manila like Santa Ana, *was the only North American port open for trade with Asia. Alejandro Ruffoni, 1628.*

Early morning sun confused their eyes as it reflected off the crests of the white-capped waves, but all aboard strained their eyes to distinguish the unknown sails from the low-hanging clouds on the horizon.

Then, just as swiftly as the excitement had erupted, panic replaced it.

The ships had raised the blood-red Cross of Saint George. These, it seemed, were English heretic pirates, intruders in Spanish waters.

Christopher stood and gazed at the distant but fast-approaching ships. They were like none he had seen before, smaller, perhaps, than a Chinese junk, but sleek and deadly looking. Speedy too, certainly so when compared with *Santa Ana*'s unwieldy hulk.

The men and women around him conversed in hasty, breathless Spanish revealing their dread fear of the English ships, and Christopher, in turn, was chilled to the bone. There would surely be no quarter from these devils.

The most senior priest on board, the Canon of Manila, Father de Armendariz started forth, bellowing out a passionate prayer, "Anima Christi," his hands held to the sky, imploring his God to intervene and save them.

Captain Tomás de Alzola ignored the priest and took matters swiftly into his own, worldlier, hands. In the galleon, stacked up in every available nook and cranny, were millions of pesos of goods. A large portion of that was his due, the rest was either the king's or belonged to crew and passengers proportional to their rank. He, and they, would not go down without a fight.

But *Santa Ana* was utterly unprepared for battle; what simple arms she possessed were nothing to the enemy's cannon. They had never expected to fight.

The few swords, bucklers, spears, and halberds available were issued to the crew. One of the captain's servants, Antonio, an enslaved Filipino youth, helped him don his armor. He personally took up the only two muskets they had with them, instructing Antonio to keep them ready and loaded—only enough powder for four shots remained.

Next, he ordered the three priests on board, Fathers de Armendariz, Juan Zorrilla de la Concha, and Francisco Ramos, to disguise themselves as merchants. English heretics did the Devil's work, and were known to harm, often kill, any holy men who fell into their hands.

Those merchants and officers who had armor fetched it at a run.

Christopher strapped the merchant into his spotless cuirass, offering him his proudly polished morion, and then followed his master back on deck. While the Spaniard headed for the captain's side, Christopher sought out his compatriot Cosmus, valet to the Canon of Manila, who seemed unable to take his eyes off the enemy ships.

They paused in the whirlwind of panicked action and nervous energy around them. The two were not particularly close, circumstances as much as a shared homeland had brought them together, but right now a surge of camaraderie swelled their hearts to quell the fear. They were going into battle.

Father de Armendariz was visibly piqued at having to disguise himself. He shouted angrily for his boy, and Cosmus took his leave, heading down to the cabin. The priest stomped down after him shortly afterward.

The ship's drum beat the call to action stations.

Orders came thick and fast.

Noncombatants below. Douse the mess fire. Extinguish all lamps. Man the bilge pumps. Bring the ballast stones on deck.

On board *Desire*, Michael Sancius, in conference with his commander, Thomas Cavendish, in the Great Cabin, had heard the lookout call "a sail, a sail" from his perch on the spar at the highest point of the topgallant mast.

Desire and her smaller partner, *Content*, had been lingering for nearly a month off Cabo San Lucas at the southern tip of California. Awaiting their prey, the Spanish treasure ship which was to make them all rich beyond their wildest dreams—and here she was.

He, Michael Sancius, was the man who had set this hunt in progress, and he now stood at the door to the armory with a wry grin on his face. He was a Frenchman, long in the service of the Spanish as a pilot along these coasts, but as the years had passed and he had seen the rivers of American gold and silver flowing by, he had continually asked himself why he should not receive more of the wealth that he did so much to facilitate.

Popinjay noblemen, fresh out of Spain, made fortunes in months without even breaking a sweat. Without the likes of Sancius, they would be lucky to get a mile beyond Acapulco Bay before swiftly foundering and meeting a nasty end on the treacherous coast of this New World.

Now it was his chance to wreak revenge. The English had taken his ship four months before, and although he had supposedly been taken prisoner, he was a highly willing captive. Without seeming too keen, he had little by little released information to the pirates about prizes and opportunities along their route north up the South American coast.

His first tip-off had borne no fruit. The pearl ship that the English hoped to take at Puerto de Navidad had already sailed. Cavendish's men were furious. In an incandescent rage they destroyed the diving settlement, and burned two, as yet unfinished, ships.

A second raid inland to the wilderness behind the tiny coastal settlement of Chacala, led by Sancius in person, had been more successful, food and supplies for repairs were looted, and a much-needed carpenter captured.

But even before this, Sancius had proved his loyalty by informing Cavendish of the treasure galleon from Manila, expected sometime in November at Acapulco. The Englishman had whooped a great cry of joy tinged with relief; he had not come halfway round the world only for the glory of the thing. He had come to get rich, and so had his men. A Spanish galleon, loaded with Asia's wealth, was the opportunity they had all been seeking.

Cavendish headed northwest and arrived in good time off California to lie in wait for his prey.

A month later, their patience was going to pay off, and Michael Sancius of Marseilles would receive his share. God damn the avaricious Spaniards.

Christopher, in the company of Cosmus and dozens of the other enslaved voyagers, made a human chain and heaved great piles of ballast stones from the depths of the galleon to the top decks. Their task completed, they squatted in the black of the lower decks waiting for battle. They would man the bilge pumps, the last line of defense against the ocean that pressed hard on *Santa Ana*'s hull.

It was difficult to see anything; this ship had no cannon

ports, and the only feeble light came through two grates in the floor of the main deck, filtering down stairways through several decks to where the noncombatants waited, crouched in the tiny spaces between the chests of Chinese silk in the hold, unable to influence the battle above them, but facing inevitable death if the ship foundered.

Sharing the floating coffin were people from the Philippine islands, Africa, the Spice Isles, Borneo, and New Spain. Anywhere where King Philip's multiethnic global empire traded or raided.

With the incessant squeak of the heaving pumps as a backdrop, prayers were muttered to a multitude of gods.

Wails and whimpers pierced the dark.

An African sang a soft mournful dirge in his mother tongue.

Alphonso the Manilan, barely fifteen, muttered "Áve María, grátia pléna, Dóminus técum" over and over again. He did not know the rest of the prayer.

Santa Ana did her best to flee, but the English ships closed slowly in. Gradually the murmurs belowdecks were replaced with a foreboding silence. All concentrated on the eternal thud of sea against the hull and the creak of the ship's dark timbers. A few inches, and the whine of the pumps, was all that stood between them and the afterlife.

For four long hours, the lumbering galleon tried to throw off the nimble English ships. If they could just gain the safety of darkness, and slip away from the heretic predators...

Those belowdecks knew little of what was going on. They had their orders, and disobeying would have meant terrible punishment, a savage whipping at best. In any case they could not escape. The nets that covered the decks during action had them snared as effectively as any fish.

It probably occurred to Christopher that he should appeal to Mazu, the Goddess of Seafarers, the Heavenly Mother deity of his Japanese and Chinese seafaring comrades. Christopher would have desperately wanted to see her red light shining at the masthead to reassure himself.

Then evil arrived in a roar of cannon fire, muffled, but petrifying for those who remained, unseeing, in the depths of the wooden ship. It was followed by a swift lurching of the vessel and the pop, pop, pop of small shot smacking into the wood of the upper reaches. As the galleon swayed irregularly from side to side, they rolled with it, the close-packed squatting men and women, sweaty with heat, fear, and panic, fell into a pile of thrashing limbs and bodies, desperately grasping out for any handhold.

Above them, fire from the two enemy ships had taken a terrible toll. From the shouts, they could hear that the African Antonio and Spaniard Cristóbal were dead. The Filipinos Lázaro and Artiaga had lost limbs, and lay bleeding their last on the deck.

The main mast had taken a direct hit.

Still connected to the rigging, it swung like a threshing tool, sweeping the defenders aside with every oscillation before it at last snagged and remained still.

Another African lost his arm, and slumped aghast, caressing the stump as the scarlet blood pumped down his naked, emaciated chest to collect in a pool beneath him.

Mere minutes later came a brutal lurch as the enemy ship rammed *Santa Ana*…and then came the thump and scratch of men climbing the outside of the hull.

Desire and *Content* had slowly but surely caught up with their prey. As soon as Cavendish could be sure of a chance of hitting his mark, he fired a broadside aimed at the superstructure of the ship. A volley of small shot from the swivel guns and muskets poised on their forked supports swept the decks. Longbowmen in the fighting tops sent down a hail of arrows.

Most of the ordnance ended in the sea, defeated by the swell, but several defenders were down, and a lucky cannon shot had severed the mainmast.

Around thirty Englishmen braced for impact against the ship's sides, weapons at the ready. The chief pilot, Thomas Fuller, steering by whipstaff in the armory, performed the delicate maneuver that rammed *Santa Ana*, just hard enough to throw the defenders but not hard enough to damage his ship.

On impact, four African and three Spanish sailors, perched precariously in the rigging, tumbled screaming to watery deaths in the foaming seas.

English mariners hurled their grappling irons upward and pulled.

The rocks that Christopher and his comrades had transferred from below now came into their own as the defenders hurled them down onto the much smaller English ship tethered alongside.

Craning his neck, Sancius watched as struck by stones, an attacker tumbled into the sea; others held on grimly with wounds gushing blood. As more and more of them gained the enemy deck, the stone throwing petered out, to be replaced by the clash and clang of steel and the dull, empty thump of swords on wooden bucklers.

The onslaught of the battle-hardened English was terrible. The defenders fell back, edging up the ladders to the higher placed forecastle and poop deck, but they were not only fighting for their lives. Every man owned a portion of the cargo, for most it was what they had worked their whole lives to scrabble together. Some had even mortgaged family property, or pawned heirlooms to invest in this voyage. The Spanish were desperate and held out with an almost suicidal bravado.

The English began to lose the ground they had won, until one by one they were pushed back to the rails and overboard. As the Spanish frontline advanced, a mangled body fell in its wake.

Cavendish had counted on shock, speed, and the fatigue of a crew who had had no respite during the five-month voyage, but the Spanish fought tooth and nail.

Desire's men ran, jumping down to their ship, and cutting the ropes which bound them to *Santa Ana*. The terrible hail of stones now resumed with a vengeance.

Two Englishmen had died and five were badly injured, for three Spanish dead and a number wounded. A considerable butcher's bill for the English force that had started the voyage with 123 men, but through disease, accident, and death in combat now comprised only sixty on the other side of the world.

Santa Ana rolled viciously again as the English ship disengaged and fled. Everyone on the galleon cheered, those belowdecks staggered as they shouted the loudest.

Christopher's relief did not last long. The English ship was turning swiftly, far faster than the Spanish behemoth could have managed, coming around again to take up a firing position. The Spanish captain promptly issued several orders. They were to keep at the pumps. Shorter shifts. Double time.

But not all of the Englishmen had left the galleon. Unseen by anyone, one of the assailants had gained the heights of *Santa Ana*'s rigging and was cutting through what ropes and snagged sails remained to hold up the swaying main mast. If he succeeded, the deck would be enveloped in sailcloth, rigging, and spars. The defenders would be snared like fish, thrashing helplessly, unable to repulse another boarding.

Christopher, down in the ship's depths and gazing up through the grilles as he awaited his turn on the pump, could just see the captain take aim with his musket. The resulting thump on the deck above his head suggested that the shot had met its mark.

The English ships lined up for the next attack; small shot from both vessels again raked the upper decks, and the heavier cannon concentrated their fire on the galleon's waterline.

It seemed as if *Santa Ana* was stuck in a strand of *Desire* and *Content*'s web, flapping her few remaining sheets like wings, but only succeeding in going around in futile circles while the deadly ships circled slowly, ever closer down silken threads.

As far as Cavendish was concerned, if the English could not take the ship, then neither would King Philip keep it to reap the profits on her cargo, gains which would be used to fund attacks on his native land. *Santa Ana* would be taken or sent to the bottom.

Below *Santa Ana*'s decks, wicked splinters of wood exploded into the frantically pumping men, mutilating exposed flesh. The metallic smell of fresh blood, sweat, and an intangible pall of fear filled the air.

Again and again, gaping holes appeared above the waterline, spent, but still scorching cannon shot rolled around dangerously. Beams of sunlight pierced the dim interior, revealing the abattoir that *Santa Ana*'s lower decks were fast becoming.

Somewhere the vessel was aflame, smoke started to billow and waft, adding its choking stench to the battle reek.

The enslaved desperately pumped the crimson-dyed water for their lives.

It was brutal and exhausting work. When their shift was over, they left the hull to find whatever space they could, sitting, panting in their soaking and blood-splattered clothes.

The ship remained afloat—just.

Christopher checked his hunger with soggy hardtack and slaked his desperate thirst with rancid water from the dregs of a barrel. Now he was resting, for the first time he noticed a cheery trumpet tune skimming over the waves from the enemy ship. The upbeat notes seemed otherworldly compared to the carnage that engulfed him and his comrades in *Santa Ana*'s depths.

Sancius, pacing the decks of *Desire*, was overcome with rage. The Frenchman wanted revenge for a thousand slights he had suffered at the hands of his erstwhile employers. Why did they not surrender? The day was clearly lost. The English guns continued to boom and while only a few missiles from each volley hit their mark, the *Santa Ana* still floundered ever more. It was only a matter of time. Soon the ship would sink, and his long-anticipated fortune would disappear with it.

Damn the haughty, arrogant, stubborn Spaniards. Damn these barbaric English, so consumed with battle lust that they threatened to sink the prey before they could reap the rewards.

He jumped on to the bowsprit at the very front of the ship and screamed,

Demons, why are you acting as the Devil's own? Why do you not ask for mercy now, for when you get to the point when you will, it will not be given.

Something of Sancius's words must have hit home. Shortly after his outburst, five hours since the action had begun, and after an hour of constant, lethal bombardment, Captain de Alzola indicated the surrender of his command with a white flag of surrender.

As the vermilion sun sank into the sea to the west, Captain de Alzola and Father de Armendariz, and *Santa Ana*'s other leading men, were desolately rowed over to *Desire*. Christopher may well have been one of the oarsmen. The rest of the exhausted and depleted crew and passengers looked on from the tattered remains of the deck.

The respite did not include the pumpers who remained below *Santa Ana*'s decks. With the ship in imminent danger of sinking, they were its last line of defense. The several dozen survivors of the action belowdecks remained organized in shifts, manning the bilge pumps until their blisters burst and the raw skin bled.

Santa Ana's humbled dignitaries came aboard *Desire* to prostrate themselves at Cavendish's feet. The arrogant struts and haughty airs Sancius knew so well were no more. These curs were beaten.

The pirate introduced himself politely, if nonchalantly, with a bow as "Thomas Cavendish of Trimley."

Cavendish, laughing, then shouted that they were safe now, and he personally guaranteed their lives would be spared if they treated with him fairly. The Englishman motioned at a lank-haired, one-eyed sailor next to him to interpret his words, waited a minute while the message was relayed, and then turned to usher de Alzola into his personal cabin.

The other vanquished notables were left standing on the deck, heads bowed in defeat and shame in the middle of a crowd of rowdy, leering Englishmen. The victorious sailors had been issued with a special ration of wine, and pinkish stains mingled with the oil and soot of battle on their filthy smocks as they idled around and taunted the vanquished foe.

Presently the pirates lost interest and the prisoners were herded into a cabin; Christopher, standing, leaned his head on a low roof beam, while his superiors sat, slumped on the floor, their backs curving against the side of the ship, heads hanging.

The wooden door uttered a sonorous boom as it swung shut and was firmly barred.

2

English Orientations

In an age when travel was arduous, expensive, and often deadly, when nautical charts were unreliable or nonexistent, and marine technology was rudimentary, Christopher and Cavendish had come together more than eight thousand miles from where the Japanese sailor had started out from his home. The English mariner had traveled over double that distance.

This fortuitous meeting had been several centuries in the making.

Until the late fifteenth century, the only known routes to the Far East and the Pacific from Europe involved voyages by ship to the eastern ends of the Mediterranean, or Black Sea, or through the freezing Murman Sea (modern-day Barents Sea) and via river southward to the Caspian Sea. Wherever they disembarked, travelers then had a long overland trek on foot, horse, or camel, through Central Asia.

Since the collapse of the highly effective Mongol policed transport network, known today as the Silk Road, in the fourteenth century, Europeans had an extremely arduous pathway east. The routes were either controlled by powerful, rich, well-organized, Muslim realms who each jealously guarded their monopolies, or restricted by conflict and ice through Muscovy (modern-day Russia).

As a result, most of the people who lived on the Atlantic Ocean or the seas which led into it—western and northern Europeans, the isolated cultures of the Americas, and southwestern Africa's powerhouses like the Kingdom of Kongo—remained, to their great detriment, almost or totally cut off from the globe's major cultural, manufacturing, and economic centers, Ming China, the Indian subcontinent, and Timurid Persia.

They were hemmed in by extremely challenging land exits, and the terrifyingly stormy waters of the Atlantic, which could not be navigated due to ignorance, insufficient technology, and impossible-seeming (or undiscovered) exits into the Pacific and Indian Oceans.

The exceptions were the wealthy Atlantic-facing Muslim empires of Songhai and Mali, who enjoyed supplies of luxuries and from their Middle Eastern coreligionists via the busy cross-Saharan caravan trade. Some maritime Mediterranean people also had limited seaborne access to the Indian subcontinent, and hence could transship Asian goods via Mamluk Egypt. They had no need to take the extreme gamble of braving the uncharted and no doubt dangerous hypothesized route around Africa to get there, and therefore stuck to the ways they knew.

With no outsiders inclined to enter the perilous and seemingly unprofitable Atlantic Ocean, it was up to those who were trapped there to find escape routes from the tempestuous watery borders that confined them.

One pioneering African attempt was in the early fourteenth century, when Mansa Muhammad ibn Qu of Mali having somehow heard news of lands over the seas, and beyond the horizon, is said to have fitted out three thousand vessels and voyaged to the fabled realm.

He was never heard of again.

During the following century, it was the inhabitants of Europe's westernmost peninsula, Iberia, who became the most determined to navigate outside the Atlantic to China, and Japan, or as they called it, "the Indies" and "Cathay."

Contrary to popular belief, fifteenth-century European navigators were well aware that the earth was round, and there was a widespread belief that China, the fount of luxuries, technical wizardry, and advanced medicine, would simply lie on the other side of the Atlantic. Japan to China's east, so the reasoning went, should therefore be closer to Europe and a far easier target destination.

Many contemporary scholars such as the Florentine Paolo Toscanelli, basing their theory on an ancient myth, stated that there was another island, called Antillia, fifty degrees to the east of Japan. An even more convenient stop on the route westward to the East.

While we remember the Genoa-born Cristoforo Colombo, (Columbus), aiming for Japan and China, as the first European to have reached the Americas (the Vikings did, but they do not seem to have been aware of the continent's extent), in Christopher's time many credited João Vaz Corte-Real of Portugal, who discovered the rich cod-fishing grounds off modern-day Canada in 1472.

The Portuguese did not capitalize on their discovery as they were probably too focused on their evermore daring attempts to navigate down the west coast of Africa, and it was left to Columbus, supported financially by Queen Isabella I of Castile, to cross the Atlantic by a more southerly route, and be revered throughout the ages.

The Genoan initially assumed that he had arrived at the eastern extreme of Asia, but it soon became clear that he was drastically mistaken.

Shortly after Columbus's second voyage to the Americas, and

after fifty years of ever-improved vessel designs forged and honed in the stormy Atlantic cauldron, Vasco da Gama's Portuguese-funded mission was the first to actually reach Asia, breaking into the Indian Ocean around the southern tip of Africa in 1497.

The motivations for this feat were not only economic, but were also inspired by the myth of the Christian king Prester John, who was said to rule somewhere in the East, and might be an effective ally in Portugal's unending conflicts with Islam. The Portuguese never found Prester John, but they certainly found wealth and trade beyond compare in Africa and Asia, and, pushing ever eastward, eventually became the first Europeans to develop their own maritime routes to China in 1513, and Japan in 1543.

In 1521, the Spanish also escaped their Atlantic prison.

Under the leadership of the Portuguese-born Fernão de Magalhães (Magellan), they found a strait into the Pacific Ocean and then continued to what would later be known as the Philippines, for King Philip of Spain. However, Magellan's icy strait suffered from frequent cruel storms, and Spain decided to concentrate on their recently conquered North American territories, which provided far safer overland access to the Pacific Ocean and Asia.

The Portuguese and Spanish agreed not to encroach on each other's spheres of influence and so these two opposite escapes from the Atlantic and approaches to the East Indies became their "exclusive" navigations.

The English and others were to be annihilated if caught attempting an oceanic breakout.

Thomas Cavendish was not the first English adventurer to make an audacious bid to reach Japan and China. Prior to him there had been ninety years of maritime attempts.

Not one had been successful.

Initially, following Columbus's lead, English missions tried to find the fabled Asian lands that they believed lay across the

Atlantic. In 1497, a mission funded by King Henry VII and led by Venetian Giovanni Caboto (John Cabot) assumed that it had found China, "the country of the Great Kahn," but had in fact made landfall in Newfoundland. A follow-up voyage in 1499 or 1500 by William Weston was the first to actually be led by an English captain.

In 1508 or 1509, Cabot's son Sebastian followed him, across the Atlantic "to Cathay," but was foiled in his attempt by mutinous sailors who rightly feared freezing to death long before they reached Asia.

The pioneering English state-sponsored voyages to North America were not to be repeated for decades, although some low-key privately funded expeditions, such as that of Richard Hore in 1536, did occur.

This less-than-proactive interregnum was later criticized intensely, most notably by John Davis, one of the era's most professional, experienced, and theoretically inclined mariners, in his 1595 work, *The Worldes Hydrographical Description*:

> *Such is the slowness of our nation, for the most part of us rather joy at home like Epicures, to sit and carpe at other mens hassardes, our selves not daring to give any attempt.*

> *This conceipt is the bastard of ignorance borne through the fornication of the malitious multitudes that onely desire to hinder when themselves can doe no good.*

When the Ottoman Empire, Europe's major power in the East, conquered Egypt and Baghdad for direct Indian Ocean access, the Turks and their African subjects joined the Spanish, and Portuguese in forging ahead in Asian maritime exploration. From the 1530s onward, they found keen allies there, particularly in the Muslim Sultanate of Aceh in Sumatra (modern-day Indonesia).

England fell further behind.

The English were not yet fully aware of where the exits discovered by the Portuguese and Spanish were located but knew that attempting to find them would provoke the wrath of those stronger nations. They believed that they had to find a new, exclusively English passage, and in the words of Roger Barlow, a merchant advisor to Henry VIII, "there resteth this waie of the northe onelie."

From this point on, a route through the icy wastes above modern-day Canada or Russia, sparsely populated and free of Portuguese or Spanish claims, became the English Holy Grail. The "Great Khan of Cathay" became a kind of English Prester John, presenting the possibility of a panacea for England's woes.

This obsession with "the Indies," existed despite the factual particulars being largely a mystery. Even geographical terms were unclear, and it was still common in 1586 for English books to refer to "Cathay and China," assuming that they were places distinct from each other. Some writers suggested that Cathay was above China, others that it was an island to the east of China, i.e., Japan.

"Cathay," like "the Indies," was essentially a catch-all term for the whole unknown vastness of East Asia.

One of the best sources of information available in the early sixteenth century was still the anonymous *Travels of Sir John Mandeville*, a fourteenth-century treatise which claims to be the story of an English knight's travels through Asia. Today we would recognize it as romanticized tall tales, giving a credulous readership what they desired—a mysterious, titillating world of romantic castles, fantastical flora and fauna, endless gold and untold luxury—perhaps vaguely based on carefully selected fact, but so warped as to be unrecognizable to reality.

Marco Polo's famed travelogue was not translated into English until 1579, although many English speakers would have read of his Chinese exploits in other languages prior to this.

There had been a vague, if very confused, conception of

"Japan" as an entity distinct from Cathay or China since ancient times. Pliny the Elder, a Roman authority on geographic matters, wrote slightly incredulously that

> *Beyond the mouth of the Indus are the islands of Chryse (Land of Gold) and Argyre (silver), abounding in metals, I believe; but as to what some persons have stated, that their soil consists of gold and silver, I am not so willing to believe that.*

Dionysius Periegetes described "Chryse" as an island "at the very rising of the sun." Over time, this "Land of Gold" and "Japan" became the selfsame place, to the extent that the world's oldest surviving globe, Martin Behaim's 1492 *Erdapfel*, indicates it in Japan's actual geographic position. The word "Chryse" was still in use during the seventeenth century, long after English people had actually visited Japan.

The Persian classic, *One Thousand and One Nights*, which was introduced to Europe in 1285, mentions the fabled islands of "Waq-Waq," to the east of China, where trees with fruits in the shape of human heads grow and people live off fish, shellfish, and tortoises but have no gold or ships. The women adorn their hair with ivory and pearl combs, but nothing else. Other legends mention conversely that the land is rich in gold, is ruled by a powerful queen, and peopled only by females (a possible reference to the Japanese shaman queen Himiko of the third century CE who was said to be attended by one thousand females, but only one man).

Although Waq-Waq has been equated with other regions of the world besides Japan, etymology could provide the answer. An old word for the peoples of Japan was "Wa" ("Wo" in Chinese), and the Arabic sound "q" ("k" in English) could easily be a garbled version of the Japanese word "koku" (pronounced similarly in some Chinese languages) meaning country. It is easy to see, therefore, that "Wakoku" could easily transmorph into

"Waq-Waq" during a long-distance game of broken telephone across Eurasia.

Marco Polo called Japan "Cipangu," temptingly describing it as a land rich in gold where the dead were buried with giant red pearls in their mouths and the ruler's palace was roofed and floored in gold two fingers thick.

Although by the sixteenth century many educated readers would have been aware that not all this information was entirely dependable, most people had no other frame of reference. For them, these medieval fantasies were as close to reality as they got.

Whatever their name, these islands were China's close neighbors, and sixteenth-century maps, some produced by close acquaintances of Cavendish's such as Emery Molyneux, showed Japan as twenty times larger than the already large and vastly rich Indian subcontinent. This only added rocket fuel to the idea of a potentially enormous and thriving Japanese market.

The English were still not certain how they could navigate to the Far East, but after an interregnum of around half a century, the *Mysterie and Companie of the Merchant Adventurers for the Discoverie of Regions, Dominions, Islands, and Places Unknown*, later the *Muscovy Company*, the world's first attempt at an organized, joint-stock–funded exploration, was established in 1551 to push to the Far East overland. Hence, in 1553, Sir Hugh Willoughby set out for "Cathay" via the "Scythian Seas," and the hypothesized Northeast Passage above Tartaria (modern-day Siberia).

Everyone on two of his three ships perished in the bitter snow and frozen seas, and only one returned to report they had discovered not Cathay, but Muscovy, and hence another possible way to the East via that region's rivers.

The Muscovy Company's merchants succeeded in traveling down the Volga to the Caspian Sea and Safavid Persia, to access Eastern goods far more cheaply than in Europe. It seemed like England had at last found its longed-for exclusive access to Asian trade, and petitioned Ivan the Terrible to make it their monopoly.

However, Muscovy was still in the process of fighting for its independence from the Tartars (Mongolic peoples) who had controlled it for so long, and in 1571, an alliance of Ottomans and Crimean Tatars torched Moscow. The flames claimed twenty-five English merchants and their worldly goods, a tiny proportion of the sixty thousand local casualties, but a huge loss to England's meager resources, and a hefty blow to the newfound commercial and navigational confidence.

A further setback was Ivan the Terrible's revocation of the Muscovy Company's license to trade. He had not been impressed by the idea that other European merchants should be banned from his realm, and to make matters worse, Queen Elizabeth had not accepted his generous proposal of marriage.

It was back to square one.

England's only serious natural resource at this point in history was the perfect damp climate for rearing sheep, and hence industrial output was largely limited to wool and its derivatives. In medieval times, a wool-based economy had been perfectly respectable, but now that England's direct competitors and enemies could supercharge their treasuries with plundered riches from the Americas and the fruits of Asian trade, it was not enough.

The court cosmographer and alchemist, John Dee, who Elizabeth called her "noble intelligencer," was commissioned to conjure up solutions to the delicate problem of securing overseas possessions to support the English economy. He was particularly happy to perform this task because he thought it would also help him realize his personal dream of reaching China to acquire advanced knowledge and technology, or at least the sixteenth-century equivalent—magic, alchemy, and the secrets of the cosmos.

Dee called his project the "British discovery and recovery enterprise," and despite the slim hope of any continental territory actually coming under English rule, he went back a millennium to the mythical King Arthur, to find "legal" claim to European lands to which he could give his Queen title.

Then he went further, imagining a new extra-European Empire in various writings during the 1570s and early 1580s, "confirming" Her Majesty's legitimate title to Greenland and Estetiland (probably part of modern-day northeast Canada, though some believe it might be Iceland) and looking further beyond even the New World, for more potential additions to the imperial realm.

To convince the many who questioned his logic and methods, Dee provided a visual prompt, painting a portrait of Queen Elizabeth enthroned before a world map. To her left was China, fount of trade, to her right the Americas, "unclaimed" territory. Below her feet was the Strait of Anian, a hypothesized but as yet undiscovered body of water on the Pacific side of the also long-hypothesized but as yet undiscovered Northwest Passage. Above the Queen's crown, central to the whole artwork, was Japan, "Land of Gold." Dee confidently stated that these four entities were the key to England's future prosperity and power, Japan's gold above all.

Dee, who is credited with inventing the term "British Empire" (*Brytanici Imperii* in Latin), had literally rendered his conjured ideas into pictorial reality.

Dee's fertile imagination inspired the great and good of England to redouble their efforts to reach the Far East, not only in practical endeavors like those of Cavendish, but in theoretical fashion too. Eventually hundreds of books and letters about the Far East were published in the early modern period.

These treatises followed a common thread.

For example, Sir Humphrey Gilbert's 1576 *A Discourse of Discoverie for a New Passage to Cataia*, advocating navigation via the Northwest Passage, described civilized countries,

> *where ther is to be fouud great aboundance of gold, silver, precious stones, Cloth of golde, silkes, all maner of Spices, Grocery wares, and other kindes of Merchandize, of an inestimable price.*

In 1595, John Davis summed up the argument that he had been promoting since the 1570s:

from England there is a short and speedie passage into the South Seas, to China, Molucca, Philippina, and India, by Northerly Navigation.

Where:

Gold, silver, stones of price, juels, pearls, spice, drugs, silks raw and wrought, velvetts, cloth of gold, besides many other commodities with us of rare and high esteeme, whereof as yet our countries is by nature deprived, al which [Asia] doth yeld at reasonable rates in great aboundance, receiving [our products] in the highest esteeme, so that hereby plentry retourning by trade abroad, and no smale quantitie provided by industry at home...

And that to engage in this trade would mean:

her majestic and her highnes successors for ever, should be monarks of the earth and commaunders of the Seas, through the aboundance of trade her customes would bee mightily augmented, her state highly inriched, and her force of shipping greatly advanced, as that thereby shee should be to all nations most dredful, and we, her subjects, through imploiment, should imbrace aboundance and be clothed.

The English believed that Asian contact was the key to English affluence and power. To put it in modern terms, engaging in trade, and attaining science, and technological knowhow, would bring a sorely lacked international respect, immense wealth, and galvanized military strength to England and its blessed Queen.

It would be a salvation. A panacea for the nation's ills.

It was with a renewed verve, in 1576, that the mariner Martin Frobisher returned to the idea of finding the Northwest

Passage, and with moral support from the Queen, and financial support from the Muscovy Company, attempted to travel above northern Canada:

> to Cathay, supposed to be on the north and northwest part of America: where our merchants may have course and recourse…with greater benefit than any others to their no little…profit.

The mission failed in its primary objective of reaching Asia but seemed to have found a plentiful source of gold in Newfoundland. A Cathay Company to be formed after the Muscovy Company model was eagerly mooted, and steps taken to find investors to exploit these riches and support the continuing attempts at forging a path to the East above North America.

Adding fuel to the fire, in 1577, Richard Willes's *The history of travayle in the West and East Indies* provided the first reliable English-language description of Japan. Drawing on recent eyewitness Jesuit missionary accounts, it described the Japanese as:

> tractable, civile, wyttye, courteous, without deceyte, in vertue and honest conversation, exceedyng all other nations lately discovered.

Seemingly ideal allies and trading partners!

That same year, and in the following, many of the great and good of England poured money into Frobisher's follow-up missions. The Queen even stumped up £1000, a vast sum for the age.

It was all a pipe dream.

The "gold," brought back in huge quantities by the second and third missions, was actually iron pyrite, "fool's gold." Worth nothing.

The whole venture was a huge financial disaster for the English upper class, and the Cathay Company, which had never been formally incorporated, collapsed.

The English, even the Queen, had been willing to put normal prudence and credulity aside and believe in even the flimsiest of evidence if it promoted their dreams of riches available for easy exploitation in America, and a simple route to the Far East where even more lucre awaited them.

Reality had intervened in Dee's reverie.

A British Empire during Elizabeth's reign would be constrained by the simple necessity of survival in the war against Spain, a moribund economy, serious military shortcomings, and the reluctance of Elizabeth herself to countenance the huge financial outlay that an ambitious imperial project would have required.

Dee, and his attempt to forge a "legal" basis for empire, fell swiftly out of favor.

If national strengthening was difficult by "legal" means, there was a far less palatable but more immediately practical solution available. Violent seaborne crime. Piracy, or in polite language, privateering.

English privateering had been occurring for decades on a small scale, but by the 1580s, the Queen herself was so central to the system, that she lent her ships to piratical excursions and took large shares of the profits above and beyond the normal customs duties due to her treasury anyway.

Ironically, this criminal activity would lead where the attempted "legal," if imaginary, means had not. To a real-life seaborne empire in the next centuries.

Queen Elizabeth saw several distinct advantages to legalizing piracy against certain enemies.

Firstly, it was a lot cheaper than employing a permanent navy. Elizabeth did own warships in her "Navy Royal," but they did not employ fighting men permanently for the most part and relied on a mixture of part-timers and impressed crew.

Secondly, in theory, privateering focused criminally minded energies on the enemy rather than the friendly shipping that more traditional pirates were wont to target. However, in practice, privateers were not overly discerning about the difference between "enemy" shipping and "friendly" shipping. The attitude was "might is right," and ships of all nations, including England, suffered terribly. Furthermore, privateering bred weakness, corruption, and criminality in the government officers who were supposed to control it. Often a large bribe was all that was needed for the authorities to ignore transgressions, which only encouraged more thuggery.

Thirdly, the risks and consequences were entirely privatized. If the ships never came back, the losses were not borne by the crown, and in the event of atrocities, the Queen could deny knowledge of them. Whether the denials were believed by foreign governments or not was another matter, but any attack on foreign shipping or coastal communities could at least not be construed as a declaration of war. The principle was identical to modern states covertly supporting rebellion and terrorism abroad to weaken enemies who could not otherwise be touched.

Fourthly, in the midst of the Spanish trade blockade with hostile enemies patrolling the seas, it kept ships and ports operational. Without privateers' activities, vessels would have rotted, and harbor facilities decayed, bringing with it long-term consequences for national defense.

Fifthly, the loot was taxable; the more plunder, the more tax. Customs duties were paid at 5 percent, and an additional 10 percent was paid in kind to the Lord High Admiral, the head of maritime forces, providing him with a large source of income without expense to the state.

Privateering provided the Queen and her officers with a handsome income and became an indispensable part of the national essence. But it also further sullied England's international reputation.

The result was that most foreign goods in the shops were laundered plunder, a large proportion of state revenue came from thieving, and the maritime armed forces consisted of co-opted pirates. Robbery of foreigners, even friendly ones such as the Dutch, was glorified and excused.

England was despaired of and despised by her neighbors as a troublemaking rabble rouser.

England's future imperial projects were built upon corrupt, rotten, exploitative, and xenophobic foundations.

People all over the world know this as the Golden Age of England—successful government propaganda has a long shelf life.

Around the 1570s, by means of bribes, treason, treachery, and increased privateering activity in waters close to the Americas, the details of the secret Spanish and Portuguese navigations via southern Africa, the Strait of Magellan, and across the Isthmus of Panama, became known to the English, and one privateer went further than any had before.

That man was Francis Drake.

In 1578, he and his men managed with great difficulty to slip through Magellan's frozen strait at the bottom of South America into the Pacific Ocean. He then took a southern route through Asia via the Spice Islands (in modern-day Indonesia), the source of commodities such as cloves (which were literally worth their weight in gold), and returned home via the Cape of Good Hope to complete England's first circumnavigation.

He was knighted by Elizabeth for his feat.

Drake and his men had pioneered both the Atlantic's southern openings for England and lived to tell the tale. He had even landed near where San Francisco is now, and claimed the land for Elizabeth, naming it New Albion, nearly three hundred years before English speakers actually settled California.

Soon, reflecting the more sophisticated understanding of East Asia that English mariners had developed, came the first voyage to explicitly name Japan as a target.

In the same year that Drake returned, Charles Jackman and

Arthur Pet attempted the northeastern route once more, not through the conflict-riven river systems to the Caspian Sea, but above Tartaria through the Scythian Seas. They failed, but they did return to tell their tale.

In 1583, Ralph Fitch and a few companions, partially reverting to Marco Polo's overland blueprint, set out with colleagues via the Middle East, both by sea and on land. In 1586, when Cavendish left, nothing had been heard of him for years.

Fitch eventually returned empty-handed in April 1591. He too had attempted to reach China but had to be content with a series of misadventures, which included a horrific torture session at the hands of the Portuguese Inquisition, and an audience with Akbar the Great, the Mogul emperor of much of the Indian subcontinent. He eventually visited Malacca via what is now Myanmar, and possibly reached the Spice Isles.

The fame which his daring travels brought even ensured that he achieved Shakespearean immortality. The first witch in *Macbeth*, referring to a mariner's wife, says, "Her husband's to Aleppo gone, master of the *Tyger*," the ship upon which Fitch sailed from England.

These men were feted in the same way we celebrate astronauts today.

3

Lords of the East

Then to great fanfare, Japan visited Europe. In serious and unforgettable style.

The Tensho Embassy which traveled between Japan and Europe and back between 1582 and 1590 was the first formal diplomatic contact between the two ends of the Eurasian world.
The legates did not act for Japan as a whole, for in this time of
war there was no unified state to represent. Instead, the mission
was sent by three Catholic lords, Otomo Sorin, Omura Sum-
itada, and Arima Harunobu. Its purpose, to pay obeisance to the
Pope, demonstrate the civilized nature of the Japanese people
to eager Europeans, celebrate the success of Jesuit proselytizing in Asia, and upon return to Japan itself, spread knowledge
of the magnificence of Europe to a highly skeptical populace.

The Jesuit who originally conceived of the project, the Visi-
tor (inspector) of Missions Alessandro Valignano, knew well
from firsthand experience that European knowledge of Japan
was often woefully lacking; the overhyped myths and legends
from previous centuries combined with recent inaccurate as-

sumptions, and sweeping judgments from limited sojourns by mainly Portuguese missionaries abounded.

On the one hand, Portuguese merchants and Jesuit Catholic missionaries reported cultural and social highlights, such as palatial castles, impeccably behaved children, and great artistic prowess, but on the other hand, Japan was said to abound in base heathen ways such as ritual suicide to atone for misdeeds, acceptance of sexual diversity, and divorce on roughly equal terms. Some commentators, including Valignano himself, held that they were the most civilized people on earth, others said that they were an incomprehensible, idol-worshiping, two-faced race of piratically inclined ruffians.

No consensus as to Japan's true nature had been achieved through actual contact.

If Europe had insufficient knowledge of Japan, Japanese knowledge of Europe was even more woeful. Although imported Korean maps showed its existence, and there had been a few sixteenth-century Euro-Japanese encounters on Asian seaways, direct and recorded contact only began when a Chinese pirate ship with several Portuguese crew members was blown ashore on the southern island of Tanegashima in 1543.

This momentous event set the tone for the next century of communication. The Portuguese guns were a hit with the local samurai, while the Japanese girls were a hit with the Portuguese. By local legend, the first in a long line of European-trafficked Japanese youngsters—Christopher's spiritual ancestor—the daughter of a swordsmith, left Japan with one of the strange barbarians.

In exchange for a gun of course.

Her father and his clan reverse engineered the weapon to start a gun-making industry that was so successful, that for long afterward muskets or harquebuses were simply known by the name of the island on which the Japanese had first encountered them, Tanegashima.

The Portuguese were then in the process of trying to establish a base at Macao in southern China, and trade with Japan became the foundation stone on which the success of the outpost was built. Soon Portuguese ships, crewed mainly by African, Indian, and Chinese sailors, brought munitions, Chinese silk, in-demand Asian commodities, and word of a strange new god.

Over four decades of trade and missionary work, the Japanese had formed mixed impressions of the curious voyagers from afar. They had good gadgets, possessed awe-inspiring geographical knowledge, and were useful purveyors of rare foreign goods, but they were ignorant of correct behavior, went unwashed, ate with their hands, consumed impure foods such as meat, and their fanatical, intolerant beliefs were beginning to contribute to the violent strife that embroiled Japan.

The Tensho Embassy was supposed to be a step toward righting the "incorrect" and "ignorant" impressions on both sides.

Four noble-blooded legates of around fourteen years of age, Ito Mancio, Hara Martinho, Chijiwa Miguel, and Nakaura Julião—all Catholics and known by their baptismal names—were selected as legates. They were chaperoned by at least three other Japanese Jesuits and servants as well as European Jesuits.

Their first European landfall in August 1584 was at Lisbon, one of the most multicultural and cosmopolitan cities on the continent thanks to Portugal's contemporary status as the most active of Europe's maritime nations. People from afar who might have turned heads in most cities were commonplace in Lisbon, and so the Japanese youths initially went relatively unremarked.

That all changed, however, when they were received and feted by King Philip's viceroy in Portugal, Cardinal Albert, and others among the nobility promptly followed his lead. Catarina de Bragança took such a fancy to their Japanese garb that she had her servants work through the night to produce a kimono in which to dress her younger son. She then sent word to the legation members that one of their fellow countrymen had unexpectedly arrived in her chambers.

The four boys took the joke in the good-natured way that it

was intended. Cultural appropriation was not a sixteenth-century concept.

Her eldest son, the Duke of Bragança, accompanied by one hundred and fifty retainers, proceeded to host a grand hunt in their honor at his lodge, the Tapada Real.

This set the pattern for the rest of the Grand Tour. During their travels through Portugal, Spain, and the Italian Peninsula to Rome and back again, they met with numerous rulers and dignitaries, and were received within some of the most sumptuous palaces and castles on the European continent.

Everywhere the Japanese emissaries were accorded the pomp and splendor customarily reserved for royalty. They would be met outside of town by large contingents of local nobles and a guard of honor, then conducted through the streets in horse-drawn carriages to the great acclaim of huge crowds straining to get a look at the "exotic" youths.

In many places, they were held in something like spiritual awe. In Assisi and Perugia the people tried to touch their clothing "as if they were sacred." There were even rumors among the common people that the four boys were Magi, akin to the three kings who had attended Jesus after his birth.

Their aristocratic hosts acted with a little more decorum, but were equally eager to descry their magnificent kimonos, hear the Japanese language spoken, behold the use of chopsticks, and learn firsthand about the distant land from whence they came. It was not only their "Japaneseness" that impressed. They dazzled with their facility in European languages, including Latin, and delighted with their knowledge of courtly customs such as social dancing. Valignano had prepared them well.

At Pisa, the duke and duchess embraced the legates in their private chambers and conversed in depth about Japan. Later, at a ball in their honor, one of the boys amused all present by gallantly asking one of the more senior, and less nimble, court ladies to dance with him. The chivalrous invitation was politely declined.

Besides this rather charming gaffe, the emissaries performed their dignified roles with panache. Upon being told to choose whatever gift he pleased from the study of the grand duchess of Tuscany, Ito, the chief legate, chose a portrait of the duchess herself, "so that in his country the women may see how much these [European ladies] exceed them in beauty and style."

It is not recorded whether the Japanese ladies to whom it was eventually shown swooned at the sight of European feminine allure.

Later, at the Garden of Pratolino in Florence, the Japanese emissaries were so fascinated with the fountains and water features that they spent a day studying the hidden mechanisms which powered them. Their guide on that occasion, Raffaello de' Medici, noted that "no trace of barbarism" attended his charges.

No doubt thanks to Marco Polo's tall tales, and also due to the respect with which they were hosted, rumors of a vast wealth which they carried with them slipped out. This not only attracted throngs of beggars wherever they went but caused the individual rulers who had responsibility for their safety to be greatly worried about bandit attacks. Hence, particularly in the Italian peninsular states, they were provided with heavily armed escorts, which only increased the locals' excitement and expectations.

In actual fact they traveled with only the presents that they were due to bestow on those who welcomed them, among them a gift of folding screens from Oda Nobunaga, the preeminent warlord in Japan when they left. The magnificent works of art, to be presented to the Pope, depicted Nobunaga's Azuchi Castle, but would not have matched reverie of riches that the Italians dreamed of.

In Rome, the legation was accorded the great honor of having Pope Gregory XIII come out to meet them personally in procession. They later reciprocated by kissing the Pontiff's feet in an act of public homage. The sacred moment when "all Japan" submitted to the Holy See was recorded for posterity.

It did not go unnoticed that the conversion of an island nation at the end of the Eurasian landmass would neatly replace the English souls so recently lost to brute heathenism.

The fragile Pope Gregory was not long for this world, however, dying from a fever on April 10, 1585.

A new pope, Sixtus V, was elected two weeks later, and promptly elevated Ito and Hara to the European nobility by knighting them. Tapped on the shoulder three times with a golden sword, they were appointed papal knights in the Order of the Golden Spur.

The Roman Senate followed with the honor of citizenship for all four of the legation.

In the end, the young legates were sent fondly on their way laden with gifts for the Japanese mission, and for the lords of Japan, upon whose continued favor Jesuit proselytizing depended.

COURTESY OF FONDAZIONE TRIVULZIO, MILAN.

Ito Mancio in the clothes of a European gentleman. Tintoretto, ca 1585.

The vast swathes of Europe that missed seeing them in person got the next best thing. Hundreds of portraits and pamphlets were published finding their way to all corners of the continent. It was the sensation of the decade.

The arrival of the Tensho legates had not escaped scrutiny in England.

A green-eyed Queen Elizabeth insisted on frequent updates on their feted progress through Catholic Europe and received almost biweekly reports between March and August of 1584. A letter from Madrid informed her that:

They are white and of very good intelligence, and when they return to their own land it is hoped they will be much benefit to Christianity.

This information is nearly word for word how various English accounts later described Christopher and Cosmus.

They traveled back to East Asia, via Africa and the Indian subcontinent, starting in 1586. The weather conditions were at times appalling, as Christopher, while traversing the same seas the opposite way around the globe at exactly the same time, also found.

The return odyssey lasted four years, and on arrival in Japan in 1590 they were so much changed from the samurai boys who had left eight years before, that their own mothers had difficulty recognizing them.

Valignano, now head of all the Asian missions, chose to make the occasion of their return a grand diplomatic event. Officially dispatched as the representative of the Viceroy of Portuguese India, he became the first state-appointed European ambassador in Japan to the court of Toyotomi Hideyoshi.

In Miyako (modern-day Kyoto), vast crowds turned out to see the exotic and gorgeously dressed procession of strange foreigners. The focus was the four boys returned from the other side of the world, dressed in black and gold robes gifted them by the Pope, and looking for all the world like Southern Barbarians, as Europeans were known in East Asia.

Valignano, a master of spectacle, would have expected no less. Nine years ago, on his first visit to this same city, the missionary had also managed to orchestrate huge throngs of similarly fascinated onlookers. That time he had paid obeisance to Hidey-oshi's predecessor, Oda Nobunaga, on behalf of the Jesuit mis-sion in Japan and was attended by his giant bodyguard, Yasuke.

This African man, the subject of a previous co-authored book of mine, *African Samurai*, proved a sensation and later became the first documented samurai of foreign origin in Japanese his-tory when he entered Nobunaga's service.

This time, Valignano genuflected himself three times before Hideyoshi in the magnificent Jurakudai Palace, and presented him with a giant Arabian stallion, two suits of the finest Mila-nese armor, swords, muskets, a royal battle tent, gilt tapestries, a finely illustrated world atlas, and a clock.

These were gifts fit for the supreme ruler of a great realm, the highest-class tribute that Europe could furnish.

Had Thomas Cavendish, a man planning to pay obeisance to the ruler of Japan, known what was expected of a supplicant from a foreign court, he may have balked at the extreme cost of the required tribute.

England herself, let alone an independent privateer, would have had great difficulty in providing such princely gifts, partly because the parsimonious Queen would not have parted with the funds, and partly because contemporary English craftsmen could not equal the quality of the Italian manufactures.

Valignano no doubt had a potential English incursion in mind when he chose his gifts. If they ever did arrive, he wanted to be sure that he had outdone his enemy and had Hideyoshi's ear.

The four boys, now grown to men, astonished the Japanese court with performances on European musical instruments, ge-ography lessons demonstrated on cutting-edge globes, and col-orful descriptions of all they had seen. The fact that this came from the mouths of fellow Japanese aristocrats greatly enhanced the trustworthiness of the information, and as the Jesuits had hoped, raised the esteem of all things Catholic in Japanese eyes.

The exoticness of European clothing even kick-started a decade-long fad for wearing "barbarian" garb, a harbinger of things to come in one of the world's most fashion-conscious countries.

Valignano was well pleased with the resounding success of the project, and all four ambassadors were accepted into the Catholic priesthood. The first Japanese people to be permitted ordination.

4

Desolation and Famine

The Tensho legates' triumphant tour of Catholic Europe, observed keenly from a distance, only whetted English appetites further.

John Davis was the next to attempt to find a way, via the Northwest Passage in 1585. He was sure he had managed to sail a long way into the passage, past a land that he named "Desolation." Contrary winds, however, forced him to turn back.

Mere weeks before Cavendish himself sailed to meet Christopher, on May 7, 1586, Davis had departed yet again to find a way above North America.

Despite not finding the long-desired passage to Japan and China, the firsthand detailed geographic, climatic, and botanical information he and others gathered was to stand England in good stead when John Dee's dreams of empire started to become a reality in future decades and centuries. For the ultimate destiny of these territories was to become vast swathes of modern-day Canada.

English horizons were expanding and England's endeavors heating up.

Thomas Cavendish chose the Strait of Magellan, not the Northwest Passage, for his planned circumnavigation. Despite its dangers, it seemed the easiest path.

But *easy* is a relative word.

After Magellan himself, a 1525–1526 Spanish mission had just managed to struggle through, only to have all the surviving ships destroyed by the Portuguese in Asia. Another voyage succeeded in making it as far as Peru in 1540–1541. Then, in 1557, an attempt to traverse the Strait from the Pacific side was made from Chile.

Only the captain and two men made it back alive.

In response to Drake's incursion, the Spanish sent a navigator called Don Pedro de Sarmiento from Peru to destroy the English if they returned through the Strait. (Drake chose instead to complete the circumnavigation, and so slipped through the net.)

Sarmiento, though, managed to cross the Atlantic to Spain, where puzzlingly, perhaps out of excessive pride, he reported that conditions were quite mild. He returned in 1581 with the biggest fleet ever assembled by Spain for a long-haul mission, twenty-three ships with five hundred colonists to protect the Strait against any other European nation that tried to pass. It took three years and the loss of most of the fleet to achieve anything, but they eventually established a settlement at a place Cavendish later named Port Famine in the modern-day Chilean region of Magallanes y la Antártica Chilena.

The sorry settlers perished in the bitter cold, in attacks by Indigenous people, and from extreme hunger.

Virtually no one survived.

The Strait of Magellan was fraught with danger for Cavendish and his men as Spain's multiple misadventures and the massive death toll had shown.

However, his eventual successful passage and entry into the

Pacific brought about the fateful meeting with Christopher in the tumultuous seas off California.

Now we turn to how Christopher came to be sailing on a Spanish galleon off California.

5

A World of Chaos and War

Japan in this age was far from the land of milk and honey that Europeans imagined.

Christopher was born into an era which is simply referred to as *The Age of the Country at War*.

It lasted through much of the fifteenth, the whole of the sixteenth, and part of the seventeenth centuries. This very long sixteenth century was a time of upheaval, destruction, and terror. Warriors, bandits, monks, pirates, peasants, and ninja fought both to dominate the archipelago, and just to survive another day.

The shock waves that emanated from the Japanese conflicts and the disorder they spawned had, by the 1580s, spanned much of Asia and would later wash up, like Christopher, on beaches far, far away.

Yet, a century or so before, Japan had not even been a player on a global stage; the epicenter of the Eurasian world lay somewhere between Beijing and Istanbul on one of the much-frequented cross-continental routes that reached from Ming China, via Central Asia to the Persian Gulf, and Ottoman Anatolia.

During the previous century though, as the wider world experienced an economic upturn and shipping technology improved, a maritime system centered on subcontinental India's seaports started to take center stage. Ships and merchants from all corners of the world met to trade spices, jewels, bullion, textiles, and trafficked people.

In 1500, Japan was on the very eastern extreme of this maritime world, connected, but only just, through China and Korea.

Within a few decades however, civil war caused the Japanese, who, according to Gonzalo Ronquillo de Peñalosa, governor of the Philippines, were a "turbulent people, much given to fighting," to travel far further abroad than their traditional trading destinations of Korea and China, to the modern-day Philippines, Vietnam, Malaysia, and Thailand. They packed their ships full of locally mined commodities, largely silver and sulfur, to form armed trading bands; if legitimate commerce was hard to come by, they swiftly turned smuggler or pirate, pillaging and slaving to recover their losses.

These feared sea bandits found ready allies across the South China Sea and beyond. Japanese lords gave them safe bases from which to operate in exchange for access to luxury goods. Chinese gentry and Southeast Asian merchants encouraged smuggling to increase their profits. Peasant folk on all coasts were willing to harbor the pirates if they would only pick on other victims and leave their hosts in peace.

Over time, the makeup of pirate crews became less and less Japanese, perhaps only 20 to 30 percent, and Chinese seamen came to form the majority.

Using words for nationality in this age though is deceiving. This era preceded the nation-state, and what we now think of as Chinese or Japanese people were in truth far more bound by tribal and local ethnic ties, some of which reached across the seas, than any national feeling. Koreans, Africans, and Europeans with similarly ambiguous ethnic and tribal identifications also signed on, eager to reap the piratical rewards.

These seas became the happy haunts of perhaps the most multiethnic marauders in world history.

The sea rovers devastated wide swathes of coastal East Asia, plundering property and people. Tens of thousands, mainly children, were ripped from their families and enslaved. Many thousands more died by the sword or from the hardships that followed in the wake of the chaos.

Wako pirates mainly attacked Chinese and Korean coastal communities, plundering goods and taking slaves. This portion from a Chinese scroll depicting pirate attacks shows Chinese villagers (on the left) fleeing as pirates burn and plunder their homes.

The Chinese and Korean governments called these pirates *wako*, "Japanese bandits," a title which conveniently glossed over the fact that their own subjects were key players and placed the blame elsewhere. The fact that there was no effective Japanese government to contest this, or prosecute the pirates, only confirmed the continentals in their firmly held opinion of the Japanese isles' barbarity.

Japan, like England, had become an international pariah, and Ming China, like Spain, forbade its people to have any interaction with their island brethren.

By the 1550s, the Portuguese had made their presence felt in seas near Japan, bringing to the islands' knowledge of a once-fabled antipodean world of strangely tinged, hairy people. Europe.

The Portuguese, and, to a lesser extent, the Spanish, had been making nuisances of themselves in the seas between Japan, China, Java, the Philippines, Malacca, and the Indian subcontinent, attempting, by means of extreme and ruthless violence, to wrest control of long-established maritime trade routes, build forts, enforce their alien beliefs upon people of other faiths, and engage in piracy and slaving.

So, in later decades, when English mariners came to Asia with letters stating that England was the enemy of the Portuguese and Spanish, the principle of "my enemy's enemy is my friend," came to the fore. Elizabethan trade and alliances would strengthen both sides against their mutual foe, and neither was overly bothered about religious differences as long as they hurt their mutual Catholic foes.

Japan was no exception, and the first English visitors were warmly welcomed. Their subterfuge, and drip-drip of anti-Catholic intelligence, would later be key in giving Japanese governments a reason to expel Roman Catholic missionaries, Iberian merchants, and mixed-heritage families.

One startling aspect of sixteenth-century geopolitics is that, despite the distance, Japan and England had much in common and were well suited for a mutually beneficial alliance.

Both were sizable island-based cultures not too far from a continental landmass.

Both continued to look up to the nearby "classical" cultures that emanated from their continents—the Italian Peninsula, and France, on one hand, and China and Tenjiku (modern-day northern India, the birthplace of Buddhism), on the other.

England's national feeling had been growing over the previous centuries as the English crown steadily lost all its mainland holdings. The monarchy therefore ceased focusing on the wealthier continental territories, forcing England to "become English," rather than simply a part of a larger multiethnic mini empire.

Japan had enjoyed unity at times in its history, but just as

often, north and south, east and west were engaged in internecine warfare. But by the time Cavendish set out on his voyage
in 1586 the great hegemon Toyotomi Hideyoshi had almost succeeded in imposing his rule on the whole country and Kyoto
was regaining its status as a grand national capital in fact, not
only in name. Japan also was feeling a new "national" wind.

Both Japan and England had been rejected economically by
the dominant powers on their nearby landmass due to piracy.
Their vernacular languages and cultures were also largely dis-
dained by continentals who, in both cases, saw the islanders as
peripheral, vulgar, barbaric, and dangerous, something which
both the Japanese and English obviously found offensive, and
further reason for anger and violence.

Finally, both relied on smuggling and piracy to access the
trade that powerful mainland players controlled and excluded
them from.

Whether the English of the time were aware of this or not,
John Dee's theorizing, even if it had failed in actually furnish-
ing an empire, had helped the English settle on a basic tactic
for growth.

From their mortal Spanish Catholic enemies, the Protestants
would steal. From their potential but unknown friend, Japan,
they would coax wealth in trade.

Christopher, one of the enslaved victims of rapacious pirates
and civil war, would live his life on the crest of this wave.

6

American Pioneer

By flickering lamplight, a party of twenty English sailors left *Desire* and rowed steadily toward *Santa Ana*. The peacock-like figure of their commander, Cavendish, sat bolt upright in the center of the skiff, the lonely silhouette of the Spanish captain slumped beside him. Christopher and Antonio crouched behind them in the bowels of the boat, the three of them released from captivity to guide the English.

Cavendish marched onto the ship as if it were his own, his scrutinizing, avaricious gaze taking it all in.

He headed straight for the captain's cabin, threw open the door, ducked his head slightly and entered. De Alzola and the interpreter trailed behind him. The other Englishmen remained on guard outside the cabin, swords drawn, and halibuts grounded.

The victor's bright blue eyes surveyed the narrow space. Solid wooden chests lay to the sides, and richly embroidered tapestries hung on the walls. In the far corner stood a portable Japanese desk, black lacquer varnished and wrought with mother of pearl and intricate gold inlay, a true work of art.

Cavendish bounced into de Alzola's great chair at the head of the table, reached his arms backward over his shoulders to cradle the back of his head, and set his feet up onto the table. A man at ease in his surroundings.

De Alzola, still standing while the pirate made himself at home in his cabin, murmured for Christopher and Antonio to wait on the enemy.

Cavendish held out his tankard and settled back with a slow, easy smile of victory.

"Señor, I desire to know how much this prize is worth."

De Alzola crossed to the ingeniously exquisite desk, opened the lid and took out the sewn-up pages of the ship's manifest from the main draw.

As he cast his eye down it, the Englishman could barely contain his glee. Occasionally he brought his head up to ask a question of the captain or check the meaning of a Spanish word with his interpreter. Christopher stood in attendance to his right, refilling his tankard time and again as it was absent-mindedly held out.

There were millions of pesos worth of goods recorded in the ledger. Gold, silks, damasks, musk, perfume, pearls, and a long list of minor treasures.

Such were the legendary riches that the English had dreamed of.

Cavendish let out a low whistle, mopped his brow, and took a large draft of wine to help him think further.

This was probably the biggest prize ever taken by an English privateer. A huge fortune, likely worth far more than his Queen's entire annual budget. All of it sitting here underneath him on this one ship.

The power and wealth of the Spanish were breathtaking. Awe-inspiring. Fearsome, if you thought about what the profits from this ship could do to England.

Cavendish could not do much about the rest of King Philip's treasury, but he could deny this portion to his enemies.

He sighed. There was too much to load on board the two English ships, most of it would have to be destroyed. But they would take the best of it. If they were lucky, they might manage a little over a tenth.

It was too dark and the sea too rough to carry out this delicate exercise right now, but Cavendish knew that the English sailors would not be able to contain themselves. He would need to sate their post-battle lust immediately or there would be trouble.

The chests, which doubled as benches around the walls of the cabin, were securely locked. He ordered de Alzola to give him the keys, and the captain, with a huge sigh, passed them to Christopher. This was his own personal wealth. He had mortgaged himself to the hilt to invest in this cargo which would have fetched many times what he had paid for it in Manila.

Christopher took the keys respectfully from the captain and handed them to Cavendish who shouted for the English sailors outside to enter and descry their loot. They rushed in, pushing and pulling at each other to be the first to set eyes upon their destiny.

With a flourish, Cavendish opened the chests one by one, running his hands through the golden contents, tossing gleaming coins around the cabin.

The English mariners grabbed for them, grubbing around the floor in a free-for-all. They shoved at each other, then kicked and hacked with a primeval rage and avarice at the unopened wooden chests. This was the desperation of men who had had little but suddenly stumbled upon many lifetimes of riches. They danced and cavorted in the golden showers like fairies in a sunlit glade.

It was chaos. Dangerously so. Cavendish had clearly lost control. No account could be taken of this; it was pure bedlam.

Santa Ana, now securely under English command, sailed to Cabo San Lucas on the very southern tip of California. It was a remote and secluded spot; no passing Spanish ship would waylay them there.

The following day Cavendish gathered all the galleon's people and declared that he would now collect any valuables that they might be carrying on their person. Should anyone dare to hide anything from him, their lives would be forfeit.

To emphasize his threat, a team of heavily armed men stood guard outside de Alzola's former cabin, and several awaited each supplicant within.

One by one *Santa Ana*'s passengers trooped in and made a declaration about what they owned, to be checked carefully against the manifest. Jewels, musk, perfumes, spices, and gold coins found their way out from pockets and traveling chests to be recorded in a ledger by the one-eyed interpreter before being stowed away carefully. These would for the most part not see the light of day again until landfall in England. Legally, privateers were supposed to leave their treasure trove intact until customs was cleared.

Relieving the passengers of their burdensome possessions took the whole day.

The next morning, most of *Santa Ana*'s one hundred ninety newly poverty-stricken passengers and crew were put ashore.

Christopher sat in the rear of the small craft as others strained at the oars. They glided past gigantic white rock outcrops, one formed like a colossal stone gateway, toward a large, wide sandy beach through waters as clear as a beautifully polished mirror. Below, multicolored fish darted through underwater rock cities and great kelp forests.

As he set his feet upon the golden beach of Cabo San Lucas, framed within parched-looking scrubland, Christopher became the first recorded Japanese and East Asian person on North American soil.

7

Interrogations

In the wide-open surroundings of Cabo San Lucas, the process of transferring the booty and any remaining provisions from the floundering Spanish galleon to the two smaller ships took nearly two weeks.

The English kept only the most valuable and portable of items. The rest of the plunder was consumed by fire or consigned to the sea's depths.

As a bonus the sailors were all issued lengths of fine thick damask for sleeping mats. Considering the crew ordinarily slept on the hard deck, this was a true luxury and one which the men would bless their commander for on the long voyage to come.

Cavendish himself took Captain de Alzola's beautifully lacquered Japanese desk. The gold within it alone would have set up a man for life, but the artwork was what made it truly stunning. It would make a fitting present for his Queen.

It wasn't long before fights broke out. *Content*'s men were convinced that they were being shortchanged. Cavendish regained control in thundering tones, ordering that the rule of law be upheld. He as captain would receive two-thirds from which he would pay other shareholders in England. The men would have the rest divided according to rank. As the law stipulated, it would be distributed on arrival in England after customs duties had been paid.

The rebellion quelled, Cavendish put his mind to other advantages that could be taken from the *Santa Ana*. It was not only with gold and jewels that she glittered. She was a floating mine of crucial intelligence.

Firstly, all letters and dispatches were appropriated.

One, taken from a passenger called Sebastián Vizcaíno, gave the Englishman what he thought was his first eyewitness glance at the country he had dreamed of for so long:

> It is the goodliest countrey, and the richest, and most plentifull in all the world. For here are great store of golde mynes, silver mynes, and pearle, great store of cotten cloth: for the countrey people weareth nothing else but fine cotten cloth, which is more accepted then silkes. For here is great store of silkes, & they are good cheape. All kinde of victuals, as bread, flesh, wines and hennes and all kindes of foules, are very plentifull. Here are great store of fresh rivers. The people are very loving. Here are very faire cities and townes with costly buildings, better then those in Spaine. And the countrey people go very richly apparelled both in silkes and gold.

Cavendish poured over the letter again with his interpreter. The tales of Japan were true after all, this man claimed to have seen it with his own eyes.

Then he interrogated the crew and passengers to find men to replenish his depleted roster, help navigate the unknown Pacific waters, and aid in future voyages.

Two Dutchmen and three African volunteers were welcomed. Then another African who had been in the Spice Islands and spoke the local language was recruited. His language skills would be invaluable in the coming months.

The chief Spanish pilot, who gave his name as Thomas de Ersola, had been speared in the action. The wound was festering, and he feared for his life if he were abandoned at Cabo San Lucas. The best chance of survival was in the Philippines with Cavendish, so he requested passage and begged the English captain to let him bring his Manilan servant, Francisco, to nurse him.

Cavendish had already planned to take the pilots anyway, and Francisco would also prove a language asset in his native islands, so he magnanimously granted this petition.

He also had word that a Portuguese navigator called Nicolás Rodríguez had sailed extensively in Chinese, Japanese, and Philippine waters, and even had a chart of the seas around China. It would be the first real map of East Asia seen by an Englishman if Cavendish could get his hands on it.

Reluctantly, Rodríguez presented himself to the Englishman, furled map in hand.

The chart, worth many times its weight in gold, was duly appropriated, and Rodríguez took his place on board *Desire*.

Eventually the English captain got to the enslaved, who were now technically liberated as English law did not recognize slavery.

In theory these men and women could now determine their own destiny. In practice of course, life is not so easy. Humans cannot eat freedom, and while Cavendish would take the most able of the formerly enslaved as sailors, the rest were left to revert swiftly to bondage.

Cavendish had his eyes on those who could be of use during the voyage or make the biggest splash in London. One by one he interrogated them, and chose three Filipinos: fifteen-year-old Alphonso; the Spanish captain's thirteen-year-old manservant, Antonio; and a handsome young lad of nine who had no language in common with anyone else, so everyone simply called him "Boy."

Among the enslaved people, he found a lad of Japan and, his

interest kindled by the letter of Vizcaíno's that he had read earlier, he knew he would have to take this one along.

The seventeen-year-old was called Cosmus, and he was just what Cavendish had been looking for. Good-looking, well comported, the trained valet of a high-ranking priest, even literate in his own language. This youth could be presented at court with no qualms, and London's scholars would be ecstatic.

Literacy, in the modern sense of the word, was not very common in England in this era. With the growth of Protestantism, the need to read the Bible oneself rather than trust spiritual matters to a Latin-reading priest had grown exponentially. However, few could actually write more than their own name, and reading and writing were actually regarded as separate skills, as opposed to how we integrate them today.

The same was true of literacy in Japan where only the upper classes or particularly gifted children were given the chance to study with a priest or other learned person. Fascinatingly, however, Japanese children learned to write first, reading (a far more difficult skill in Japanese) came later.

To a contemporary Englishman, the ability to write the complicated and highly mysterious characters used in Japanese would have only increased the mystique surrounding Cosmus.

Jesuit missionaries were notable for their belief in education, and in the areas of Japan where they propagated, community schools were opened to educate common children. Although it is impossible to say for sure where Cosmus learned his letters, it was probably in a mission school.

Lastly, Thomas Cavendish called in Christopher. The commander had more doubts about this man, Japanese or no. He was old for starters. Twenty.

What could this sailor do for him?

8

Trafficked

Although the story of Japanese slavery has been virtually forgotten, indentured and trafficked people in fact represented the majority of Japanese people outside Japan in Christopher's time.

While the vast majority of enslaved people stayed within the country, in the 1580s, around one thousand enslaved children each year were sold to Portuguese human traffickers and traded through European and Chinese trade networks to destinations as far away as Europe and the Americas, as well as everywhere in between.

They were the victims of slavers for various reasons. There were those who were sold to pay a family debt, those whose parents sold them to spare them from famine, hoping that the buyer would invest in their purchase and nourish them, and those kidnapped by bandits. However, the largest number were victims of the incessant warfare that plagued Japan, both captives and orphans.

The Jesuit missionaries, in Japan since 1549, were deeply complicit in this trade and issued licenses legalizing and regulating sale by certifying that the enslaved person had been taken in a "just war," against a non–Catholic enemy. Becoming Catholic through baptism saved the victim's soul for heaven, so enforced servitude was justified as a benign act. Furthermore, the missionaries' clerical fees, charged in addition to the enslaved person's price, funded more propagation, so for the Jesuits it was a win–win situation.

Enslaved people were key members of the communities where they lived; without their services and skills, society would have broken down. Many trafficked people were taught specialist skills, being employed as sailors, mercenaries, musicians, entertainers, and craftsmen. The majority of girls suffered sexual exploitation, some as specialist concubines or sex workers in brothels, and others simply as domestics who were assaulted as and when the master fancied. Those with the means could have numerous trafficked young females, and males, to use as they wished.

Although it sounds strange to the modern ear, enslaved people often had a degree of what we would see as freedom. They married, earned money, owned property (including their own chattels), and could purchase their own liberty. It was also customary to free enslaved people upon the death of their owner, but not all followed this unwritten rule.

On occasion, manumitted people became important merchants, politicians, soldiers, or professional guild members. However, the fate of the vast majority was far less exulted; many were simply worked until they dropped, at which point less scrupulous owners abandoned them to die on the streets.

The story of two enslaved Japanese people, uncovered by the researcher Lúcio de Sousa, provides a fitting end to this chapter.

In Lisbon on February 5, 1573, two manumitted Japanese people celebrated a felicitous occasion.

In the presence of two witnesses, Father Bastião Pereira and Carlos Neto, the bride Jacinta de Sá married her fellow national Guilherme Brandão. Nothing more is known of these two early Japanese residents of Europe. Neither their Japanese names, nor their fate.

A few years later in 1580, the plague made one of its regular visits to the area of Lisbon where they lived. The most likely conclusion to their story is that they, and any children, perished and were buried in unmarked communal graves.

Far from home, they simply lived and died in the shadows.

Japanese slavery was outlawed in 1587 by the same Japanese hegemon Toyotomi Hideyoshi who welcomed home the Tensho legates. But it simply metamorphosed into a system of indentured servitude.

In practice, once an indentured worker had been trafficked from Japan, there was little that the Japanese authorities could do to repatriate them. Many suffered the same fate as their formally enslaved brethren had prior to 1587.

The traffic of Japanese people overseas would not fully stop until all Japanese citizens were forbidden from foreign travel in the mid-1630s. The ban was not exclusively meant to counter human trafficking, but that was one of the motivations. It was a drastic measure, but an effective one.

9

Collateral Damage

Cavendish bore in mind the crucial advice he had been given by Richard Hakluyt, the geographer, intelligencer, priest, and prolific chronicler of English navigations, before departure, "every nation is to be considered advisedly and used with prudent circumspection with all gentleness and courtesy." He also thought on the further advice to make a person "drunk with your beer, or wine, so you shall know the secrets of his heart."

The confiscated Spanish wine flowed plentifully that day.

Christopher stood in the Great Cabin, the English commander sitting only feet from him at the head of the table that filled most of the narrow space. Cavendish was inebriated and getting more so.

In broken Spanish he asked the Japanese man to tell him everything about himself. Cavendish nodded at the initial answers and occasionally gestured to the ever-present interpreter beside him for fuller explanations.

Christopher had no idea what this man wanted to hear, but the obvious place to start seemed to be at the beginning. The wine was strong and had a speedy effect on the looseness of his tongue.

He told his story.

For more than a century, Japan had been at brutal, bitter, internecine war from the icy capes of northern Mutsu to the balmy coasts facing China. Generations had grown up knowing nothing but conflict and chaos. Christopher was no exception and it had defined the course of his life.

Christopher could not remember his parents.

His first memories were of the sea. He worked on a ship, running any errand in exchange for just enough food to survive. He slept on deck or curled up in the corners of huts on islands where the ship berthed.

He did not run. He had nowhere to go, and besides, all the others on board led a hard life, not so different from his. They were all the family he had.

Christopher's pirate crew haunted the coasts and seaways of the seas to the west of Japan and south of China. He became a hardened seaman and fighter. He was a pirate because that is what he was. It was no conscious decision. He simply was.

The ship's Chinese pilot and custodian of Mazu's flame, the *huǒ cháng* (fire keeper), a wizened old mariner, saw promise in the orphan lad. He taught Christopher the art of writing characters, the ocean's ways, and, most importantly, instructed him how to tend the goddess's flame. It was a near mystical art involving invocation of the divine and magic, for the spirits and deities of the sea decided the fate of the men who lived their lives on water. They needed to be treated with the utmost respect and awe.

Christopher's last pirate voyage was at fourteen.

The ship pulled out of the choppy but well-protected Fukabori harbor at the mouth of Nagasaki Bay where Christopher's band of sea rovers had made camp for the cold months. Pink-tinged clouds floated above them, and the water sparkled in the late spring sun. They were bound for Luzon, where they would trade with visiting Chinese merchants and the island peoples.

Heavy Japanese silver, in exchange for feather-like Chinese silk, the greatly prized local ceramics, and saltpeter to make gunpowder.

They were headed to Cagayan, a thriving settlement where more and more pirates and smugglers from across the region were congregating. There were rumors that it was being developed as a safe port by one of the most powerful pirates, Lord Tei, and he planned to found a new realm conveniently placed at the crux of all the trade routes.

Their Nagasaki Bay camp faded into the distance behind them, only to be replaced by other islands and promontories, big and small, which after several weeks sailing eventually led to the large mountainous island of Takasago, and thence to Luzon. All through the voyage, the old pilot kept up his lessons with Christopher, pointing out landmarks, shoals, birds, distinctive weather patterns, the differing taste of salt on the air, and use of the compass.

As in all ships, Mazu's flame in the pilot's cabin was never allowed to fade. To have let it die would have been to lose her heavenly protection.

Arriving in Cagayan, they lodged in the rapidly growing settlement and settled down to handle their business, planning to return to Japan with the autumn winds.

The sound of the morning chorus accompanied the sun as it slowly rose above the low hills on the other side of the Cagayan River, its piercing fiery light reflecting long in the strong fast-flowing waters, in which Christopher's small boat lay tugging at its stone-weighed anchor.

A light breeze wafting from the direction of the sea kept things cool enough this morning, but later it would be blisteringly hot and sweaty.

The river teemed with flashing, plump quarry, and his mouth watered in time to the grumbling of his stomach.

Far up the muddy riverbanks, on the slopes emerging and rising gently from the river, stood Lord Tei's palisaded town of stilted bamboo houses thatched with cogon grass and surrounded front and back by large verandas. Women could even now be seen chatting, fetching water, sweeping, setting fires, and setting out food for the morning meal. Bananas, rice, yams, and soft *oropisa* potatoes. They lived a bountiful life here and food was always plentiful.

Chickens pecked and pigs rooted within the bamboo fence, there as much to keep the animals in as to keep anyone out, but also useful against river attack from the warlike local Ibanag people if needed.

There were several lookout towers, and a drum alert would be sounded in event of need, but in truth the pirates believed themselves safe here, far from the Chinese warships that hunted them in waters further north.

Beached in the mud of low tide along the river were twenty medium-sized vessels. These were shallow-hulled coastal crafts, powered by oars and a battened woven bamboo sail, for trading with settlements around the islands. They also made excellent river attack craft to harry hostile local warriors upriver. A squadron of men, armed with swords, spears, grappling hooks, bows, throwing bombs, and harquebuses, could be deployed speedily, bloodily, and mercilessly.

Recently, there had been rumors that the Southern Barbarians who had made a colony to the south in Manila were planning an attack, but Christopher wasn't worried; although men said they were formidable warriors, Lord Tei's men were surely more powerful.

Fish were landed in quick succession, and dropped, still thrashing, into a bamboo leaf basket. As Christopher slipped through the shallows to glide his skiff back to shore, a black butterfly brushed his face making him recoil in involuntary reflex.

Black butterflies were harbingers of death.

Trying to forget the omen, Christopher pulled the fishing skiff up the muddy bank and headed to the settlement for breakfast.

Gazing on as he climbed was the lord's Number One Cagayan Wife with her ladies, bodyguards, and palanquin carriers.

Having a wife here showed the world that Lord Tei was settled and in charge even if he only visited a few times each year. In the lord's absence his wife's word was law, and the four African bodyguards who accompanied her everywhere enforced it unquestioningly.

Mistress Tei was dressed gloriously, befitting her status as queen of a multicultural pirate fief. She wore flowing robes of smooth, stunningly embroidered Chinese silk. Her long, untrammeled hair shone like polished black jade, and her elegant nails, normally encased in ornate guards, were painted red and black.

She was carried everywhere in a lacquered palanquin inlaid with golden dragons, which looked very out of place here on the scruffy riverside so far from the centers of civilization that inspired her attire.

When she smiled, the sun was reflected in her black-lacquered teeth.

Christopher adored her.

The young man performed a kneeling bow as her entourage passed him by, his eyes down until the palanquin had passed. Then he raised his head, and gazed after her; luckily no one looked back, they were engaged in some joke or other, and a shriek of infectious laughter rang out.

Mistress Tei's loud peals were abruptly cut short by the deep sonorous booming of a lookout drum shattering the peace of the morning.

Christopher looked round to see the prow of a huge Southern Barbarian galley, her mast stowed, speedily rowing round the bend to bear down upon the riverside pirates.

Following the galley around the bend came five local *karakoa* warships, their sails also stowed, the outriggers manned by Indigenous oarsmen wielding their paddles at a fierce rate.

Karakoa were warships used by Indigenous Filipino peoples. They included fighting platforms for warriors and were armed with lantaka guns. Bartolomé Leonardo de Argensola, 1711.

Then, suddenly, the galley oars reversed to expertly reduce the vessel's momentum. It glided to a gentle halt, and following a pause of a few seconds, fired its front-mounted swivel guns.

The settlement had suddenly come to life around Christopher. Leaders barked orders in several languages as hundreds of armed men appeared from their sleeping mats. They leaped and bounded down to the boats, slipping and sliding through the mud in their haste to push off to counter the attack.

In the surprise of the moment, few pirates had more than their swords to hand, even fewer were dressed for battle, the majority wore only the loincloths they had woken in.

The enemy vessels were all within range now, and it was not only the four galley-mounted swivel guns, but also the double-barreled local *lantaka* guns on the five *karakoa*, which spat lead at the pirates tumbling down the riverbanks.

The nearly seventy-year-old Spanish commander, Juan Pablo

de Carrión, King Philip's Admiral of the South Seas and the Sea of China, had planned the ambush well.

On land, he would have had to send in his handful of troops for hand-to-hand combat, something which would have resulted in severe losses against superior numbers and concerted gunfire. On the river, he could pick off the surprised, unprepared, and lightly armed enemy with relative ease.

Once clear of the shore, the boats made some headway, bearing down upon the large galley and smaller *karakoa*. If they reached his vessel, the battle would surely be theirs; few men could stand up to a ferocious pirate boarding.

The pirates kept their heads as low as possible, but their rowing became ragged and out of time as oarsmen fell, the dropped oars hindering the others and slowing the boats' progress.

It was not long before Mistress Tei removed a white silk kerchief from her voluminous sleeve and waved it in the air above her palanquin.

Simultaneously, the largest of her African guards bellowed the order to halt. His deep sonorous tones carried across the river, ringing even above the sound of the slowing guns. The enemy hoisted a white flag in reply, and the firing ceased.

Wounded pirates struggled up the mud banks to the settlement. Others lay where they had fallen.

It was still smoky, and the filthy tang of gunpowder—rotten eggs, urine, and devil's brimstone—hung heavy in the air.

The galley and the *karakoa* stayed where they were, cutting off any escape to the open sea, but a number of skiffs put out from the enemy ships and landed a short way downriver; two others approached the pirate settlement.

Mistress Tei waited while they approached. Some of the pirates grouped around her, and others moved back surreptitiously toward the fortifications. They would be arming themselves properly this time.

Christopher abandoned his fish basket and took his place in the group around Mistress Tei.

What a foe!

Despite the heat, the enemy were clad in shiny steel from head to knee, straight swords hung from their belts, and they wielded long-bladed pole-weapons, something akin to a *naginata*.

But the strangest things were the faces which poked out from under the shiny peaked helmets.

Above beards of red, orange, black, and yellow, stuck noses like birds' beaks. Above that lay deep-set round eyes under bushy eyebrows. Any exposed parts of their faces were either a pale sickly color, as if they were about to vomit, or ruby red as if about to burst into a rage. To Christopher, they looked fearsome, wild. Demon-like in fact.

From one of the boats which had approached Mistress Tei's position, a man in ornate, black-lacquered armor called through an interpreter for the pirates to surrender.

Mistress Tei refused and told him her husband would soon be arriving to deal with them.

The Spanish leader laughed out loud and informed her that he had sunk Lord Tei's ships and killed him, his son, and their followers at the place known as Bojeador.

Mistress Tei did not flinch; instead she attempted a bargain. Gold for a quick and bloodless exit.

Flicking his well-kempt salt-and-pepper hair, the enemy refused outright. It was surrender unconditionally or be destroyed. His orders were clear. He must deal with this existential threat to Manila.

Mistress Tei stretched her elegant, pale swan-like neck one way and then the other; she raised her fan languidly to cool herself.

A shot pierced the air. The fan had been a signal to attack.

From the fortress, the phut, phut of harquebus fire rang out, and telltale lazy puffs of smoke appeared above the palisade. Two men in the enemy skiff fell, and one of them bounced onto the outstretched oars; the body rose with the sweeps as the oarsmen bent their backs to get quickly away, flitting between the oars like a coin in a trickster's fingers before splashing into the swift waters below.

But the *wako* had not been the only ones preparing for the next round.

The Spanish had roughly fortified a position downriver around tripod-mounted swivel guns which now targeted the fort where the remaining pirates had taken refuge. The Japanese guns had a shorter range than the larger tripod guns, so unless they charged the position, the Spanish could bombard the fort with near impunity.

Christopher and his comrades could not stay behind their palisade forever.

There was no realistic escape; the river was cut off, so were the land routes toward the sea. The rear was thickly forested, and the pirates were sea people; they could not navigate the tropical hinterland.

Mistress Tei slipped a nail cover on and off the first finger of her right hand, betraying her nerves. Then, decided, she raised a black talon to her mouth and drew a line around her rouged lip. She brought it down slowly and made a slitting gesture across her throat. In an almost petulant voice, which was all the more terrifying for its girl-like pitch, she stood and screamed a fearsome war cry.

Christopher and hundreds of pirates leaped over the palisade armed with swords, knives, and spears, to charge pell-mell in a ferocious head-on attack downhill toward the enemy guns. Handguns were of little use in a running attack, so they left them.

Above and around the enemy guns stood a small group of several dozen pikemen, their grounded and regularly placed weapons facing upward and glistening with oil to prevent the attackers getting a grip.

The vessels in the river continued to target the charging warriors from the side. Scores fell, but momentum and weight of numbers kept the survivors running. As the slope meandered downward, Christopher and his comrades came ever closer to the Spanish line.

When they were nearly upon the enemy, the Spanish soldiers moved forward as one to present a well-ordered hedgehog of sharp, deadly, pointed steel. The men at the front knelt with the butts of their weapons firmly lodged in the earth. The second rank presented their pikes straight, in the charge position.

As the pirates approached this unfamiliar defensive formation, many jumped, landing on the shafts and forcing them down, dispatching the defenders with swords. Others ran straight onto the long blades, forcing them aside with their own bodies so that their comrades could pass through unhindered. Still more timed it just so that they could grab the thrusting points, only to find the oiled shafts pulled back by the pikemen and swiftly thrust forward again, to deadly effect.

The initial ferocity of the attack began to flounder as those at the rear crammed forward, pushing and crushing those at the front against the impaling pikes. Their limp bodies formed a wall of protection for the pikemen and the crush of pirates behind were rendered even easier targets for the boat-mounted guns.

The Spanish line wavered but held.

Christopher knew the day was nearly lost.

Those at the back started edging away from the maelstrom. Then the rearward movement turned into a flood as the survivors ran from the murderous, stabbing pikes. A small mountain of bodies lay like sandbags before the Spanish line.

Mistress Tei stood with her Africans at the palisade. Observing the carnage.

She had dressed gloriously for battle. Her dark hair rustled under a helmet of deep carmine lacquer above steel-scaled Chinese body armor. Two tasseled swords hung at her belt.

The fleeing warriors took one look at her icy stare and turned to charge back once more toward the place where their comrades had met their end.

The Spanish had lost many men, and their line was shorter now, but interspersed among them were the gunners, all firing at will. The attack regained its forward thrust as Mistress Tei, screaming a spine-tingling howl of rage, joined her pirates.

The ship-borne bombardment was unceasing and to deadly effect. As the riverside flank was decimated, the survivors veered landward, and the battle became a massacre.

Some pirates fled, some collapsed to the floor. Mistress Tei remained statue-like, waiting for the Spanish approach.

Christopher's spear had broken long ago and the sword he had picked up, a cheap and poorly forged *dao*, had snapped at the hilt. Two large Spanish soldiers with grim scowls approached him. One punched him in the face.

He passed out briefly but came to in the churned-up battlefield to find three soldiers, laughing and jesting as they used his body for kicking practice. Despite not understanding a word they said, he felt their jibes, knew he was nothing to them. He ceased moving to the pattern of their blows, letting his body go.

Eventually the troopers tired of the tormenting and trussed him up like a slaughtered chicken.

Mistress Tei now stood alone in the middle of the battlefield, still looking glorious, but with her queendom shrunk to no more than the ground she stood upon. The African bodyguards lay dead at her feet.

Carrión removed his helmet to reveal ruffled hair, lank with sweat. He smiled a leering, victorious grin.

Two men grasped the former queen by the arms as he turned his back on her.

It was a quiet end to a brutal fight, but as Carrión walked

away, the first of her captors stripped Mistress Tei of the final dregs of dignity that remained to her.

By the time they had finished, she was broken and sobbing. Her fine burnished armor was cleaved from her body, her exquisite nails were broken stubs, and her long hair was a bloody, matted mess. All that remained of her finery was a few shards of silk hanging dankly from the still-intact embroidered collar around her neck.

Christopher never saw her again.

The Cagayan base probably had a population of around one thousand and at least two-dozen ships were based there, more during trading seasons. It would soon have come to rival Manila, only recently and precariously established as capital of the new Spanish colony.

In size and power, it was one of many Japanese or Chinese pirate settlements to compete with the Europeans as foreign oppressors of these alluring lands.

Cagayan, as with other similar settlements, had to go, and Manila had put everything into the fight. They had won.

10

Manila

Weeks later in Manila, Christopher stood in the bright interior of a wooden church thatched with dried golden *nypa* palm leaves, awaiting baptism. Once he experienced the holy rite, the portly merchant who had purchased him could have his enslaved status legalized by the Canon of Manila, Juan de Almentares.

Christopher could not understand a word of what was said, but he stood still as de Almentares, giving off a caustically pungent smell of stale sweat and vinegary wine, splashed him with water, and watched as Father de Almentares flourished his quill and carefully sanded the paper before presenting the document to the merchant with a flourish.

Christopher recalled that he had heard that the Southern Barbarians were happy to sprinkle water on people only once in their lives. Normally, they never washed, hence their stench.

What strange behavior.

He would not say his seafaring comrades had smelled of roses, but certainly no dignified person should allow themselves to be as malodorous as this priest.

In a corner of the church the priest's servant knelt, praying. He gave the newcomer a sideward glance and flashed a smile before returning to his devotions. Christopher judged by his looks that he was also probably Japanese, however, his movements seemed more like those of the Spanish. He had clearly been among them a long time.

The merchant handed the priest a small purse, then they walked through the shady courtyard, past the palisade gates, and into the dusty streets of Manila.

The new master was a Spanish merchant from Andalucía who had come to the furthest end of the empire to make his fortune. His house, like all the others in the young city, was on stilts to protect against flooding, made of, bamboo, timber, and grasses in the Indigenous *bahay kubo* style, cool and breezy in the heat, but waterproof enough to endure the rainy season.

The merchant decided to make use of Christopher's maritime skills, and transferred him to a storehouse in Manila's port, Cavite. He ferried the master when required and interpreted for him with Chinese and Japanese counterparts.

The trade goods were varied, and the newly enslaved young man learned more of the business each day, discovering grades of silks, qualities of spices, perfumes, and beeswax, and the deep but mysterious beauty of Chinese porcelain.

His situation was probably not as bad as might be imagined. Following the Iberian custom of wage-earning slavery, Christopher was likely paid around half a peso a day and he would have had plenty of company. Sailors from all corners of the earth who sometimes had little to do for months on end while they were waiting for winds to change or orders to arrive, were only too happy to pass the time in chitchat while drinking copious amounts of potent palm wine.

A year later, the settlement burned. Governor Gonzalo Ronquillo de Peñalosa had died and a candle that attended his funeral bier in the very church where Christopher had been baptized and "legalized," tumbled during the night, cremating the former governor and his city with it. Hundreds of sleeping inhabitants perished in what some saw as a sacrifice to his soul.

Christopher, absent in Cavite, had returned with the other men, and worked for days to extinguish the fires.

The new governor, Santiago de Vera, decided it was time to build a Spanish-style city, forged from stone with grand churches and solid protective walls. It was to send a message that Manila had come of age, was in solid command of the islands, and had proved its right to be permanent.

Suitable rock was found nearby, in Guadalupe on the Pasig River, and enslaved Indigenous people were put to work quarrying it. Christopher, on his master's orders, became one of the watermen ferrying materials up the river.

The call for more labor went out to all the Spanish and Portuguese settlements in East Asia, to Nagasaki, Macao, Malacca, and the Spice Isles. They had little manpower to spare for their up-and-coming rival, however, and the work progressed at a snail's pace.

Christopher continued his work on the quarry boats for another two years.

The merchant, though, had made his fortune and was winding down his business. By early 1586, he had sold off his local property, including a new town house, and announced in the spring that he would be returning to Andalucía. Christopher was to accompany him.

When *Santa Ana*, the looming six-hundred-tun galleon, arrived at Cavite direct from the shipyards of Realejo in the colony of Guatemala (modern-day Nicaragua), she dwarfed the Chinese and Japanese vessels transshipping goods bound for America, Africa, and Europe. They and their accompanying sampans looked like feeder fish shoaling around the great hulk of a shark dominating the narrow harbor's horizon.

The galleon eventually contained perhaps one of the biggest

concentrations of floating wealth under heaven, all the exotic riches, scents, and flavors of the Indies to be carried across the Pacific Ocean to other eagerly waiting worlds.

One other ship did match her for size. *Santa Ana*'s sister ship, *Nuestra Senora de Esperanza*, was to be sent on a special mission to chart the western American coast and hopefully find landfall midway between Manila and New Spain. As yet there was nowhere to rest and resupply on the voyage, a fact that made the crossing extradangerous, uncomfortable, and uncertain.

Upon arrival in Acapulco, the passengers and cargo would disperse around the colonies, or move on to Mexico City, and thence to the Caribbean. Eventually, up to two years later, after another long ocean voyage, they would reach Seville in southern Spain, the only Spanish port permitted to handle trade with the "Indies."

This dangerous odyssey across the Pacific and onward was not for the fainthearted. The travelers would be at the mercy of tempests, and prey to the diseases which incessantly stalked those on board the unhygienic and cramped vessel. Many of the circa three hundred voyagers, Spaniard, Portuguese, Chinese, Filipino, Japanese, and African alike, would never set foot on land again.

On July 2, 1587, a team of chanting mariners slowly twisted the capstan to haul up a protesting seaweed-laden hemp rope. The anchor's fluke stuck fast on the seabed causing an anxious moment as *Santa Ana* veered downward, but suddenly she bounced back as it gave way, knocking half the sailors off their feet. To laughter and curses, the crew resumed their work, inching the great metal fixture up from the seabed below.

With the anchor secured, a score of tugboats made fast their ropes, and the oarsmen set to their sweeps. The great galleon was set in motion, and presently, when the pilots judged it prudent, the tugboats were dismissed, and the stiff sails unfurled.

As cables tightened to meet the wind, the sheets gently filled with power. Long inertia gave way to sprightliness, and *Santa*

Ana moved through Manila's vast bay, distant tropical peaks attending each flank.

By the time they had cleared the islands guarding the approaches to the open sea, a red-haloed ball-of-fire sun was sinking into its watery grave. The great galleon passed in its golden wake and out into the infinite ocean.

Santa Ana tacked southeast through the archipelago past verdant forest-clad mountainous islands rising straight up from bright blue waters. After clearing the southern tip of Luzon, she veered eastward into the open Pacific, and took a course to catch the warm marine currents which would bear her northeast in a great arc, and then south down the landmass on the far side of the great ocean.

A few weeks later, from far out to sea, Christopher caught a glimpse of the majestic peak of Mount Fuji swathed in a halo of snow-white summer clouds, glimmering like polished diamonds. His heart erupted with emotion but calmed as the mountaintop seemed to turn a deep, vivid vermillion. A trick of the light, or perhaps Mazu, the Heavenly Mother's love radiating protection and benevolence.

Father Juan de Almentares's servant, Cosmus, came to stand beside him shyly. Both knew their Pacific voyage meant that they would never see the land of their birth again. Few returned from this passage.

11

Cosmus

Cosmus was a quiet lad, and his story, told one star-lit Pacific night aboard *Santa Ana*, was no less heartrending than Christopher's own.

He too was an orphan. He did not know what had happened to his parents; no one had thought to tell him.

At some point he had been taken in by the Jesuit lay brothers of a mission in Bungo domain, good and kind men who had fed and treated him well. As a child he had spent his days working in the church, a converted Buddhist temple of dark polished wood and tatty old *tatami*, under the loving gaze of Mother Mary.

He and his fellow orphans had also been taught their letters, and how to praise the One True God.

Then one day, the mission was no more.

Men came. Hard, rough, swaggering samurai on some campaign or other. They wore a hodgepodge of loose hempen clothing, bore two swords thrust through the sashes at their waists, and their faces were mostly hidden in the shadow of hard, lacquered helmets. They marched under banners bearing a white cross within a black circle, plundering and raping as they went.

The Jesuits had fled into the forest.

Any children who had not run with them were roped together with rough rice-straw cord and frog-marched to a nearby battle camp. There, a merchant so fat he had to be carried in a palanquin inspected the human wares, and instructed his underlings to poke and prod them in any place he saw fit. He took many, but any he rejected were swiftly removed. Cosmus was sure they did not survive, the fast-moving samurai army had no need for children following in its wake, they would be on a new battlefield, destroying another village tomorrow. Any child that did not fetch a price was an unlooked-for burden.

The survivors struggled through the mountains in silence, following the sun westward, sleeping on the ground, empty stomachs wailing for food.

The merchant's thugs did not hesitate to beat captives on the slightest pretext. Some of the smaller ones weakened and simply collapsed on the muddy road. Their bodies were left for the wild animals.

Cosmus staggered on to the sea. He had never seen such a vast extent of water before, nor been on a boat, but there was little time to wonder at it. He and his comrades were shoved roughly aboard, and the oarsman at the stern paddled them across a wide channel toward a towering dark green cloud-encircled volcano on the other side of the wide bay.

Upon reaching the beaches and low rocky cliffs of the far coast, the sampan hugged the land, moving south to a port called Kuchinotsu. There they found a sheltered bay dominated by a gigantic black ship, protruding island-like from the waters of the bay.

The men who sailed her, black and pink-skinned, and clothed outlandishly, were even more fearsome than the brusque samurai who had ripped Cosmus from his home. Their words sounded like barks, howls, and hisses. When they laughed, their whole bodies quaked in huge convulsing movements.

Cosmus wet himself.

The sampan disgorged the children onto golden sand to await their fate. After a few hours in the hot sun, a bamboo bucket of water was passed around and Cosmus sated his thirst with a ladle of tepid liquid.

At dusk, further up the beach, groups of sailors gathered, squatting, chatting, and drinking while small skewered fish roasted over open fires. The revelers glanced around and pointed as the day culminated with Cosmus and his rag-clad brethren being boated out to the fearsome dark ship.

A giant with black ink-colored skin watched the sorry scene with pitying eyes. This foreigner, despite the long knife he carried at his side, seemed like an island of calm in the tempest. Cosmus felt a desperate trust break through the fear, Mother Mary had sent this man to help in his hour of need.

He had nothing to lose.

Cosmus broke away from the shuffling group, tried to tell the Black man with the sad eyes that there was some mistake. But one of the slavers swiftly caught up with him. Cosmus's blood speckled the golden beach as his emaciated body fell, sprawling headlong into the sand.

As he looked back from the wooden craft where he had been thrown, he saw the giant bow his head and turn away. It may have been a trick of the firelight, but Cosmus could have sworn he saw a hot tear descend to the sand.

By candlelight, the boys and girls were separated and shackled to brackets on the wall with heavy chains. There was a bucket for waste. Nothing else.

More and more children joined them over the next weeks and months until there was no room to lie down and all they could do was squat, leaning against each other's small, frail bodies for support. One morning after a few snatched hours of sleep, Cosmus awoke to find the boy he had been leaning against dead. The body was not thrown overboard until feeding time that evening.

As the bucket filled, its contents slopped over the sides. Cosmus was lucky that he had been chained near the door and not near the bucket, those nearest to it were covered in a filth that dried quickly to a crust in the heat. Flies buzzed and swarmed.

Then the time came to set sail, and Cosmus, near the door, was unshackled to empty the overflowing slop bucket. The boy hobbled around uncertainly on weakened legs, wasted muscles straining to the maximum. Up the ladder he staggered, and onto the main deck to tip the putrefying slush over the side into the shallow light blue sea.

Cosmus's eyes gazed on the world outside his cell for the first time in months.

A shadowy haze hovered over the gentle slopes that rose above the town in the horseshoe-shaped bay; he gulped at the sweet, humid air, and reveled in the soft sea breeze caressing his face. His ears filled with the sound of chirping cicadas and the buzz of dragonflies. Every so often birds of prey swept by, their vast wings snapping in the still air. Then a fish jumped and the sudden splash as it flopped back into the water brought Cosmus back.

This moment of peaceful bliss did not last long. A slaver, club in hand, came up and beat him back belowdecks, topped off with a kick through the cell door.

He fetched a pretty price in the market where Manila sold human beings. Japanese, Christian, literate, presentable, well behaved. All fashionable and useful traits in an enslaved valet.

His new master was Don Juan de Armendariz, canon of Manila, who, since his cathedral had been razed in the fire, resided next to the partly repaired San Agustin Church.

Cosmus settled down to life as a servant to the far from saintly canon. A man who angered easily, lusted constantly, and craved money and power.

12

The Japanese "Gentleman" Privateer

Cavendish slouched in his chair spellbound by Christopher's story. He smiled a lopsided grin, ruffled his blond curls, and nodded to the one-eyed interpreter next to him to write everything down. He was deep in his cups right now and needed to have it all to hand in the morning.

The Japanese youth described the city of Manila, unwalled as yet, but boasting many guns mounted securely in strong blockhouses to defend against *wako* pirate attacks. It had nearly been overwhelmed several times but had always survived by the skin of its teeth. He also told of the two speedy war galleys mounted with large swivel guns.

Christopher then spoke of Manila's wealth. The plentiful gold mined by local people in the mountains to the north, and of the dozens of Chinese trading ships exchanging gold for New Spain's silver—weight for weight—to the great advantage of the Manilans who made vast profits.

He recounted what he had noticed of the increasing number of Japanese ships and the hundreds of Japanese residents. They also brought silver, and sometimes the wheat essential for ship biscuit, for it was not commonly grown locally.

Cavendish, slurring severely, dismissed Christopher with a flick of his hand, insisting that he take his place as a "gentleman" sleeping on the armory floor, not with the common sailors on the gun deck. He was also issued with a damask sleeping pallet stuffed with springy flock wool.

Christopher the Japanese *wako* pirate was reborn as an English gentleman privateer.

Christopher's advancement to nobility had been swift and unheralded.

We know of this fantastic promotion because Cavendish wrote in a letter that was published throughout Europe, of the "gentlemen that he had brought with him from the Indies of their own free will." Giovanni Mocenigo, the Venetian ambassador to Paris, penned an additional detail in a report to Doge Pasquale Cicogna and the senate of Venice, that they came "through a desire to meet the Queen."

Along with a new status came a fabricated birthplace. Christopher is recorded as being born in the imperial capital, Miyako (modern-day Kyoto), but few people who were trafficked overseas came from there, and it is far more probable that he came from one of the coastal towns of the south. The English courtiers who needed to be impressed would never have heard of a fishing village and Miyako would have sounded far more convincing a city for a nobleman's birth.

Today, we think of a gentleman as being a courteous and considerate man. The type of refined well-mannered person who holds open a door for a lady and engages in intelligent, inoffensive conversation.

In 1588, it meant something very different to the Europeans who heard news of Christopher.

"Gentleman," derived from the French word *gentilhomme*, and to be one was to belong to the ruling class.

It encompassed both a hereditary standing in its own right and was also the default status for higher ranking lords' younger sons. The ones who did not inherit the family title.

The term was in use in England by the mid-fifteenth century to describe the lowest rank of aristocrat, the gentry. Above it were the ranks of squire, knight, and then the most elevated such as baron, earl, marquess, and duke. Gentlemen possessed a coat of arms and, even in Christopher's time, had the right to carry a sword in public, reflecting the military origins of the caste.

A gentleman normally made a good living, likely dwelt in a large, glass-windowed house, dressed in sumptuous clothes, ate meat at every religiously permitted meal, consumed imported luxuries, employed several servants, and held public office.

The gentry rose to prominence in part due to the need to boost the standing of longer established and more senior patricians.

The highest-ranking nobles, earls, dukes, or even kings, did not employ mere commoners in their service. They needed suitably elevated retainers to meet their needs, the higher in rank the attendant, the higher the status of the employer. Therefore, for example, the person who attended the monarch at toilet and disposed of the resulting effluent, the Groom of the Stool, was a noble. Sir William Compton served Henry VIII in this role for seventeen years, and given the king's legendary dietary excesses, it must have been an unpleasant, if honorable, form of employment.

Cavendish who was himself a squire, would have claimed that his Asian guests were nobles of patrician lineages in their own countries so as to enhance his own standing and prestige.

Initially, the numbers of the English gentry were small, but they expanded considerably in the sixteenth century as "men of good name and fame" were admitted through success in commerce and increasingly in the sixteenth century through the practice of law. Of course, the status also became more attractive to aspirants (particularly those of non-martial backgrounds) as the actual need to fight in battle decreased. It was, as Sir John Wynne (who claimed descent from Welsh princes) would have it, "a great temporal blessing [for] a man to find that he is well descended."

In 1530, when there were around four hundred gentlemen nationally, the minimum qualification was £10 in land and possessions (a considerable amount of money in those times). By Christopher's time, two thousand or more new gentlemen had been appointed.

As a consequence of this vast expansion in the nobility, exclusivity was diluted, spurring those that could afford it, especially new men, to fake their ancestry and further ameliorate their pedigree. Questionable experts in heraldry could make a good living "researching" ancestors at the behest of eager gentlemanly customers.

One family, the Wellesbornes, went so far as to install a fake crusader tomb in their local church in Hughenden Buckinghamshire. They managed to top even that deed when they desecrated a genuine grave by adding a version of their coat of arms to claim a lineage to which they had no right whatsoever.

This behavior was not limited to new nobles. Elizabeth's most trusted advisor, William Cecil Baron Burghley, who was born the son of a minor knight, managed to "uncover" an ancestor who had fought on the Saxon king Harold II's side in the Battle of Hastings of 1066, thereby suggesting that his pedigree went beyond the Norman Conquest of England into the mists of ancient history.

In some ways, Christopher's fabricated status was nothing surprising in this age; Cavendish was simply doing what everybody else did. He knew if Christopher and his friends were not seen to be patrician, they would be held in little note upon arrival in England. Blue blood was everything in the sixteenth-century world.

It was not only Japanese people whose rank counted even on the other side of the world. Prior to Christopher and his colleagues' time, in 1531, a Brazilian chieftain had made the journey to England on board a ship sailed by William Hawkins. While he was gawped at for his exotic attire, bone-pierced cheeks, and foreign ways, he was honored and received at King Henry VIII's court in a manner befitting his status.

The pattern continued after Christopher's era, as well. For example, in 1616, the Native American princess, Pocahontas, known in England as Rebecca, Lady Rolfe, due to her marriage to John Rolfe, visited London and was feted by royalty and high society alike. As a contemporary wrote, Lady Rolfe "carried her selfe as the Daughter of a King, and was accordingly respected."

Once again, blue blood and social rank were the prime factors, and although Pocahontas was clearly of interest for the fact that she was a representative of a very foreign people, rank and class trumped race or ethnicity.

PUBLIC DOMAIN

Pocahontas, also known as Rebecca and, later, Lady Rolfe, while she was in England. Simon van de Passe, 1616.

As Christopher himself probably understood it, he was now of a class similar to *bushi*, or samurai, in Japan, a warrior of noble birth, with the right to bear arms and a duty to serve his liege lord in battle, or in any other way demanded.

COURTESY OF THE RIJKSMUSEUM, AMSTERDAM.

Japanese youths dressed in clothing of the type that well-to-do—i.e., gentlemen— Portuguese men wore. Detail from a Japanese folding screen. Kano School, ca 1590.

The new "samurai" may well have grinned to himself. He'd have to get a swagger in his step and an arrogant scowl adorning his face if he was to look like the fearsome men he remembered from his youth.

13

Hanging a Canon

In Cabo San Lucas, an inviting wind blew gently out to sea. It was time to make sail.

Santa Ana had been sunk, and now her hull was firmly stuck on the bay's sandy bottom. Only the top decks peeked above the waves.

Over the previous few days, the English had gotten drunker and ever more violent as the transfer of loot came to an end. They were about to set off into the unknown, across a body of water that was mightier than any other on earth. They knew the chances of survival were slim, even with the captured pilots on board.

On November seventeenth, there had been fireworks and salvoes for the twenty-ninth anniversary of Queen Elizabeth's ascension to the English throne, and by extension, a commemoration of when King Philip had lost that throne. The Spanish watched glumly as the Chinese firecrackers and rockets, which had probably been intended as a homecoming present for some notable's wife in Spain, lit up the dark sky of the cape in colorful jollity.

Those to be left behind in the scrubby surroundings of the

Californian cape were gathered in a large huddle slightly above the water line. They had been granted stores of dried garbanzo beans, split peas, and even some wine. The country teemed with wildlife and fish, and the water in the streams was pure and sweet. Not only that, but they also had the grayed and salt-stiffened sails of their galleon to make tents, and blankets.

They would probably survive to be picked up by a passing ship in the years to come.

Cavendish bid farewell to the Americas in the gloaming surrounded by twenty heavily armed sailors.

First, he gifted presents of silver to the castaway ladies, a gallant gesture that no doubt appealed to his ego. Then he gestured to Captain de Alzola, pointing out a sealed crate containing the hand weapons that had been surrendered to him two weeks before. They would have good defense against any foe. He tossed a small barrel of gunpowder to the floor in front of the crowd as a bonus.

In a typically flamboyant Cavendish gesture, he then grandly unrolled a scroll and presented a receipt for Captain de Alzola's cargo. The English commander knew how to expertly rub salt into open wounds.

Suddenly, a scuffle broke out.

Cosmus's former master, Don Juan de Armendariz, started to declaim in a sonorous but furious tone, honed by many years of projecting his voice in places of worship, that Cavendish was nothing but a heretic pirate, the lowest rung of humanity, lower even than the heathen Indians who would no doubt butcher and eat them after the English ship had taken its leave.

He added a curse in Latin.

Christopher could not understand the words, but he understood their intent well enough.

Finally, the priest raged that the English would never have captured the brave *Santa Ana* had the Spanish not been bested by the cowardly use of artillery. Any Spaniard was a match for ten Englishmen in a fair fight.

Cavendish burst out laughing, called him a popish whore and bid him hold his peace.

But de Armendariz would not cease. It was as if he had not even heard Cavendish. His voice became louder and eventually peaked in a shrill, almost rabid, wail demanding the return of his money and his fine Japanese boy. How could he be expected to live without his boy? A man of the cloth had a right to certain privileges and a boy to see to his needs was one of them.

Suddenly, he produced a knife from his sleeve and lunged at an English mariner. The sailor backed off nimbly, and de Armendariz, almost foaming at the mouth, ended up slashing through thin air. Losing his balance, he fell helplessly, slipping on the loose sand. The pathetic attack ended with the Canon of Manila face down on the beach, sobbing and stabbing repeatedly in rage, shouting for his beloved boy.

Next to Christopher aboard *Desire*, Cosmus must have gaped, gripping the polished wooden rail tightly, and letting out small gasps as events unfolded before him.

Cavendish turned away to take his leave. With contempt, and danger in his voice, he softly ordered the priest bound.

De Armendariz, tied securely and unmoving, was thrown into the boat. Christopher could have sworn that he heard bones break as his body hit the central bench and bounced off. The priest screamed a keening howl, and one of the sailors, laughing, kicked him repeatedly in his ample belly as the others around him cheered and jeered in the rocking boat.

When the wails at length stopped, the priest lay still. No trace of the haughtiness that had placed him there remained. He was like a terrified animal, frozen and waiting silently to be put out of its misery.

Captain de Alzola suddenly found his courage and shouted a protest, reminding everyone that Cavendish had given his word they would not be harmed.

Cavendish, red-faced with fury, shouted back from the boat that the priest had gainsaid the promise of clemency through his attempted murder. Humbled, scared, and defenseless in the face of all that had befallen him over the last weeks, the captain fell silent.

The only sound to be heard above the lapping of the sea and the sculling of the oars was the laughter of the excited English sailors, previous fears of the ocean crossing to come forgotten in their mounting bloodlust.

The boat did not head for *Desire*, but toward the semisunken hulk of *Santa Ana*. When they reached it, a team of sailors hauled the canon up the side, a scream burst out as he crashed against the superstructure, but it was swiftly silenced with a kick.

Cosmus's master was strung up on what remained of the foremast.

It took a long time, his face slowly turning the shade of a plum as he thrashed like a landed fish. Eventually movement ceased, and the corpse was cut down to drift into the gathering dusk of the bay.

The world had turned upside down. Christopher's master was ashore, cut off forever from his former chattel. Cosmus's now floated up and down surfing the softly lapping waves.

Food for the fish.

The sailors proceeded to scamper around the wreck of *Santa Ana* stacking charges of powder at regular intervals. When done, they set a fuse and sped away, rowing as swiftly as possible.

The explosion when it came was small, but slowly the fire caught, and flames licked speedily up and around the exposed portion of deck and leaning masts.

Christopher, still gazing at the burning *Santa Ana*, perhaps imagined that he saw Mazu's flame flickering above the stricken ship. His soul would have reached out to her, imploring her to again keep him safe on this next chapter of his tumultuous adventure.

It was almost night now; *Desire* turned her back on the carnage she had left at Cabo San Lucas, let off a farewell blast, and headed for the dying sun—westward and home.

Content remained in the bay, completing the last preparations for her voyage. She was to attempt a different route, trying for the Northwest Passage from the western end through the Strait of Anian.

Content was never heard from again.

14

Abductees and Collaborators

Christopher had been delivered from a life of slavery and was now being treated as minor nobility. Most people who found themselves in such circumstances were not so lucky.

By 1587, kidnapping, or enticing "exotic" peoples on board ship for abduction, was common practice with fine precedent. All the most famous mariners did it.

In fact, the English were comparative latecomers to this type of kidnap. Arabs and other peoples who sailed far afield in ancient times had done it for centuries, and among Europeans, Columbus himself had probably started the trend, later continued by the Portuguese, Spanish, and French.

From the foreign sailor's perspective there was good reason for luring victims away from their homes.

Many of the places that the most daring missions such as Cavendish's aimed for were so distant and unknown that anyone could make up believable stories. Indeed, many islands, countries, and even some continents only existed in theory, legend, or as errors on maps. Bringing back real live Indigenous peoples was a great way to prove that sailors had been where they said they had, and not just skulked around for a year before returning with tall tales like Sir John Mandeville's.

Furthermore, once in England, the kidnapped people could be used as publicity to drum up investment for future voyages.

Finally, in some cases like Christopher's and his colleagues', and of far greater importance to England's future prosperity, the kidnapped could be used to find out firsthand information concerning distant parts of the world, their cultures, technologies, geography, and languages.

The very first, unnamed, abductees from North America arrived in England during the reign of Henry VII in 1501. They were "clothid in bestys skynnys and ete Rawe fflesh...in theyre demeanure lyke to bruyt bestis."

The English were enraptured, and these abductees were kept at court as living proof of the existence of exotic lands. In their "bruyt" appearance and habits, they of course also acted as a foil, demonstrating to the English natives their innate civilized nature, which considering its position as a minor European power recovering from a terrible civil war, must have been a great morale boost.

Two years later, the abductees were observed in native English garb, virtually indistinguishable from other courtiers. Their end is sadly unknown.

In 1577, three people from what is now Canada were snatched by Sir Martin Frobisher on his ill-fated search for New World gold. They were a man called Kalicho, an unrelated woman called Arnaq, and her baby son, Nutaaq.

The three abductees arrived at Bristol in October 1578 and Kalicho wowed the English with displays of his kayaking and hunting skills despite broken ribs and innumerable cerebral injuries incurred during his kidnapping. These eventually resulted in his death after only a few weeks.

PUBLIC DOMAIN

An Inuit man brought to England from Baffin Island (modern-day Canada) by Martin Frobisher on his first mission to North America in 1576. Lucas de Heer, 1570s or 1580s.

Arnaq only survived him by a few days.

The race was then on to transport at least one of these amazing Americans to London to be displayed to the Queen. The baby Nutaaq was swiftly conveyed by coach to the capital with a specially hired wet nurse to attend him.

But Her Majesty was to be disappointed. The baby died en route, only eight days after arrival. Both he and his mother are thought to have perished from measles.

That Frobisher had attempted the same thing before in 1576 (with similarly fatal results for the victim) and would later attempt to do it, unsuccessfully, once more, suggests that he did not care much. Neither did his investors, who included many of the most prominent people in the country, including the Queen herself, Lady Anne Talbot, and Lady Mary Sidney. One wonders if these grand ladies pondered on the grim fate of the people that they had caused to be plucked from their Canadian homes so tragically?

Probably not. The lower classes of whatever nationality or ethnicity came and went, lived and died as pawns in the power games of the wealthy. To them, American captives were simply exotic living souvenirs, ego boosters, propaganda coups, and token successes from the largely failed North American voyages.

After all, life was cheap in this age, and the mariners who actually manhandled these unfortunates aboard also commonly perished in far-flung places, victims of woeful supplies, exotic diseases, poor leadership, and insufficient equipment.

Abductees' propaganda value, however, lived on in art. Around thirty illustrations depicting kidnapped American people are still in existence, and there were probably many more at the time.

The exotic "celebrities" of whom Cavendish would have been most aware, and almost definitely based his own plans for the Japanese and Filipino abductees upon, would have been the two Native Americans, Manteo and Wanchese. As portrayed in the Prologue to this book, they traveled to England voluntarily from what is now Roanoke in North Carolina with Philip Amadas and Arthur Barlowe in 1584.

The Amadas–Barlowe expedition was under the sponsorship of a patron of Cavendish's, Sir Walter Raleigh, and so Manteo and Wanchese were honored guests at his London residence, the palatial Durham House. Access to them was carefully controlled to create and sustain an air of mystery, but he ensured they learned to communicate fluently in English.

Raleigh used the Americans for intelligence purposes, to learn as much about their land, coasts, natural resources, and language as possible. In this he was very successful, and they rendered a huge amount of knowledge that the English were later to use in the foundation of their North American colonial endeavors. The brilliant scholar and friend of Cavendish's, Thomas Harriot, even learned the Algonquin language from them—the first known English-speaking student of an Indigenous American language, and furthermore invented a revolutionary phonetic script which he called a "universall Alphabet conteyninge six &

thirty letters," to render all the sounds of human speech, what-ever the language, recordable by hand.

As expected, the Americans proved a sensation at court. Ear-lier attempts at obtaining New World riches had come to naught, but such amazing human propaganda persuaded the great and good of England, including Cavendish, to invest in the Roanoke pirate haven. Many would later complain that they had been hoodwinked as it provided little or no return on their money.

Cavendish, a friend and mentee of Raleigh's, met the two Americans in London, and as they traveled together on the 1585 expedition back to Roanoke, which inspired the planning of the circumnavigation, he would have had the chance to deepen his acquaintance. The young adventurer would undoubtedly have been hoping to replicate Raleigh's coup with Manteo and Wanchese by bringing Christopher and his comrades to Lon-don in 1588.

Back in North America in 1585, Manteo remained a friend of the English, acting as a reliable diplomat and linguistic and cultural interpreter. Wanchese seems to have turned against the colonists, and perhaps even incited his people to conflict. He had always been less obliging to English needs, and there is some suggestion that he was actually sent across the Atlantic to gather knowledge for his own nation. It was not only Europe-ans who played at intelligence.

In 1586, Manteo again sailed to London with another Amer-ican called Towaye, returning to Roanoke in May 1587, and missing Christopher by just over a year. The last few people in Roanoke had disappeared without trace, but a few dozen new would-be settlers were determined to make a go of it.

Manteo's efforts to smooth relations between the local people and the English were unsuccessful, and conflict was a perpetual danger. He would eventually convert to Anglican Christianity, though it may have been more for show than a sincere avowal of faith as it occurred under orders from Raleigh—part of an unsuccessful attempt to raise him to puppet ruler of a local people.

Due to the Spanish Armada's attempted invasion of England and subsequent counterattacks, England was unable to mount any successful expeditions to America until 1590. The relief mission arrived to investigate the fate of those who had been left behind, only to find a destroyed settlement and a cryptic clue that suggested they had relocated to a nearby island.

The question of the latter's whereabouts has been a mystery for centuries, but it seems the survivors may have in fact simply melted into the woods to join local tribes. In the absence of resupply, they probably believed they had been abandoned. Whether Manteo stayed with the Roanoke English or forged his own path is unknown.

Other people from afar also traveled to England voluntarily. Diego Negro, a Maroon from one of the Black Caribbean states of enslaved people and their descendants who had escaped bondage, accompanied Sir Francis Drake to Plymouth in 1573, and the two men seem to have enjoyed a close personal relationship. He guided the English in guerrilla warfare against the Spanish, acted as an interpreter with Native Americans, and while in England contributed considerable intelligence to be used on later voyages. Diego lived in England for three years, and then joined Drake on his circumnavigation. He was killed in battle by a poisoned arrow in 1578 on the island of La Mocha in modern-day Chile.

Some abductees never made it to England. Thomas Cavendish himself kidnapped an African called Emmanuel from Peru and used him as a guide along the South American coast. Emmanuel clearly preferred the company of the Spanish, as he jumped ship in Puna, modern-day Ecuador, and told the Spanish all he knew of the English ships and crew. This intelligence was used to foil Cavendish and he lost men, equipment, and one of the ships in his fleet as a consequence—a setback which nearly disrupted his plans and could have changed Christopher's destiny.

A truly horrific abduction story involves that of an African woman called Maria, kidnapped from a Spanish ship off New Spain during Sir Francis Drake's circumnavigation. Her captors described her as "a proper wench," and she was "had use of" by the crew. When it was discovered that Maria was pregnant, she and two African men were abandoned with some supplies on an island in modern-day Indonesia.

The evidence of rape had been disposed of, along with two potential witnesses to the crime. Their fate is unknown.

These abductees do not include the up to three hundred thousand Indigenous Americans or equal number of Africans ripped from their homes, enslaved, and trafficked in the Atlantic world during the sixteenth century. For every positive story like Diego Negro and Christopher, there were thousands, perhaps millions, of anonymous men, women, and children who lived and died in the direst of conditions, used, abused, and discarded. Their captors and traffickers saw little humanity, only financial gain.

15

It's a Sailor's Death for Me!

Desire was a race-built galleon, one of the fastest European ships afloat with an estimated speed of eight knots (9 mph, 15 kmh).

These French-inspired vessels which enabled the English to travel the globe were surprisingly small, in *Desire*'s case not much bigger than a large modern-day intercity bus. Her original design is lost to us, but we do know that she was around 120 to 150 tuns and was probably similar to Francis Drake's ship *Golden Hinde* at around 75 feet (21.1 meters) at the waterline, 20 feet (6.1 meters) wide and 92 feet (28 meters) at the highest point on the main mast.

The two ships that had accompanied her to the Pacific, *Content* and *Hugh Gallant*, were much smaller and served as auxiliary vessels for action in shallow waters such as estuaries where *Desire* would have run aground.

A race-built galleon was not a large space to be marooned upon in the middle of an ocean with no prospect of landfall for thousands of miles. Crews were often physical and emotional wrecks when they made landfall, and mental illness was rife. Weeks from land, there was literally no escape besides death. No wonder then that the crew spent so much time in a semidrunken state. It must have been the easiest way to cope, though it caused innumerable further deaths from alcohol-induced accidents.

These were the facts of Christopher's new home.

The Japanese mariner would have seen a wooden ship topped off by a high half deck, or poop deck, at the stern in which the captain's Great Cabin and the armory were located. *Desire*'s big guns packed a punch, but the armory's racks contained the tools to actually take an enemy ship, a process that called for hand-to-hand combat.

Weapons carried included harquebuses, muskets, and long-bows, which were far more accurate than guns at medium range but lacked the noise and fear-inducing devilish smoke of gunpowder. For when things got up close and personal, there were swords, pikes, shields, and halberds.

To the front of the ship, where a prominent tower-like edifice was located on older ships, *Desire* had nothing more than a low foredeck and a spritsail protruding into the eternal ocean.

Between the foredeck and the poop at the rear was the main deck, a small area with a grilled hatch, to allow light and goods to reach the levels below.

A gaze through the grille would reveal *Desire*'s fists, over half of the ship's total complement of thirty-odd cannon filling the low-slung gun deck with their dark presence. These were the four-pound minion guns which so effectively disabled *Santa Ana* with their deadly bombardment. The remainder of the guns, spread throughout the ship, would have been lesser pieces, falcons and falconets, three pounds and two pounds respectively. There would also have been two swivel chaser guns at the rear to target pursuing ships.

It was a heavy armament for this size of ship. Cavendish was taking no chances.

The low ceiling on the gun deck, only three feet, four inches (around one meter) high, made it impossible to stand up straight.

Those working the guns in battle had to stoop or crawl about in the grease and blood that covered the decks, dodging recoiling weapons as acrid smoke billowed around them.

On the much larger and higher-ceilinged orlop below, visible only dimly through another wooden grille, piled high with hardly an inch to spare, was the majority of *Santa Ana*'s looted wealth. The sparse light was largely eaten up by the dark timbers of the ship's superstructure.

Movement yet further into the bowels of the vessel right above the keel, mere inches from the ocean itself, would have been difficult, but here Christopher would have encountered any heavy and nonperishable goods, gold, silver, and pearls, acting as ballast. Little light shone to make them glisten, but all on board knew what riches lay there, and that once home, they would be flush beyond their wildest dreams.

Santa Ana was approximately four or five times larger than *Desire*. But the vessels on which Christopher had spent most of his early life in Japan and the South China Sea were probably nearer to *Desire* in size. The largest were of several hundred tuns.

By this time, Japanese ships were just starting to incorporate the best from various Asian (mainly Chinese, later also Korean) and European shipbuilding traditions. These ships with curved white-painted hulls normally featured an almost sawn-off-looking, bowsprit-less prow, main sails of bamboo battens interwoven with thread, and far less rigging than a European ship. Steering was by a massive centerline oar-like rudder, and anchors were normally of stone rather than metal. Soon, though exactly when is unclear, cloth topsails, sometimes bowsprits, and larger cannon firing broadside rather than forward or backward, came to be incorporated along with traditional features.

Christopher would have weighed up these differences and gauged the advantages of various different styles. His English interlocutors certainly did, and it is likely that opinions were favorable, as only a few decades later, they used Japanese ships extensively in Asian waters.

Desire and her two privateering companions left England in 1586 with 123 men. Bravados recruited from all corners of the country. By the time Christopher joined, half of the men who had started the voyage were gone.

The first to die had been William Pickman who succumbed to a poisoned arrow in a revenge attack after the English had raided a West African town for supplies. It was a nasty and lingering death in which his body swelled up and his belly and groin turned black.

During more raids, the Spanish killed twelve in what is now Chile, and eight more in modern-day Ecuador, and Robert Maddocke shot himself in the head by mistake. Others were taken prisoner to be enslaved or died from disease. The smallest vessel in the three-strong squadron, *Hugh Gallant*, had to be scuttled on June 5, 1587, for lack of hands to man her.

The men who signed up for such voyages must have possessed a special kind of guts to gamble with the grim reaper at such high stakes.

There were some perks of course. During the last fifteen years of the sixteenth century, including the three years Christopher was in England, government parsimony, corruption, international blockade, rampant inflation, and poor agricultural yields meant that many Elizabethans were constantly hungry, even in some cases starving to death. During the last decade alone, grain prices rose by nearly 50 percent.

Therefore, food was a major reason why mariners gambled their lives on these extremely precarious voyages. It might have seemed better to die with a full belly and a chance at riches at sea, than from an empty one in penury on land.

At the very beginning of a voyage, privateering mariners would have been dining on reasonable quality salted beef, mutton, pork, and fish, ship biscuit (hardtack), butter, and cheese.

However, storage of food in the hold next to the cooking quarters risked penetration by damp and contamination by smoke, not to mention hungry rats, mice, and other vermin (including bats!) devouring supplies meant for humans. Within barrels, hardtack was reduced to dust by movement of the ship and could soon only be consumed as a kind of gruel, while meat sometimes became so foul that the diners had to hold their noses while eating. As victuals degraded in quality and quantity, sailors became both physically and mentally weaker, and easy prey to disease.

Therefore, strenuous efforts were made to replenish supplies with whatever local produce was to be had at landfalls (either hunted, foraged, traded, or most commonly, thieved). Prior to meeting Christopher, foods acquired by Cavendish's men included lemons, bananas, figs, baby seals, seagulls, penguins, mussels, limpets, venison, various types of fish, potatoes, maize, hares, rabbits, sugar, molasses, marmalade, goat's milk, myriad fowl, pineapples, iguanas, melons, and much more. The crew were apparently not impressed with cacao, the chocolate bean, recording it as "very like unto an almond but nothing so pleasant in taste."

The *solanum tuberosum* potatoes they found could just possibly have supplied the first seed potatoes grown in England. While it cannot be confirmed for certain, early records of potato cultivation coincide closely with Christopher's arrival.

Besides food, alcohol was a prime source of calories as well as a tonic to boost fragile morale. At the time of Christopher's joining, the crew would have been enjoying the treat of reasonable-quality wine raided in South America, but prior to this they would have been reduced to the dregs of stale and sour ale brought from England. Later in voyages, as supplies dwindled dangerously, alcohol was eked out by mixing it with, often putrid, water to form a questionable liquid which sailors simply referred to as "beverage."

In nightmare situations, sailors were forced into the penury of imbibing plain water, unrecommended because of the high chance of disease. Beer and wine were sterilized during the fermentation process, and therefore much safer.

The worst-case scenario for ships was bad beer. It was not only an unpleasant surprise, but a risk to sailors' lives and therefore to their missions. Most famously, as England awaited the Spanish invasion fleet of 1588, thousands of sailors died. Bad beer, supplied by unscrupulous merchants, is thought to have been the main cause.

Alcohol was a matter of national security.

What was missing from this diet of flesh, dairy, carbohydrate, and alcohol, was vitamin C (unless like Cavendish's men, you found fruit and vegetables on the way), a condition which results in scurvy.

Scurvy takes around a month to rear its head, but when it does, purple bruises appear, skin grows taught, gums bleed, teeth fall out, wounds do not heal, sufferers weaken drastically, and eventually death presents itself as a mercy.

Every long-distance European mariner knew the symptoms and outcomes. What they did not know was the cause, and a proven cure was to elude sailors for hundreds of years to come.

In dire straits, when the hold was bereft of supplies, sailors were reduced to drinking rainwater or even urine, and munching on hemp ropes and leather fittings. When these were gone, and only the emaciated bodies of the near-dead sailors themselves remained, the last resort was cannibalism. By maritime custom, in such situations it was considered acceptable if the person had died willingly or accidentally.

The living quarters on board a race-built galleon would have been yet another shocking experience for modern-day people.

Captains naturally had the best quarters. A small solo cabin in the stern, a bed which doubled as a seat, windows and possibly even a balcony which doubled as personal latrine. They were essentially insulated from many of the horrors of the ship, and the only ones who had any privacy.

Everyone else slept and lived on top of each other.

Christopher, as a "gentleman," would have dossed down with the officers in the armory, hot bedding as they went on and off duty. There was just enough space to stretch out, but probably not enough to be spared kicks from restless bedfellows.

The common sailors simply stretched out on the hardwood floor of the gun deck sandwiched between the cannon and stowed goods. There was no privacy, and prior to Cavendish's generous gift of damask bedding, there would have been little comfort. Mariners of all ranks provided their own covers; those who could not afford a blanket froze. Everyone sweltered in warmer climes.

There were no toilet facilities; defecation took place over the side, directly into the sea from the prow, or head, of the ship. It is thought that the phrase "hit the head" originated in this practice, and as a consequence, vessels undoubtedly enjoyed various shades of scatological pebble dash on the outside of the hull.

Elizabethan-era Europeans were not noted for their hygiene at the best of times, so lack of bathing equipment probably did not bother them overly.

As an enslaved person on *Santa Ana*, Christopher would have led a far from comfortable life, so *Desire*'s shipboard conditions, the damask sleeping mat in particular, would probably have been quite a step up for him.

To control the powder kegs of emotion, anger, and fear which onboard conditions nurtured, harsh and strict regulations derived from the ancient French "Rolls of Oléron" were enforced. They are said to have originally been introduced by Eleanor of Aquitaine, Queen of England, in around 1160.

A murder at sea was punished by the culprit being tied to the victim and thrown overboard. On land, the killer would be buried alive with the corpse.

Thieving was punished with tar and feathers, and abandonment at the next landing place. Other legitimate punishments included enforced fasting, keel hauling, and hanging weights around the neck until the back was ready to break.

Even swearing was punishable by an expensive forerunner to today's swear boxes, an ounce of silver for each transgression. If the fine could not be paid, the culprit's tongue was scraped, or the guilty party gagged.

These regulations were read to all crew members two or three times a week. There was no excuse for transgression or ignorance.

As today, personnel were organized into a hierarchy, and commanders such as Cavendish appointed by the Queen herself, to rule "both in fear and love," were empowered to "slay, execute and put to death."

However, leaders were only respected as long as they ensured full bellies, fresh beer, and ample opportunities for plunder. If they did not fulfill their side of the bargain, discontent among the crew, followed by protest, petition, and eventual mutiny was common, a consequence of captains' greed normally being greater than their leadership talents.

These uprisings did not normally take the form of outright revolution, the crew simply sought to put right their grievances and persuade or force the captain to another, more favorable, course. Captains in such situations often moved from command to persuasion, and sometimes performed great speeches of justification to win back a mutinous crew.

With the constant threat of sudden and unpleasant death, mortality was foremost in the Elizabethan seaman's mind. They dealt with this not only with alcohol, but also through the framework of religious belief, which brought discipline, hope, and a touch of fantasy into their perilous existence.

God was the driving force behind everything in a world with little understanding of economics, biology, meteorology, or medicine. Seafarers in particular were highly superstitious and evinced a deep belief in divine intervention in times of trouble. Many instances of "God's deliverance" and belief in the power of prayer are recorded in accounts of contemporary voyages. When Drake's ship *Golden Hinde* struck a rock in 1580 for example, even in immediate danger of death, the crew held a prayer service before manning the pumps. For them divine intervention counted for more than their own efforts.

Most ships did not carry a priest with them, so seamen managed their own communal services twice a day in the morning and evening. Psalms were sung, prayer books read, bible study encouraged, and occasional sermons delivered. Religion was decidedly Protestant, and worship conducted in English, reflecting habits and conventions in England at the time.

Desire was rare in the fact that she did have a preacher, John Way, aboard. Cavendish obviously believed in collecting as many divine brownie points as possible, and perhaps with all the very unholy killing, burning, and pillaging that his crew engaged in, they needed them.

Despite the appalling conditions, Christopher had joined *Desire* on the best part of the voyage. Overcrowding was down due to death, the surviving sailors had been well rested before taking *Santa Ana*, and stocks of fresh food and drink were high. Furthermore, the crew were wealthy beyond their wildest dreams. All knew they just had to get home to reap the rewards of their hard work; *Desire*'s men were in high spirits.

16

The Large Mappe of China

With the wind behind her, *Desire* veritably flew the 1850 leagues westward across the Pacific Ocean toward a place the pilots called *Islas de los Ladrones*, the "Islands of Thieves."

At forty-five days, it was the fastest ever crossing by a European ship.

Thankfully, the voyage was uninterrupted by tempest or calm, and with the liberated Spanish food and drink, the sailors were in rude health, and even better fettle.

The stage was set for Christopher's first revolutionary contribution to English and global maritime history, the decoding of the Chinese map confiscated from the Portuguese pilot, Rodríguez.

It was the English-speaking world's first true peek at Far Eastern waters, but much more than a mere geographic revelation, it was a cartographic treasure-trove including military rosters and even taxable household data. As Cavendish himself wrote,

The statelinesse and riches of which countrey I feare to make report of, least I should not be credited: for if I had not knowen suf-

*ficiently the incomparable wealth of that countrey, I should have
bene as incredulous thereof, as others will be that have not had
the like experience.*

This was a eureka moment. England had uncovered safe paths
to the Far East. At last ships would be able to navigate with
secure knowledge of the route, and a concrete idea of what
awaited them.

The problem for Cavendish was that the vital information
held within the magic map was written in indecipherable Chinese script. As luck would have it, however, written Japanese
also entailed a sound knowledge of Chinese characters. It was
Christopher's time to shine.

The Far East has a long and distinguished history of mapmaking that, in China, stretches far back beyond the Common
Era. Charts were used for navigation and control of territory,
but also for military and civil engineering purposes, with river
systems and mountain ranges accurately depicted.

Notably bereft of mythical geography such as the Garden of
Eden, which was imaginatively shown on European maps (often
tentatively placed in the Far East), these maps were depicted accurately to scale on silk cloth. As Chinese geographical knowledge of the world increased, the maps came to encompass outer
regions such as Japan, Korea, Tibet, Central Asia, Indochina,
and the nomad-inhabited lands to the far north.

The Mongol conquest of China and then the Eurasian world
in the thirteenth century incorporated the East Asian realms into
an empire that stretched as far as Poland in the west. Along with
immense wealth pillaged from subjected peoples, the learning of
Persia and Arabia's ancient libraries traveled east. This included
cartographical knowledge of the extreme west, to be added
to Chinese world maps. Fourteenth-century examples sport a
triangular-shaped Africa with thirty-five place names, and a
recognizable Europe with one hundred.

Chinese maps and techniques were transmitted to Korea in 1399, and Korean versions to Japan around one hundred years later. By Christopher's time, the higher echelons of Japanese society had also obtained European maps and globes showing the New World as well as more accurate renderings of the Far West.

A few days after setting out, Cavendish called for Christopher. The English commander was sitting in his great chair, next to him was the interpreter, and standing at the table foot was Rodríguez with a scowl on his face.

On the table in front of them, a sheet of paper was spread out, secured with golden paper weights. It was rare to see paper of such quality, and Christopher sneaked a look while he awaited Cavendish's orders. Parts of the paper seemed almost blank. The rest was a darker, browner color, and was decorated with illustrations of delicate and lifelike trees, flowers, and landscape formations. There were also the names of cities in Chinese writing. This must be a map. He had seen such things before, but only fleetingly. Pilots and captains normally kept them jealously under lock and key.

Cavendish gestured with his hand, a sweeping movement which covered the entire map, and asked if Christopher could make sense of the writing, which was on a sheet of paper next to the chart.

Now that he was free to look properly, he gazed at each part of the chart in turn. It was truly beautiful.

The writing and the written description was of place names, bays, harbors, and trade routes. On the map itself the shapes in the blank parts were islands in the vast sea.

He read "Ryukyu Kingdom," and looking further up, he saw "Goto" and "Karatsu." This must be Japan, he realized. Moving to the left, he saw "Chosenkoku," Korea! And then dominating the rest of the map, "Daimin," China. The Great Wall was clearly depicted, and north of that was empty space. The land of nomads who disdain city living and migrate with their animals.

Japan and Korea had few place names indicated, but China, clearly the cartographer's focus, was covered with them. In fact, there was barely room between them for the scenes of nature that the artist had also included. Christopher knew some of the cities, Canton, Fukien, and Peking, but others, particularly those inland, were new to him.

He transferred his gaze to the written description of the chart. It was filled with numbers and text.

Measurements of province size, taxable households, men under arms, and numbers of horses. In places there were explanations, histories, and even comments on climate. As he thought about them and got his head round the whole amazing concept of this beautiful artifact, the marks started to make more sense.

Christopher hesitated... He would need to learn English to explain it all.

It was time for him to become the first Far Eastern student of a language which would, centuries later, become the global lingua franca.

English would have seemed like a strange, guttural, unclear-sounding tongue, with some awkward sounds, very unlike the clear and precise sounds of Japanese, let alone the songlike tones of Spanish or the Manilan dialect.

His teaching aid was probably the Bible, from which came interesting stories, some terrifying, others with happy endings. All had life lessons attached. Another language means another world, and Christopher found just such a one opening up before him, knowledge revealing itself like a scroll unrolling to unveil further wonders and secrets.

One day, Christopher found he was ready to attempt an explanation of the map.

Cavendish, delighted, rolled it out on his great table, and called Rodríguez to pass comment if need be.

"The great city of Peking where the king does lie, hath eight great cities, and eighteen small cities, with 118 towns and castles; it hath 418,789 houses of great men that pay tribute."

Christopher stumbled over some of the unfamiliar terms and how he should translate them.

"It hath horsemen for the war 258,100."

Cavendish stared at him. "Repeat that!" he ordered curtly. Christopher started. What had he said wrong?

"That is surely more households and horsemen than in the whole of Christendom! And only in one city!" shouted Cavendish. He gaped.

"Keep going."

Rodríguez, who had remained silent up to now, nodded his agreement, and added, "what the Japan lad says is true. You cannot believe the vastness of China. I have not been to Peking, but I have seen Canton. It seems never ending, but they say Peking is much bigger, and filled with palaces and mansions."

Christopher continued, "The province of Fukien hath eight great cities, and one principal city, and fifty-four towns and castles, and two great cities of garrison, to keep watch upon the Japons, and is 200 leagues broad, and hath 5,009,532 great houses that pay tax, and 4,003,225 men of the king's guard."

He could have gone on for a long time, but Cavendish stopped him. "You have already proved your worth lad." He sat back and smiled broadly, exposing his rotten teeth. "Your job on this voyage is to further learn our language and to produce a translation of this map. I want you to be able to explain it when we get to London. You will be given whatever you need. This treasure is more valuable than all the gold and silks on this ship, never has such intelligence been heard of in our country."

Cavendish stopped talking suddenly, frowned, and then he scratched the stubble on his chin. "You will only work on this here in my cabin while I am present. The map does not leave. We start tomorrow."

Then he waved his hand in dismissal and sat back as Christopher and Rodríguez took their leave.

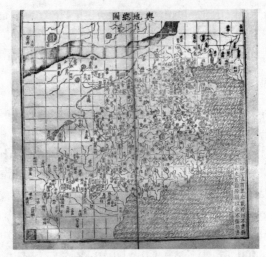

A Luo Hongxian map of the east coast of China and the western coast of the Korean Peninsula. Christopher's map would have looked like this.

This groundbreaking map of China and its surrounding seas arrived in London to much excitement.

The only people on *Desire* who could conceivably have deciphered the Chinese characters in which this map was written were Christopher and his friend Cosmus, and likely the only one with sufficient seafaring and navigational experience was Christopher.

Although Christopher's actual map is thought lost, there are a few other woodblock-printed maps with census data included that survive to the modern day in libraries and private collections.

The maps, with written data printed on the reverse side and adjacent pages, were derived from an atlas compiled by the cartographer Luo Hongxian and his collaborators in 1555. Starting in the 1570s or 1580s, large-scale charts based on Luo's atlas began to appear, and Christopher's specimen was probably one of these.

When Christopher's map arrived in England, it was exhibited to an exclusive few, probably at the Palace of Whitehall in Westminster. It blew Elizabethan minds.

A Luo Hongxian map description, published on the page following the map of the coastal regions of eastern China and the western stretches of the Korean Peninsula. The text that Christopher translated would have looked something like this.

The map revealed the size, tax base, and population of the Chinese realm—and its military strength. A figure just short of eight million men. Double the whole population of England, which had no standing army at all.

Four million of these forces were recorded as being deployed in the coastal province of Fukien to defend against attacks by Japanese pirates. Christopher must have grinned at this as he translated it.

Taxpaying households were revealed at 13,330,297, and if the qualifications for those who were wealthy enough to pay tax were similar to those in England—only a very small percentage of the population—then the total population indicated on the map could be estimated at well over 100 million.

Today, the true figure is believed to be between 100 and 160 million. England's contemporary population was around 4 million.

The obvious conclusion that any English viewer would have come to was that China, as had been believed for so many centuries, was large, rich, and powerful beyond comparison in every measure.

It wielded mighty military power and saw its most dangerous enemy as Japan. Extrapolation of this fact would mean that
Japan must be an immense power in its own right. Both were
clearly places worthy of cultivation as trade partners and military allies, exactly as those who had so desperately sought out
the sea routes to the Far East for so long had predicted.

The written description of the map, published by Richard
Hakluyt and quoted above, is sadly not credited to the Japanese
translator, but without Christopher to render the data into English, it would have only been so many indecipherable squiggles.

The next person to be able to properly decipher Chinese text
in England was almost definitely Michael Shen Fuzong, a Chinese Jesuit scholar who arrived exactly a century later. He helped
Oxford University to catalog and make sense of their Chinese
texts and wowed the courts of Europe with his sophistication.
King James II of England was so taken with him that he commissioned a portrait, and had it hung in his private chambers.

In 1588, when accurate maps and nautical charts of distant
parts of the globe were more valuable than diamonds, this was
a massive coup. Christopher's "Mappe of China" and the measurements that Cavendish and his crew collected on their circumnavigation, formed the basis of the charts used by future
English, and later American, adventurers.

The Chinese Convert *(Godfrey Kneller, 1687)* portrays *Michael Shen Fuzong. This hung in the private chambers of King James II.*

17

A Global Mystery

In 1589, Richard Hakluyt, in the same volume that celebrated Christopher's arrival and published the description of the Mappe of China, announced in great excitement the imminent publication of a:

> *very large and most exact terrestriall globe, collected and reformed according to the newest, secretest, and latest discoveries, both Spanish, Portugall and English, composed by Mr. Emmerie Molineux of Lambeth, a rare Gentleman in his profession.*

Emery Molyneux, the pioneering geographer, is known to have sailed on Drake's circumnavigation, and an inscription on his globe suggests a second planet-encircling adventure with Cavendish too. If so, he would have been one of the gentlemen adventurers who bunked down with Christopher in the armory. Perhaps even been privy to the map translation exercise.

It is therefore entirely possible that Christopher and his colleagues could have had some input into his revolutionary navigational instruments, which were the first-ever globes to be produced in England, the cause of immense national pride.

A terrestrial globe is recorded as having been presented to the Chinese court by the Persian astronomer Jamal ad-Din, in 1267, but they were a relatively new innovation in the Christian world. The earliest extant European one is from 1492, and was created by Martin Behaim in Nuremberg, a free city in the Holy Roman Empire.

In his book *The Seaman's Secrets*, the explorer John Davis described this innovative technology thus:

> *The use of the Globe is of so great ease, certainty, and pleasure, as that the commendations thereof cannot sufficiently be expressed, for of all instruments it is the most rare and excellent, whose conclusions are infallible, giving the true line, angle, and circular motion of any corse or trauers that may in Navigation happen, whereby the longitude and latitude is most precisely knowne, and the certainty of distance very plainely manifested, according to the true nature thereof.*

This cutting-edge technological advance seemed to prove, along with other recent advances such as Cavendish's successfully planned and executed circumnavigation, that English scholars and sailors were at last able to compete with Europe's best.

Hakluyt's eager announcement in 1589 proved to be optimistic. It took another three years for Molyneux to actually present his instrument to the world. However, the excitement was no less for it. If anything, expectations had increased.

And Molyneux's globe was a truly fine specimen. At two feet, one inch in diameter, it was the largest ever made and had cost at least £1000 to develop, a huge sum in contemporary terms. It beautifully presented the world known to the English in the 1590s, faithfully recording the circumnavigation routes of Drake and Cavendish among other seafaring achievements.

The Middle Temple Library in London holds the only extant pair of Molyneux terrestrial and celestial globes. © The Honourable Society of Middle Temple, 2023. Grateful thanks to the Masters of the Bench of the Honourable Society of the Middle Temple for permission to reproduce this picture.

Although they were very expensive, at around £20, globes became one of the must-have items of the 1590s, finding their way to palaces, libraries, universities, and manors. A large number of smaller versions, for use on board ships, and for people without the means to buy the larger ones, were also produced, with the price starting at a far more reasonable £2.

Globes became the iconic symbol of the late Elizabethan age.

Shakespeare even called the theater in which he invested his fortune The Globe, thus immortalizing Molyneux's achievement for as long as the Bard himself is remembered.

A close inspection of an existing Molyneux terrestrial globe in Middle Temple Library, London, does not reveal exact similarities to the map of China that Christopher helped translate; some of the spellings are different and some of the place names are omitted. However, space on the globe was at a premium, and this was an era of notoriously slapdash word rendering—

there was no standardized spelling in English until much later in history. Whether Christopher's seafaring and cartographical knowledge contributed to these globes is impossible to say for sure.

For now, we cannot count it for certain among Christopher's nautical and scientific contributions to the English-speaking world, but it is not unlikely that he had an indirect influence.

18

Gloriana

During his time on the English ship, Christopher came to know more and more about the person he was traveling the world to meet, Elizabeth, by grace of God Queen of England, France, and Ireland, Defender of the Faith.

This portrait of Queen Elizabeth I, commonly called the Armada Portrait, *painted around the time that Christopher arrived in England, depicts her with her right hand on a globe. She is touching North America, signifying her claim to those lands. In the rear, scenes of the defeat of the Spanish Armada are visible. Artist unknown, 1588.*

The Queen had led a troubled and turbulent life. Her father, King Henry VIII, had had her mother, his second wife, Anne Boleyn, executed due to lack of male issue (although the official reason was adultery, incest, and treason). Queen Anne's death had not solved that, and the king's seeming inability to beget a male heir led him to undertake extreme actions to boost his diminished sense of manhood. These included lavishing vast sums on palace building to impress foreign sovereigns and embarking on hopeless and ill-conceived military campaigns. He funded these massages to his bruised ego through massive debasement of the currency, the destruction of monasteries and the plundering of their wealth, and extensive loans from foreign money lenders. His children were left with a legacy of economic and social turmoil, and an impoverished populace.

The old king was eventually succeeded by his long-looked-for male heir, but Edward VI's reign lasted only six years. He died aged fifteen in 1553, to be succeeded by his sister Mary, who soon married Philip Hapsburg, later to become Philip II of Spain.

These were uneasy years for Elizabeth as under Edward she was implicated in the treasonous manipulations of her guardian, Thomas Seymour, and later under Mary and Philip, imprisoned in the Tower of London, England's most notorious prison, under suspicion of rebellion. A charge she vehemently denied.

In an ironic twist of fate, it was her brother-in-law who saved her life. Few accused of treason exited the tower alive, but Philip thought that Elizabeth's cousin and main rival for the English succession, Mary Queen of Scots (then engaged to France's heir) would take England into France's orbit if she ascended to the throne of Scotland's southern neighbor. He was determined that England would ally with Spain, and so ensured that Elizabeth, the last of Henry VIII's children surviving, remained alive to take the throne and become a future pawn of Spain.

Philip left England to become the Spanish king in 1556, and Mary died in 1558.

Elizabeth was duly enthroned.

In a perhaps predictable plot twist, Philip, having lost his right to the English throne when Mary died, attempted to keep it by proposing marriage to Elizabeth.

The new Queen rejected him out of hand.

His decision to spare her life was beginning to look less politic.

It was not only the King of Spain whom Elizabeth spurned. Known as the "Virgin Queen," Elizabeth refused to take a husband full stop.

In this age of patriarchy, as Caspar Bruneur, the ambassador pressing the suit of Charles II, Archduke of Austria, stated, "that she should wish to remain a maid and never marry [was] inconceivable." But her reign wore on and, time upon time, she rejected foreign royal advances. Nor would she accept a noble English suitor. It became clear that she "meant to die a maid," because she was "already bound unto a husband which is the Kingdom of England."

Her subjects were seriously concerned. No royal succession meant instability and uncertainty. It was not so long since her grandfather Henry VII, of Welsh descent with a relatively weak claim to the throne, had seized England by force of arms to end the War of the Roses, after decades of disputed succession and a tortuous conflict.

Those bleak days of civil war remained prominent in the national conscience.

The early years of Queen Elizabeth's reign were no less precarious than those preceding them. Her father's chaotic financial legacy ensured that building the economy had to take priority, but in the underdeveloped country that she inherited, her advisors had to start small, and truly think outside of the box.

Following the critical, but reflective 1549 writings of Sir Thomas Smith, secretary of state to Edward VI, lambasting his fellow countrymen for looking down on learning, rejecting the experience and advice of low-born people, and an unthinking xenophobic distrust of foreigners, William Cecil, the minister who served Elizabeth faithfully until his death in 1598, worked slowly but surely to support a series of nation-strengthening initiatives. Chief among projects considered for patronage were those which offered the prospect of financial profit for the crown, economic development, better weaponry, and employment for the swathes of poverty-stricken citizens.

Crucially, for immigrants to be granted crown support, they had to undertake to teach their new skill or knowledge to natives. In this way, lucrative industries like glassmaking found roots in English soil, drainage of mines was improved, and water wheels were installed on London Bridge, the capital's first waterworks since Roman times over a millennium before.

European know-how, and new innovations and knowledge from the farthest corners of the earth, such as Christopher's own, contributed a new forward-looking verve to the nation.

Another legacy of her father's was a country cleaved in two by the ongoing schism from Rome, and the transformation from a largely Catholic nation to an increasingly Protestant one.

As a young newly crowned monarch in a challengingly precarious position, Elizabeth attempted to sit on the fence, permitting her subjects, as far as possible, individual freedom of religion as long as they attended her Church of England on Sundays, and their beliefs did not extend to treason.

In 1570, however, Pope Pius V excommunicated her, declaring Elizabeth to be a heretic and releasing her subjects from any allegiance under threat of excommunication themselves should they obey her.

It was a defining moment and transformed her remaining Catholic subjects into an existential threat, playing directly into the hands of those opposed to rapprochement, and accelerating England's journey away from Rome.

Several plots against her life were uncovered and the culprits executed. The common thread was that most would-be assassins

seemed to have either French or Spanish support, foreign interference which only strengthened support for the Queen among
her subjects at large, few of whom were prepared to be ruled by
a continental sovereign whatever their own religious convictions.
England had spent centuries under the rule of French-speaking
monarchs, and aversion to continental hegemony was still raw.

Furthermore, during the 1570s, news from the continent only
strengthened the English anti-Catholics in their convictions.

Dutch Protestants declared independence from the Hapsburg
Spanish crown, forming a new republic, while the Ottoman Empire's conquests encroached ever more on the Italian city-states
and Eastern Europe, both Protestant coreligionists and Muslims
proved welcome allies for isolated England.

After all, the enemy of my enemy is my friend.

French internal religious conflict culminated in the massacre of their Protestant Huguenot minority in a 1572 Parisian
bloodbath. It was witnessed in person by one of Elizabeth's key
advisors, Francis Walsingham, and he did not fail to use it to
strengthen her resolve to resist.

Finally, the young, vibrant, and militant Portuguese-funded
Catholic missionary order, the Society of Jesus, or *Jesuits*, zeal-
ous soldiers for the Roman Church, put their whole being into
destabilizing any nation or people who refused papal primacy.
As far as they were concerned, the Kingdom of Heaven was
built upon Roman foundations. Elizabeth declared them trai-
tors, and deported, imprisoned, or executed those missionaries
who were captured.

England had not always been in such a tumultuous state.

The approximate territory that Queen Elizabeth's government
now controlled had three times been part of continental empires.
The Roman Empire, a short-lived Anglo-Scandinavian Empire in
the tenth century, and after 1066, when Duke William launched
a successful invasion from Normandy to take England into the
French-speaking world.

Over the following half millennium, England and large swathes of what is now France, including at times parts of Ireland, were ruled over by England's monarchs.

Territorial possessions on the Continent waxed but mostly waned during the fifteenth century. The very last mainland bastion, the Port of Calais in northern France, was lost to military conquest in 1557 as a consequence of Philip II of Spain, still king of England at the time, warring with France.

The tiny Channel Islands, just off the French coast, were all that was left of England's former vast continental holdings. They remain so to this day.

And so, at perhaps the lowest point in England's history, Elizabeth's government attempted to revert to the idea of a transnational empire with which to relaunch England.

In the British Isles, the Isle of Man, Cornwall, and Wales, from whence Elizabeth's Tudor dynasty originated, were more or less under English control, though the native languages still flourished in all three places.

The reconquest of Ireland, lost to England's crown during the fourteenth and fifteenth centuries, had long been a deeply held ambition. However, despite huge outlay and massive bloodshed on all sides, pacification and settlement attempts had met with limited success. The Irish, with Spanish support, were determined to frustrate English conquest.

Scotland to the north was an independent nation, and despite extensive English attempts at domination, remained so determinedly. France was an ancient ally of Scotland, and Scotland's Queen Mary, imprisoned in England since 1567 as a result of her rival claim to Elizabeth's throne, was the widow of the French king Francis II.

If unification of the British Isles looked unlikely, hopes of a continental empire were also bleak. Elizabeth had neither the financial nor military means, not to mention the ruthless will and determination to prosecute a war of imperial conquest.

John Dee's *Brytanici Imperii* project was clearly doomed, and so her advisors urged a more proactive maritime policy instead. There seemed no other way to strengthen the nation and preserve independence.

And so, following in Portugal's and Spain's footsteps, maritime endeavor was fostered to establish external trading opportunities, find exploitable natural resources, and seize territories "unclaimed by Christian Kingdoms."

To achieve this, the Queen unleashed seaborne fury. Privateer pirates.

A scourge and plague on all other houses.

The crippled country, starved of trade goods and bullion alike, boomed upon the stolen fare that was fenced in London and countless other ports around England's coasts.

In 1585, Elizabeth went a step further, ceasing her policy of not dispatching armies outside the British Isles by sending an expeditionary force to support the Dutch rebels against their former Spanish overlords.

This, predictably, infuriated King Philip; as far as he was concerned the Netherlands were as much his land as Wales was England's.

If England was outright invading his territory, he could no longer wait for economic collapse or fifth column assassins to produce victory.

When Cavendish and his men departed England in 1586, Spanish invasion fleets were expected on the horizon any day.

19

Singeing the King of Spain's Beard

On January 3, 1588, amid general rejoicing at the miraculous Pacific crossing, a string of small atolls, gray at first, then browner and greener, rose out of a glittering silver-gilt sea, to meet the cloud spirals that Christopher knew indicated their presence. Eventually, the "Islands of Thieves" (the modern-day Marianas) came into view as vivid low, green, sand-encircled specks in the azure ocean, every detail bathed in sunlight.

As the English ship approached close by one of the larger islands, a fleet of sixty or seventy sleek red, white, and black outrigger canoes, seven yards long and half a yard wide, swarmed outward, running swift circles around *Desire*. Triangular woven-reed sails stretched their length, peaking at the top of the mast in the middle, and each boat sported a devilish looking prow-mounted figurehead.

The nimble agility and pace at which they skimmed the waves as they approached reminded Christopher of a pod of dolphins. One second, they were on the way, the next they were there, the six to eight crew members grinning up at *Desire*'s men a couple of yards above them.

And what humans they were. Compared to the thin, wiry, weathered Englishmen and their Asian and African colleagues, these near-naked muscle-bound people with smooth tanned and oiled skin, their long silken black hair either flowing down their backs or bound high in a topknot, were pictures of health. While they were clearly friendly, welcoming their unseasonal visitors warmly, they carried businesslike spear harpoons, sported war slings wrapped around their bodies, and carried pouches of ammunition on woven palm leaf belts.

This illustration from the Boxer Codex *shows a Manila galleon arriving at the Mariana Islands, "the Islands of Thieves." The exchange of food for scrap metal via fishing lines can clearly be seen. Artist unknown, ca 1590.*

The islanders held up baskets of green coconuts, knobby fat roots of myriad colors and shapes, and shiny plump fresh fish, some still thrashing about in the woven containers. *Desire*'s crew drooled.

The Spanish pilot, de Ersola, explained that these islands had no natural source of metal, and hence any old iron would trade for vast quantities of food. He also recounted Magellan's experience, that if islanders were allowed aboard, they would pilfer anything.

Cavendish had prepared, and the men lowered old scraps down by fishing line to the grasping hands below. Christopher joined in the sport, directing a bent old nail a couple of yards downward into the hands of a colossal islander. The man eagerly grabbed the iron and sent up a long, purple-skinned potato in its place. Repeating this a few times provided a feast of roots and fruits to add to the communal pot.

Desire never dropped anchor, and never ceased her forward movement, but that did not stop the deftly handled canoes weaving in and out of each other, displaying their seamanship for the strangers' appraisal. Even when the boats were empty of food to trade, they continued to expertly ply the blue-green waters that frothed and heaved around *Desire*.

Several canoes collided with each other and smashed into *Desire*'s oaken hull, their crews diving gracefully overboard to avoid a braining by the English ship. Despite their corporeal bulk the islanders swam almost as nimbly as their boats to surface, bobbing and laughing several yards beyond the maelstrom. *Desire*'s sailors, few of whom could swim, leaned on the ship's rails gawping and pointing at the satisfied warriors who reveled in their admiring gaze.

The canoes seemed attached like strings to the fleeing English ship and would not take their leave. Christopher could see Cavendish getting agitated, perhaps worried about the islanders' light-fingered reputation. It was a reasonable concern; while the canoes could not match the English ship for bulk, they were far faster, and as *Desire* lay deep and heavy in the water, a warrior could easily have boarded with a leap from one of the fearsome figureheads.

Eventually, Cavendish strode into the armory and passed out six guns before grabbing one himself. The English loaded and placed the guns on the firing forks before lighting the matches and touching the pans as one. At the sudden explosions, alien in this idyllic archipelago, the amicable atmosphere fled, and the canoe crews dived overboard to escape. Christopher wondered if any had been hit. It was hard to say who had dived and who had died.

The men and women of the Ladrones vanished into the dusk behind them as *Desire* forged ahead once more into the rapidly setting sun.

Three hundred or more leagues and eleven days of uncooperative winds and foul weather later, they again spied the cloud formations which forecast land.

At their first sight of the Philippines, the vast, wooded peak of Cape Espiritu Santo on Samar Island, hearts soared. They would soon be on dry land once more.

De Ersola, still limping, navigated them steadily through the choppy currents of the San Bernardino Strait, past the mountains of Samar, and the low-lying, verdant, southern reaches of Luzon. From there, the going was slow and steady in the breezy, but humid climate of the islands.

Desire eventually made landfall in shallow water on the southwestern shore of the small island of Capul on January 15, 1588. A thin beach, hemmed in by rocky spits giving way to sturdy anhaw trees dripping with fruit, greeted them.

Upon burning-hot sand, Christopher set his shaky feet on dry land again. The sun beat down, untrammeled now by the cooling open ocean winds, but the young Japanese man basked in the sweat that pooled on his skin and soaked his clothes. After so long at sea, he was back in a land of soft, tropical green.

It was a long way from the more northern latitudes where he had been born and grown up, but it felt familiar, warm, and almost like a homecoming.

The islands which now form the Philippines had been active in East Asian trade long before the Spanish arrived. Some local states paid tribute to the sultan of Brunei, others recognized the Chinese emperor as their overlord, and Muslim, Japanese, and Chinese mariners had been trading there for centuries. The Spanish jumped in to usurp the local rulers, enforce their alien religion, and seize the trade profits for themselves.

The first Spanish mission to reach these islands, in 1521, was Ferdinand Magellan's. He met a lingering end on the blade of a poisoned spear as he tried to enforce conversion to Catholicism.

Half a century later, in 1571, Spain seized the settlement of

Maynila as a back door to the long-sought wealth and power of Asia, and a base for the first-ever regular and direct trade route to connect every known inhabited continent on earth—the Manila Galleon, or "Galleon of China" as the Spanish called it.

This transpacific trade route transferred silver mined in the Americas to Asia, where it was exchanged for commodities such as gold, manufactures like silk and porcelain, and enslaved people. These made their back way to New Spain, and thence on to trade routes in the Atlantic to fetch a fortune on American, European, and African markets. The profits supported the Spanish crown, and the silver which flowed in the other direction kept the eternally bullion-thirsty East Asian economies, in particular China, monetized, facilitating high standards of living for vast populations.

Neither could have thrived without the other. Eurasia's two extremes had become well and truly globalized via Manila and the Pacific.

The great fire of 1583, probably experienced by Christopher, destroyed the first Spanish Manila which had been built of wood and thatch in the manner of prior Indigenous settlements. It was rebuilt in stone, with grand walls, churches, and administrative buildings befitting its new status as an international trade hub and as a warning to anyone else who had designs on the islands. The rebuilding took decades to complete, and Christopher would have seen only the initial stages.

The Spanish population of Manila in the 1580s was between five hundred and one thousand, most of whom were engaged in trade of some sort, although they were also supposed to be available for militia service when needed.

With only around fifty Spanish women, many foreign men bought Chinese or Japanese women and girls as "local wives." This resulted in a large mixed-heritage population, common throughout Spanish controlled territories, which only grew as the years went by.

There were thousands of Chinese people, known as Sangleys, in Manila, especially during the trading season. This couple portrayed in the Boxer Codex *is dressed sumptuously. Artist unknown, ca 1590.*

Thanks to China's ban on direct trade with Japan, there were a number of Japanese residents also looking for Chinese products in exchange for silver. However, the vast majority of the colony's inhabitants were Chinese, perhaps four thousand in Christopher's time, many of them based in the port of Cavite.

During peak trade times, seven thousand extra Chinese mariners and hundreds more Japanese traders would flock in dozens or even hundreds of ships to Manila to tap into the wealth that transshipped there.

However, Manila was far north of the point where Cavendish and his men first landed in the Philippines at Capul, and hence, in this immense and diverse archipelago, there was not much of a Spanish presence to threaten their passage.

The reception committee was swift to approach.

Through shallow rock-strewn lagoon waters teeming with shining tropical fish and gently swaying sea grasses, came one of the Indigenous chiefs of the island to welcome them in person. Assuming the English were in fact the Spanish, he had his people offer up lush green coconuts filled with fresh, succulent coconut water, and myriad potato roots in all the colors of the rainbow as tribute gifts.

There were hundreds of Japanese people in Manila, especially during the trading season. This couple portrayed in the Boxer Codex *is not rich, their clothing is of the type that common people wore, but the man carries a long sword. He may be a wako-type mariner. The lady wears non-Japanese shoes, and her sash is tied at the front. This traditionally signifies that she is a sex worker. Artist unknown, ca 1590.*

The English grasped at the coconuts over the side and gulped down the cool and refreshing liquid. Christopher would have felt his body lift as the smooth honeyed juice made its way down his throat. The sugary nectar boosted him both spiritually and physically, and a feeling of elation would have spread throughout his body.

Cavendish ordered that the presents would have to be paid for in linen which he presented in person to the fascinated chief aboard *Desire*. It was time to reveal that they were not Spanish and announce that they came in peace to aid the islanders.

This is where politics came into play.

Subverting Spanish power among their Asian vassals had the potential to foment rebellion, disrupt flows of bullion to Europe, and promote English influence. Following his orders from Elizabeth, Cavendish had raided in Africa, pillaged and plundered in the Americas. Now, he had arrived near China, it was time for different tactics to plant the seeds of the Anglo–Cathayan alliances that John Dee and others in England dreamed of.

The Capul nobleman lifted aboard on the shoulders of two of

his men was a walking work of art, the like of which Christopher had probably never seen before, even during his years in Manila.

The man's tanned body was covered in both tattoos and intricately carved scars. He went almost naked, a simple strip of cloth woven from leaves hanging from his waist and tied behind his rear. It was supposed to cover his member, but when it slipped, it exposed the most fantastic and astonishing decoration of all. The local lord did not appear at all ashamed by this but was more than happy to show his marvelous organ and its appendage to the curious and horrified foreign sailors.

Desire's mariners gasped as it was explained exactly why the man had a huge gilt metal nail pushed through the head of his circumcised penis.

They heard how the women of the island insisted that their menfolk, who had in the past been partial to intercourse among themselves, wore this ornament to allow their energies to be retained for their wives' needs. When the urge arose, the women permitted the men to remove the nails. If done without permission, the offender was ostracized.

The metal pin, with spear-like points or bolts at each end, and a hole in the middle for urination, was apparently first inserted during infanthood, with the operation repeated at various intervals until the lad was old enough to need it kept in permanently. It was claimed that it did not cause pain, something that Christopher seriously doubted.

Man-on-man love was perfectly common where Christopher came from, especially among the pirate warriors he had grown up with. He could understand the local ladies' frustration, however, but still...the nail seemed a drastic measure.

Soon, other chieftains and their vassals came to greet the English, bringing with them more baskets of vegetables, fruit, woven crates of squawking chickens, and several plump pigs trussed upside down and howling with rage on bamboo poles carried between two burly men. Cavendish diplomatically paid for it all, and *Desire*'s crew and the islanders settled down to a beach feast of stuffed and tender bamboo pole–roasted pork, cinder-baked potatoes, and juicy fruits. Stocks of Spanish wine from *Santa Ana* flowed freely in the lantern-lit, balmy January evening.

Christopher joined in the festivities and enjoyed a prominent place near Cavendish on the smooth sand, not far from the roaring pit fires over which the butchered pigs slowly roasted.

One evening, as darkness fell, Rodríguez approached Cavendish and asked to speak with him in private. His attitude and bearing had changed considerably, and he now apologized for his previously recalcitrant behavior and swore to serve Cavendish faithfully.

Cavendish magnanimously bade him sit and listened to his story. Rodríguez told how the pilot de Ersola was plotting to warn Manila of *Desire*'s presence and bring down Spanish wrath upon them. He was writing a letter, which he planned to have the islanders deliver in secret, giving word of *Santa Ana*'s capture and the mischief which Cavendish was getting up to by fomenting rebellion in Capul and the islands nearby.

Cavendish stood immediately, demanding the man be brought before him.

Astonishingly, they found de Ersola on *Desire* in the act of actually writing the letter, and he was rowed ashore with the incriminating evidence to be hauled before Cavendish. It was a done and dusted case, there was no denial and there was no groveling or begging from de Ersola. He stood proud, straight, and silent despite his wounded foot, glaring at his captor. When he saw Rodríguez standing in the shadow of the flames, he spat a huge gob into the fire. He knew his Judas.

Cavendish had no patience with dissenting Spaniards.

It was death at dawn.

De Ersola's corpse was cut down, wrapped in his sleeping mat, and thrown into the sea with a cannon ball to weigh it down. The macabre bundle glided slowly down to the coral below. Fish of a million colors surrounded it, and the hanged pilot was lost to view.

They stayed on the island for nine days, restocking food, watering, and making repairs. *Desire* also made a small foray to chart parts of the San Bernardino Strait. Such information would be vital for future English missions, and de Ersola would certainly not be there to guide their passage next time.

Before and after this sortie, chieftains from numerous other islands came to gaze at these curious new foreigners who were neither from distant islands in the locality, nor Spanish, nor even Chinese. They brought tribute, and again Cavendish insisted that it was all paid for fairly. This was a charm offensive which reached its culmination on their final day, January 23.

By the light of gently swaying palm leaf lanterns in the trees fringing the beach, the English commander, probably using Christopher's colleague Alphonso as an interpreter, made a grand speech to the islanders, telling them that he was English, and displaying the flag of Saint George. They and the Spanish were mortal enemies, he explained, and he would be back in two years to aid these islanders against their overlords. The chieftains and their people were rapturous in their cheers, and effusive in their thanks.

As *Desire*'s men prepared to leave, the island boats swarmed around, bidding the Englishmen farewell. Cavendish attempted one last propaganda coup, firing off a cannon, to be greeted by much whooping and cheering from the islanders.

The anchor was displaced from its lodging on the seabed and slowly winched up the side of the ship. The boats were deployed to tug their mistress from her rest, and inch by inch, *Desire* edged out toward the open sea and northward toward the jewel in the Philippine crown, Manila.

20

A Game of Cat and Mouse

Without the Spanish pilot, *Desire* was sailing blind.

Everyone was on edge.

Christopher, who had voyaged south through these islands less than a year ago, knew how perilous the channels and shoals were.

They got as far as the island of Masbate, surveying, plumb lining, and observing as they went, before Cavendish lost his nerve.

As tempting as a raid on Manila might be, it risked the failure of the whole mission. *Desire* was full to breaking point with loot, they had ample provisions, and more awaited them in Java where Drake had been a decade before. Making for the south would put them in waters far less dangerous than these.

Reluctantly, Cavendish ordered a change in course.

Christopher likely breathed a sigh of relief; he had no wish to return to the site of his former life. He also knew that *Desire* might not make it away from there. The defenses were not as strong as they should be, but they were still more than a match for one small English ship. It would have been foolhardy in the extreme to risk an assault.

The sun had risen, and *Desire* was preparing to weigh anchor when there was a shout from the lookout in the fighting top. A small Spanish vessel had been spied, emerging from the lee of two islands.

Desire took an excruciatingly long time to get underway, and by the time her prow was plowing the waves, the Spaniards were disappearing off into the blue. But the chase was on, and as *Desire* got up speed, the distance lessened.

The enemy ship played to its smaller size and moved close into the shallow water of the shore fleeing into the mouth of a half-hidden cove-cum-estuary, where the larger English ship could not pursue.

Then suddenly the wind dropped, and the Spanish ship put out oars. Despite the crew's toiling she was caught by the tidal flow, and slowly swept out to sea again.

Desire dropped anchor in shallow waters in the late afternoon. They were still far from the shore, but the enemy vessel was now only about four miles away. It was time to take to the oars.

One of the ship's boats was lowered, crewed, and got underway. De Ersola's former servant, Francisco, joined as interpreter.

Fish teemed, shoaling together this way and that, changing color with each ray of the afternoon sun as the fresh rowers edged through the clear waters, avoiding coral and submerged rocks. But *Desire*'s skiff could not catch the Spanish boat. It darted once more into the river mouth.

Christopher watched from *Desire*, straining his eyes. Suddenly, three small outrigger canoes danced out from the forested shore, then just as quickly turned and sped back to be replaced by a huge Indigenous *viroco* warship, crewed by dozens of warriors and sporting a number of mounted guns.

The English boat, now turned prey, struggling desperately to evade the hunter, ran aground on a sandbank. Two men jumped out, and, heaving with all their might, pushed the boat off before vaulting back in.

Just as the *viroco* caught up with them, *Desire*'s boat ceased fleeing and went in for the attack. As the two boats were about to collide, grappling hooks were thrown and the *viroco* was hauled in.

The shocked Indigenous mariners abandoned ship, striking out for the beach, leaving the sole Spanish occupant to the mercy of the English. He could not swim.

The audacious role reversal had worked.

Almost unnoticed by the celebrating English, Francisco dived and swam like a fish to swiftly gain the shore just as a column of around sixty fully armored soldiers under a proud Spanish ensign advanced confidently out of the forested hinterland.

As they approached the shore, the soldiers let off a hopeful volley in the direction of *Desire*'s boat. The shot fell short to little purpose, leaving only a great cloud of dirty pale smoke hanging limp in the humid air.

The small vessel that they had been chasing all day appeared again at the river mouth, now bristling with guns. Once more, *Desire*'s boat became the prey, and turned tail to flee.

Cavendish ordered *Desire*'s cannon to cover the retreat. The gun crews rushed to their stations, charges and shot were rammed down, the barrels run out. The sailors crouched, matches smoldering, awaiting further orders.

As soon as the English boat reached the cover of *Desire*'s guns, the Spanish scuttled back to safety.

The captive, Lope de Arjoma, was a simple man. Trembling incessantly, he could barely string a sentence together, a state which was not helped by the fact that he thought he was about to die at the hands of heretics.

It transpired that he had only recently been judged well enough to resume maritime duties after a long illness and had been sent here with sixty comrades—the men on the beach—to take possession of *Santiago*, the gigantic successor to *Santa Ana* which was being built in a shipyard located just up the river. The irons to attach the rudder had been delivered a matter of days before and she would soon be seaworthy.

The shipyard lay vulnerable with a whole new galleon ripe

for destruction and immobile within. Cavendish pondered, then drained his tankard of ruby-red wine.

On the island's shores huge bonfires had appeared. Lope de Arjoma's comrades were showing their strength. Cavendish heard their message loud and clear, and once more, reluctantly, ordered a tactical withdrawal.

Sunrise saw *Desire* heading southwest. Once she was well clear of the Spanish base, Cavendish ordered the ship's boat hauled in from where it bobbed behind, and Lope de Arjoma was rowed ashore. He would find his way back to his people easily enough, and now he carried an important letter from Cavendish addressed to Governor Luis de Santiago de Vera.

The missive requested politely that Manila increase its stocks of gold, so that when Cavendish returned in a few years, he had something to plunder.

Unbeknownst to Cavendish, Manila was already festering with revolt caused by his presence.

A rebellious Indigenous ruler, Rajah Muhammad Zahir al-Din, fuming over countless insults to his dignity and honor, had somehow heard that the English were coming to throw the Spanish into the sea. He enlisted the help of Juan Gayo, a Japanese pirate who would provide weapons to the rebels and enter the colony with his cutthroats in the guise of peaceful traders.

They would all rise up to exterminate the Spanish when Cavendish appeared in Manila Bay.

In one of history's cruel twists of fate, Cavendish was utterly unaware of all of this, and what is known as the Tondo Conspiracy was betrayed before a shot could be fired.

The ringleaders were hanged, and their heads displayed in cages as a warning. Their properties were confiscated and plowed with salt to render the soil infertile.

Cavendish, in sad ignorance, headed toward Java.

It was January 29, 1588.

21

Java

Since leaving California, reasonably fresh food and good wine had ensured the health of *Desire*'s men. Aside from de Ersola's hanging, only one of the Dutch recruits from *Santa Ana* had died. But as they sailed south past the Moluccas Islands, toward Java, disease reared its head.

First to die was the cooper John Gameford, who languished in extreme agony for a week before he succumbed. The body was wrapped in his sweat and blood-stained damask bedding, speedy prayers were said for his soul, and the long bundle headed over *Desire*'s side.

Gameford's demise heralded an epidemic.

Three days later, on Ash Wednesday, Captain Havers, second-in-command to Cavendish, breathed his last. He had been in the grip of a fearsome ague for a week, burning up, keeping nothing down, and thrashing about in his own vomit. By the end, his skin had taken on a yellowish hue, and he had been in a coma for two days.

Cavendish himself presided at the ceremony before the assembled crew.

A farewell gun salute pealed across the vast ocean, and the body, wrapped in bedding and sailcloth with a cannonball added for weight, broke the waves for the last time.

Soon, many of the crew were falling to this pestilence that Rodríguez called *mal de Luanda* (the Luandan disease), and some others seemed to think was *mala aria*, "bad air." For a month or more, Christopher's sleeping quarters in the armory overflowed with writhing victims. The sailors on their gun deck closed up all ports and grilles to keep out fresh air. Everyone knew that it carried disease-laden vapors.

The ship, never the most fragrant of places, now became a putrid prison. The only way to escape the worst of it was to evacuate to the open deck where the healthy slept under the bright stars, their celestial glow undimmed by the human tragedy unfolding below.

There was no known medicine for this malady other than prayer.

Christopher, when he inevitably succumbed, would have suddenly felt the need to urinate and staggered to the side of the ship.

To his horror, he would have seen the urine was tinged black.

The knowledge of what was to come would have overwhelmed him, and as pain slowly spread through his joints and muscles, he already probably felt like death was at hand.

Body burning, he likely curled up on his sleeping mat, and writhed in delirious torment, waking later to shivering and intense cold.

But Christopher was strong.

Within a few days, he became able to keep down water and a little food. A week later he was probably back at his duties.

Miraculously, there were no further deaths. One by one, the sick recovered and somehow returned to work.

Using a combination of Christopher's Chinese map, Drake's

incomplete charts from the decade before, and Rodríguez's experience, the navigators charted a course southward.

Strong currents and winds flowing from the Pacific to the Indian Ocean drew them rapidly past Mindanao toward the Spice Isles, then through the Banda and Flores Seas to the great island of Java, which passed by in a mirage of white beaches, rocky outcrops, great towering forests, and in the very distance, gigantic mountains scraping the sky.

Desire eventually came to anchor in a wide bay in a sparkling, wave-flecked sea among a host of fishing boats which swiftly fled landward. Upon reaching the shore, the fishermen hauled their craft up the beach and melted into the forest.

Cavendish ordered *Desire*'s boat brought alongside, and with the African man who spoke a local language, he rowed close inshore. The interpreter called out that they were friendly and meant no harm. They simply wanted water and food.

One of the fishermen must have passed on the word, because three days later a *kora kora* outrigger boat delivered a local pilot, barefoot, bare-chested, and clad in a colorful sarong to conduct them to the local ruler's city.

Under the pilot's supervision, *Desire* proceeded to a large settlement of wooden houses with a prosperous feel to it. Chinese ships lay at anchor, and hundreds of smaller, brightly painted Javanese craft of myriad types buzzed about their business. Christopher reflected that it was the first town he had seen since leaving Manila.

Desire anchored, the pilot went ashore, and soon a splendid *kora kora*, rowed by dozens of straining men and armed with swivel cannon, brought the king's chief vizier to greet them. The nobleman, resplendent in a brilliantly dyed turban with a short sarong about his waist, his chest sporting an arrow-shaped scar, was accompanied by a light-skinned Portuguese interpreter in local dress.

It transpired that there was a Portuguese presence in the kingdom and the interpreter was the son of a European man and a local woman.

Cavendish put on the best display he could, wining and dining the vizier and his interpreter while the crew put on a musical accompaniment. When it got dark, he offered the minister his own bed in the Great Cabin for the night. The hospitality was readily accepted by the tipsy visitors.

In the morning, the drowsy vizier was awoken by every member of the crew firing his harquebus into the air. In startled fear, he bounded out of the cabin, but laughed delightedly when he saw that the salute was in his honor.

Clearly charmed by all this exotic entertainment, the minister ordered the English provided with whatever supplies they needed.

A few days later, just after dawn, ten heavily laden crafts approached *Desire*. The delicate job of lading, via an elaborate getup of ropes and pulleys, took all morning.

Crates of live chickens, ducks, geese, pigs trussed with twine on bamboo poles, and two huge oxen in sturdy frames were slowly loaded. Vast baskets and bundles of short bananas, sugarcane, coconuts, oranges, limes, salt, and sweetmeats were stacked on deck, and best of all, they were accompanied by copious quantities of potent palm wine. By the afternoon, the ship felt more like a farm than a seagoing vessel.

That sweltering tropical night, punctured only by gentle snores and lapping waves, Christopher may have gazed up at the mere shard of a moon, curved and shiny as a Japanese blade, and taken his first draft of the clear spirit.

It was like nothing he had ever experienced before.

The southern stars shone all the brighter, and his head seemed to clear, although he could not remember it being foggy. An enormous feeling of euphoric comfort and satisfaction descended upon him.

He had survived the *mal de Luanda* and all the other perils of the last year.

How blessed he was to be here, alive, in this beautiful place, freed, well-fed, and held in respect.

Before they left, Cavendish invited several of the kingdom's Portuguese traders aboard. They were desperate for any news from Europe, despite it being years out of date.

Disgust at Portugal's continued subjugation by Spain was tempered by news that the English had offered asylum and support to their true king, Dom António.

The men toasted their motherland and drank death to Spain, drunkenly assuring Cavendish that Philip II's new subjects in the East had no love for him and would happily rise in rebellion with English support. They would, furthermore, ensure that the local warriors, valiant, fearless, and loyal unto death, were at Cavendish's disposal.

Cavendish gleefully accepted their pledges and soaked up this golden intelligence. Neither Elizabeth nor the Portuguese pretender in London knew anything of the festering resentment on the other side of the world. In fact, they knew little or nothing about politics in Asia, nor how it could aid their own struggle against Spain. Cutting off King Philip's riches here would start dominoes tumbling around the globe. The disruption would eventually reach Europe, and Spain's gigantic navies and vast standing armies would crumble and fade.

The merchants' pro-English sentiments were richly rewarded with the gift of a number of church ornaments for their lovingly tended chapel.

It is to be assumed that they were unaware of the provenance of their new treasures, nor that the South American holy sites to which they previously belonged had been reduced to ash.

The small group of Portuguese merchants were long established in this out-of-the-way kingdom on Java for the same reason that Drake had returned to England this way and not via China or Japan, despite the further renown it would have ensured him.

Spices.

In our modern world, where global commodities are freely available everywhere, it is hard to believe that thousands of lives and gargantuan effort was expended to simply supply spices such as pepper and cloves to European dinner tables. But the men who risked their lives to traverse the world and satisfy cravings for spices could make profits of up to 32,000 percent on their cargoes.

Three of the most profitable seasonings, cloves, nutmeg, and mace, could only be found growing in one place on earth, the Moluccas Islands, which became known simply as the Spice Islands.

The traditional spice trade routes westward involved a host of middlemen in subcontinental India and the Middle East, who sold their heavily marked-up wares via merchants of Venice and other Italian city-states to the continent. Europe, which had few products of value to trade with, had to pay in scarce silver or gold, thereby leaking the crucial commodities on which monetized economies were based, lessening the money supply and distorting wider financial systems.

However, the Portuguese seaborne escape from the Atlantic world in 1497 brought Europeans into the center of world trade, the Indian Ocean, for the first time. The large Portuguese vessels were able to cut out the middlemen and trade for large volumes directly in subcontinental India, thereby undercutting Venice to dominate the European spice trade.

With numerous ships and an increasingly secure Asian foothold, they reasoned that if they could find the source of the spices, they could lower their costs even further. By 1511, they had navigated a route to Java and then the Moluccas Islands, and immediately started to establish themselves by making local alliances, setting up remote trading posts, and building forts in easily defendable positions.

The trade in Asian spice to Europe carried on as Portugal's exclusive monopoly for more than sixty years, enriching the formerly poverty-stricken, peripheral country, and enabling it to reach around the globe, even to China and Japan.

In 1580, when Spain unified with Portugal, King Philip II forbade English ships to dock in Lisbon, thereby cutting London's supply of spices. Fortunately, and providently, Francis Drake, having completed his circumnavigation, appeared almost immediately with a huge cargo of cloves and the priceless knowledge of how to reach the Spice Islands for more. He had bought his spices with looted Spanish gold, and hence he was a twofold hero.

Desire, the second English ship to reach this region, was already so weighed down with riches that even spices did not tempt Cavendish, but the feat confirmed, once again, that it was possible to navigate there across the Pacific.

In the coming century, with Dutch and English shipping arriving in earnest, wars with devastating local and global consequences would be fought here, but in 1588, it was still a world of sleepy Portuguese outposts, long-established Chinese and occasional Japanese trading hubs, and powerful local rulers.

Despite the bond of Spain and Portugal under King Philip II in the Iberian Union, the extra-European territories remained separately governed, so Cavendish's Portuguese friends were tasked with passing on a letter which would reach Europe via Portuguese India.

As in Manila, Cavendish mischievously stated that he would be back soon, and warned his enemies to make ready more plunder. Christopher smiled. The Spanish, his former masters, would be white with fury.

In positive spirits after the Javan welcome, *Desire* weighed anchor on March 16, 1588. This time there was no wowing of the locals with gunnery; cannon here were often far bigger than anything the English carried.

Java faded beyond the horizon as they swept out into the Indian Ocean toward Africa.

22

The Last Leg

They could tell Africa was growing close as the currents changed, and albatrosses, with their vast black wings, started to appear high among the scuttling clouds. Christopher would have known this bird. In Japanese it was called *ahodori*, "idiot bird," because it was so easy to catch on land. He probably chuckled to himself.

After six weeks, on May 1, Africa appeared at last as a vast low-lying land bordered with brown sand, but as they approached, the seas got progressively rougher, shoaling waves throwing the wooden ship hither and thither.

Ten days after sighting land, as the shoaling worsened, a storm raged out of the west to further pummel little *Desire*, pushing her eastward, away from the Atlantic, back toward Asia.

The beleaguered crew fought valiantly against the roaring wind and towering waves that rose higher even than *Desire*'s mainmast, enveloping the ship. Visibility was zero, and the unrelenting creaking of the timbers told of a ship threatening to rip apart at the seams.

It was madness to attempt to make headway in this typhoon,

but Cavendish could do little else. To try for land would be to suicide on the rocks clearly marked on Rodríguez's Portuguese charts.

These were the worst conditions that Christopher had encountered since the action off California, and as in that battle, he had to take his turn at the bilge pumps, living a soaked and shivering existence for an interminable day and night. He would have prayed constantly to Mazu, to deliver him from this forsaken place.

On the second morning, the gales blew out to leave a calm, almost waveless sea. The ship was battered, the sails tattered and gray. But she lived, they lived, to fight another day. Cavendish ordered a man aloft to the fighting top to assess their progress.

It turned out that they were sailing just fifty leagues southeast of the Cape of Good Hope, the landmark that signified entrance into the Atlantic Ocean, and heralded the last leg of their voyage.

But *Desire* lay adrift, buffeted by the waves and unable to make any headway, impotent without wind to fill the sails.

At midnight, the wind picked up and by the light of a full moon, *Desire* inched slowly westward until morning when the breeze dropped off once more.

Two long, tedious days and nights they lay, becalmed, while a disorienting thick fog rippled around them. In these little-understood waters, Christopher knew they were playing with death. Some crew members had been this way with Drake a decade earlier and they recalled the hidden rocks that waited to impale unsuspecting ships that lay at the mercy of contrary currents.

On May 14 at around three o'clock, the fog suddenly cleared to reveal land before them, surf foaming in anger as it smashed the rocky shore. They knew they were approaching the Cape now because of the three distinctive peaks standing beside each other above the low-lying shore.

On Saturday, May 21, nine weeks after leaving Java, *Desire* rounded the Cape of Good Hope and the pilots judged by the waters that they had passed into the Atlantic Ocean. The path to England was now clear.

At the same time, far to the North, the Spanish Armada was making its final preparations to leave Lisbon's port and put an end to England's independence.

The east wind did not cease, and *Desire* flew before it. Fresh water was needed desperately, but the gale was too strong to resist, and they passed the Cape, tantalizingly close, but unable to reach its safe anchorage.

It was not for another eighteen days, having been borne northward by the stormy winds that continued to billow in the tired, discolored sails, that they managed to anchor safely in a drizzly, secluded bay on the northwest side of a remote green smudge in the endless ocean, the Atlantic island of Saint Helena.

In the steep valley leading inland from their anchorage, the search parties stumbled upon a vine-covered Portuguese hamlet, beautiful in its simplicity, and the first true buildings Christopher had stepped inside since leaving Manila.

Built upon a gushing stream, at its center was a small whitewashed church complete with bell and a neatly tiled stone cross. A miniscule slice of the divine on this far-flung isle.

The crew had not seen a place of Christian worship since South America, and not left one unmolested since England. This time however was different. Despite the fact it was a Catholic sanctuary the men gave thanks before the wooden crucifix and icon of Christ's mother for their deliverance thus far.

At length, the statue of Saint Mary, a figure often equated with the goddess Mazu by Asian seafarers, radiating love and compassion, may have prompted Christopher to implore this Heavenly Mother to preserve him on his odyssey.

The sailors rose from prayer, and spread out to investigate the little settlement, kicking in doors and forcing open shutters.

Cowering in one of the houses were three Africans and a

Javan. All four had been abandoned to tend to the island's crops until Portuguese ships arrived clamoring for fresh food and respite from the harsh travails of the homeward voyage.

The abandoned men, although scared out of their wits by the rough Englishmen, had no compunction about guiding the invaders around the island. They also reported a narrow miss. Five large Portuguese carracks of at least eight hundred tuns, laden with Indian cloth, pearls, and jewels, had left only three weeks before. Although it would have been a risky business, Portuguese Indiamen were normally only lightly armed, and to capture one and sail it home would have been an amazing scalp with which to cap off the voyage. Sadly, it was not to be, the carracks would already be halfway to Europe by now.

From the church, cobbled paths led up the valley along whispering brooks to where the narrow valley opened into a virtual Garden of Eden. Orchards of lemon, orange, pomegranate, fig, and date trees bathed the valley in cool shade, and only petered out high on the steep slopes where the ground became brown and barren. The confused trees, unaware of seasons in this equatorial region, bore blossoms, ripe and unripe fruit, all at the same time.

Among the seasonless orchards, in the sweet, moist cover of the trees, lay patches of great orange pumpkins and plump green melons. Myriad herbs—parsley, sorrel, basil, fennel, anise, mustard—and radishes flourished. Fluttering, running, and flying among the verdant woods were light brown striped partridges, red-necked pheasants and black turkeys.

Neither Christopher nor his comrades had ever seen the like. They marveled at the birds' size and abundance, not to mention the beauty and taste of their eggs. The luscious savor and sweet liquid richness of the raw eggs in his mouth and throat would have been a sensation which stayed with him for a long time.

The landing party took a score of birds for their meal that day and then kept killing. The prey seemed to have no sense of danger, for although they fled at the gunshots, they quickly returned, oblivious of the fate that awaited them.

It had been eons since the crew had had fresh food of any kind, but that night they would feast on roast fowl and delicate herb-flavored eggs.

Christopher would have watched in disbelief as great herds of four-legged beasts, the size of a donkey but with a horselike mane and long beard, gamboled over the impossible cliffs and paused on the sheer outcrops at the top to observe their rocky kingdom.

They seemed to be a type of goat, and the juicy yet firm meat which they later provided confirmed it. The crew took great numbers of the beasts, but still the herds swarmed like bees high up in the hills.

Another source of nutrition was the swift and powerful, gray-colored wild pig.

Warier than either the goats or game, they sensibly stayed well away from the men who sought them, but when captured and stewed with island onions, tubers, greens, and any number of aromatics they fed *Desire*'s hungry men for days.

The English took what they could, gorged themselves, refilled their casks, performed sorely needed repairs on the damaged ship, shaved, washed themselves and their clothes in the pure mountain streams, and then left the castaways to their lonely watch.

On June 20 at eight o'clock in the evening as dusk transitioned to night and an elegant moon rose silver and pure from the ocean, *Desire* caught the wind. It blew her north and onward toward her final destination.

England.

The abundance of Saint Helena was not merely the result of bounteous nature and an excellent climate. The Portuguese are thought to have originally discovered the uninhabited island in May 1502 and established it as a victualing station, a place of rest and refreshment before the last leg of the long voyage home from the Indian subcontinent. Sick mariners were left there to recuperate and wait for other ships, who in turn left their sick, and boarded those fortunate souls who had been healed by the island's magic.

Christopher would have wondered how many trafficked Japanese people, borne ripple-like upon the shockwaves of civil war at home, had found respite here on their way to Europe. Was he the first of his people to come this way? It was unlikely.

From Christopher's time onward, the area had become a hot spot for English buccaneers waiting to pounce upon tired Portuguese merchant ships, until, later, in the seventeenth century, with their sea power more established, the English decided to go a step further and seize control of the island itself. They used it in much the same way that the Portuguese had done but expanded operations to form a fully-fledged plantation colony with enslaved Africans to tend the crops. The island would later go down in history as Napoleon's final prison, so remote that even the legendary French emperor could not escape. He died there in 1821.

Upon departure, *Desire* made good time. The occasional windless days were more than made up for by fair gales which thrust them ever onward. Smelling London on the breeze, they crossed the equator again, and saw the night sky return to its reassuringly familiar northern hemisphere norm.

By August 23, they had reached the Azores, and altered course for the English Channel.

In the Bay of Biscay, they came upon a Flemish merchantman and heard tidings of the spectacular failure of Spain's attempted invasion of England. The Flemish sailors could give few details, but such an attempt had been threatened for as long as any of *Desire*'s crew had been alive, so they would not have been surprised. The circumstances of England's delivery from foreign threat would become clear when they arrived, but for now it was enough to know that they had homes to return too.

That day, *Desire* celebrated in relief and thanksgiving.

Christopher was well used to English drunkenness and frolics by now, but this was something else. After prayers had been said and suitable thanksgiving offered unto the victorious English God, the final barrels of Javan spirit were tapped, and Cavendish ordered double rations. Hardly a man on board could stand, and most slept where they fell.

The tempest which smashed into them just two days from port hit like a spiteful, vengeful divinity. They had been granted riches beyond their wildest dreams, survived against the odds, and sped on their way for a whole year, and now all their hopes were threatened as they came within sight of home.

The wind howled as thunder roared and the rain beat the tired vessel this way and that. The hull timbers wailed, solid spars snapped like twigs, sails rent as if they were paper, and rope as thick as a man's arm snapped like twine.

Desire seemed ready to succumb to the beckoning depths of the ocean that had borne her so far. In mortal terror, the crew resorted to the only remedy they knew, prayer.

Probably all Christopher could think of was the bitter irony of having sailed the globe, only to arrive as a pale, limp corpse on an English beach.

Then as suddenly as it had blown up, the storm fled, leaving a clear, clean, fresh summer's day, with the screech of seagulls on the breeze to foretell land.

To hoots of glee and yet more prayers of thanksgiving from those around him, Christopher got his first sight of England.

23

Plymouth Ho

The Biscayan tempest had shaken the exhausted men to their very core, but the elation of deliverance from the storm, and reality of surviving the epic voyage brought them within sight of the British Isles with singing hearts.

Desire was headed for Plymouth, a harbor in the very southwest of England.

Christopher would have gazed with intense interest at the scraggy shoreline of Cornwall, just west of Plymouth as *Desire* sailed eastward.

He saw sheer, crooked, rusty-brown and dirty-green rocky cliffs with wind-battered plants and clumpy flowers hugging their heights. Beautiful golden beaches blossomed here and there at the foot of the jagged cliffs, while hook-beaked seagulls glided overhead and squawked perpetually like a screeching choir in the ship's wake.

Occasional stone forts and towers, camouflaged against gunmetal-gray cliffs, betrayed the presence of humans. Whether the fortifications were to guard against pirates or belonged to the sea marauders themselves, Christopher did not know.

However, the late summer sun shone bright, and Christopher relaxed, cradled in its soft warmth. He would have reflected that in the sunlight, the Cornish coast's wild, untrammeled beauty was more welcoming than both the misty and mysterious California coast, and the storm-swept southern African shores, but lacked the peaceful warmth and verdancy of southeast Asian islands.

Presently, the land culminated in a spiked headland and unfolded to reveal the mouth of a wide opening in the coast. *Desire* seemed nothing more than a speck in the blue-green immenseness as she turned to enter the bay which the men called Plymouth Sound.

They continued past steep wooded slopes and rocky promontories, which funneled toward a grass-topped cliff in the dead center of the bay. As *Desire* moved further in, to the right of a fortified island, Christopher spied two giant white figures carved into the green. The crew said they commemorated an ancient battle on this spot between humans and the giants who had lived here before the advent of men.

Above the giants stood the beacon to be lit in times of trouble. It had had plenty of use recently.

Desire rounded the cliff to the right of the giants, where perched on the edge just above needles of rock was a formidable gray castle of stone with four towers. The outermost tower, above the harbor mouth, was sheathed in a dull gray lead, and great guns poked their snouts over the ramparts. It was as formidable a fortification as any Christopher had seen in his life, unquestionably the strongest since Manila fifteen months before. It announced in no uncertain terms that this was an abode of proud warriors and mariners, prepared and ready to defend their land.

Desire anchored in Cattewater, just beyond the safety of the stone-walled Sutton Pool harbor.

An illustration of Plymouth much as Christopher would have encountered it. From A True Mapp and Description of the Towne / of Plymouth and the Fortifications there, with the workes and approaches of the Enemy, at the last Seige A.o 1643. *After Wenceslaus Hollar, seventeeth century.*

A peal of cannon fire and church bells greeted them, echoing over the waters. Once more an English ship had returned from unknown realms and Plymouth celebrated.

It was September 9, 1588, and the town was in a state of high excitement. Only weeks before, God had delivered them from the "Great Enterprise Against England." The Spanish Armada, one hundred thirty ships, eight thousand sailors, and eighteen thousand soldiers, was so large, it had taken two whole days to leave Lisbon's port in late May before sailing northeast to its date with destiny.

Queen Elizabeth's Navy Royal was not strong enough to repel the invasion alone, and so, it was that on July 20, 1588, the men of Plymouth, with their hearts in their mouths, had sailed hastily to meet the invaders. These fathers and sons, volunteers all, England's first line of defense, fought under the gaze of anxious mothers, wives, and children gathered on Plymouth Hoe. What ensued was a whirlwind of tacking English ships, puffs of smoke, and the delayed retorts of cannon fire.

The battle for England had begun.

The English held off, attempting to bombard the huge crescent-shaped galleon battle formation from afar while the Spanish simply tried to ignore the English attacks, batting the smaller enemy ships away like flies while doing their best to stay in line.

Little damage could be caused at long range, and the defenders' tactics simply whittled down the already short supply of gunpowder. The English ships followed in the Armada's wake, pouncing on vessels which fell out of formation and grasping at any opening for an attack.

The Spanish plan was to meet the Duke of Parma's army further up the Channel, and then conduct a decisive amphibious assault on Southern England. As the rendezvous point got closer, the English harassment became evermore desperate and daring, concluding in a fireship assault, and a narrow victory off the Northern French coast near Gravelines.

It was enough.

A seasonal tempest blew King Philip's ships away from the target, and eventually forced them so far north that contrary winds and currents put paid to any ideas of invasion.

What was left of the great Armada was then drawn by the elements around the treacherous coasts and craggy islands of northern Scotland, where many met their doom on the rocks.

The great enterprise had been foiled; England was safe.

Now, only months later, Cavendish had returned to Plymouth after two years riding the world's oceans. He was not a local man like many of the great sailors of the age, but he was English, and his triumph reflected on them all.

At first sight, Plymouth must have been, in a way, deeply familiar to Christopher. It had many similarities to the other ports and bases where the young Japanese man had spent his whole life. Like Manila and Nagasaki's bays, it was a fine natural harbor, and fortified with gun emplacements. Like those places too, it was a town that owed its very existence to maritime trade and, to an even greater extent, piracy.

But in most ways, it was highly exotic.

The Japan of his youth was timber-built. His time in Manila coincided with the cusp of stone construction after the great fire, but little had yet been completed when he boarded *Santa Ana*, never to return. The main landfalls during his voyage to England—Capul, and Java—were also lands of timber and bamboo.

The buildings on the inside of Plymouth's port, though only just visible to Christopher through the mast-filled harbor, were very different. He saw an eclectic mixture of edifices of gray stone, wooden beams, and white plaster, some with many stories, creeping up the steep sides from Sutton Pool to form one of the largest settlements he had ever seen. The population of approximately five thousand was growing rapidly, not harmed at all by the Elizabethan boom in legalized piracy, and the city was just starting to play a key role in world history as the main jump-off point for English activities outside Europe, particularly to the New World.

It was from here that Drake had sailed to claim California for the Queen, from here that the Roanoke ships, including Thomas Cavendish's vessel *Elizabeth*, sailed, and from here that most of the raiders of King Philip's territories bid England farewell. Eventually it would be from here in 1620 that the religious fanatics on *Mayflower* would see their homeland for the final time before voyaging to New England where they founded a settlement called Plymouth.

Christopher spent a tiresome night aboard *Desire* along with the men tasked with guarding the treasure. All in the town guessed what that ship contained and many eyes, green and hungry with envy, gazed longingly from the shore.

But Christopher and his comrades were not on guard duty, they were now part of the treasure.

Cavendish had been fearful that the town might be in the

midst of plague and had had no wish to risk their lives unnecessarily. He remembered only too well the fact that Frobisher's Americans had perished quickly, even if the Roanoke men, Manteo and Wanchese, had thrived and returned home.

The privateer also wanted nothing left to chance in his bold claim that they were "gentlemen." The people of England were to be gobsmacked by the spectacle of these civilized, literate, English-speaking noble bloods from so far away, and Cavendish meant to control access to his charges carefully.

Cattewater, where *Desire* anchored, was just outside the fortified Sutton Pool, situated in the lee of a peninsula opposite the Hoe. Toward nightfall, pinpoints of light emanated from the buildings and streets on shore and faint noises of chatter and laughter drifted over from the town where the sailors who had been granted first shore leave were drinking, eating, and fornicating to their hearts' content. The sounds of raucous and bawdy celebration mingled incongruously with the peaceful, steady lapping of gentle waves around the ship anchored safely at last in Plymouth Sound.

The next morning, Cavendish returned to escort Christopher and his colleagues ashore.

Alighting from the boat onto a solid stone quay, while curious onlookers looked them up and down, they became the first documented East Asian people to land in the British Isles.

24

Anglo-Japanese Pioneer

Cavendish led them first through a throng of curious dockside bystanders to the customs house, a four-storied stone building at the end of the dock. This was where he was to declare all his liberated riches and pay the duty due to the crown.

The men inside gaped at the visitors from afar as Cavendish made the introductions. Onlookers from the quay had followed the action, and now a small gaggle of people was gathered outside, pushing and shoving to get a glimpse through the tiny windows. The hubbub drew more folk, and soon it became a crowd.

Later, Christopher and the others, amidst the ringing of more bells, were led up the steep and narrow cobbled alleys past shiny new houses and less blessed tatty, run-down hovels toward Saint Andrew's Church where they and the other crew members were to give thanks for their deliverance.

The men in the ever-multiplying crowd were dressed very differently from the sailors who Christopher had known for the past year.

The ragged but tough and tarred protective marine smocks

gave way to shapeless, dull-colored shaggy coats, leather smocks, loose shirts, and brimmed hats or caps. Although ununiformed in this age, most of the men were clearly soldiers, posted here from afar and probably soon to be demobilized after the invasion threat had truly passed.

But what really would have caught Christopher's eye were the women who made up the majority of the crowd. These were the first English women that Christopher had seen, the first women he had seen in a whole year since California, and he could not help but be curious. Poking out from under their modest head coverings, he saw thin hair the color of sun-dried straw, prominent noses, long faces, cheeks rosy from the sea air, and a pinched, thin look about them. They used few cosmetics and wore faded or drab browns, light blues, and grays. Even in the late summer heat, they wore long dresses, hats, coifs, caps, or bonnets.

Despite the fascinating human traffic, as he moved further into the town, it was the smell that would have overwhelmed him. The teeming streets were open sewers, but even the almost engulfing stench of ordure could not fully overpower the stink of rotted fish. Records tell of it permeating everything. The vast open spaces of the eternal sea where he had largely been spared the olfactory assault of dense human settlement, had given way to these narrow, dark, and claustrophobic alleys. The mixture of vigorous fetors almost made him retch in disgust.

His fellow sailors were clearly in the same boat, but they and he would all be used to it soon enough.

Of all the strange and wonderful stone buildings that Christopher saw in Plymouth, Saint Andrew's Church was probably the most dumbfounding. He had likely never before seen such a large space enclosed with a roof.

And what a roof it was. Shouldered on the back of colossal stone columns, it seemed to reach to the very heavens where its distant ceilings were shrouded in darkness.

St. Andrew's Church in Plymouth, where Christopher and his colleagues would have given thanks for their safe arrival. From Old Plymouth *drawn by Sibyl Jerram, 1913.*

Below, in the aisles, however, the church was bright. Windows of glass, a true wonder, let in the light, contrasting curiously with the darkness of the towering heights above.

The clergyman who presided over the service of thanksgiving stood behind the altar and in front of the gigantic window at the end of the chancel, dwarfed by the size of the place.

Notwithstanding the church's magnitude, it was standing room only, even the ornately carved wooden balconies were packed. It felt like the whole town had turned out to celebrate in thanksgiving.

In these surroundings, Christopher would have felt the magic of the foreign religion for the first time. Something that in all honesty had probably escaped him during the dour, interminable, incomprehensible prayer sessions on board *Desire*. The packed precincts, the congregational chanting of psalms, and the powerful voice of the preacher booming from the central pulpit, like that of God himself, might have left Christopher swaying, both inside and out.

This religion was suited here in a way it did not fit in elsewhere. It was the product of these people and this land.

What else did Christopher do in Plymouth for a month before *Desire* headed for London? There is no record of this, but the most popular entertainments were bull baiting in the ring just adjacent to the carved giants on Plymouth Hoe and drinking in the many taverns such as the smoky but cozy Minerva Inn.

Cavendish, however, got down to business.

On the day of his arrival, he wrote from Plymouth to publicize his homecoming. The original English letter is no longer extant, but French, Dutch, Spanish, and Italian versions were published in pamphlet form within a few weeks or months of arrival and news of Christopher and his comrade's arrival spread throughout Europe.

On October 8, he also wrote to Sir Francis Walsingham, Queen Elizabeth's secretary of state in London.

Thirty-six hours later, the letter lay in the hands of the chief of intelligence.

The old spy sat in bed, propped up by cushions with his sheets tumbled around him. He was thin and pale, his fingers gnarled, all color long knocked out of him by the sickness and troubles that afflicted him. His monarch could no longer call him her "Moor," a joke about his previously swarthy looks.

A pewter cup of watered wine stood on the table to his right, and three secretaries were in attendance, standing at desks around the large four-poster bed. Just because he was sick did not mean that the business of state or his own affairs ground to a halt.

The missive from the south coast, accompanied by a report from his customs officials, contained a great many platitudes which he had glossed over, and some welcome financial news:

his customs officers in Plymouth (he had bought the rights to all national custom duties from the Queen) had collected a magnificent £900 from *Desire*'s cargo.

Then came the really interesting part.

Cavendish revealed that he had kept certain secrets for the secretary of state's ears only. Walsingham lived for information; the more knowledge and intelligence he had, the better he could serve his Queen and Church. What could Cavendish have found on his long travels that was better than Spanish gold and Chinese silks?

He knew about Christopher and his companions; the news had spread rapidly along with excitement about their imminent arrival in London. Even the Queen had demanded to see them. However, he was probably skeptical about their true worth. After all, communication would be difficult, and they would no doubt be little more than a piece of propaganda for the ambitious young adventurer to catch Her Majesty's eye.

Most visitors from distant realms had sadly proven delicate and prone to speedy deaths.

Well, he would have to wait a few weeks until Cavendish arrived in person. At least the cargo the circumnavigator brought was not a disappointment. More than £125,000 of goods had been "liberated" from the enemy. A veritable Queen's ransom, and equal to a third of the whole annual Royal budget.

With God's blessings he would be out of bed and recovered by the time *Desire* arrived, curse this sickness.

25

Marked Man

Prior to their unfortunate meeting with *Desire*, *Santa Ana*'s passengers and crew had been looking forward to reaching the wooded hills and safe harbor of Acapulco Bay, the only North American port open to Asian trade.

The town was in its infancy, with only a tiny permanent population living in rudimentary housing above the beach; however, in anticipation of the galleon's arrival, the settlement had swelled with merchants, administrators, mariners, entertainers, cooks, crooks, prostitutes, donkey drivers, and a doctor from Mexico City, Cristobal Jurus. All were here to grasp a slice of *Santa Ana*'s riches. They erected a makeshift hodgepodge town of tents and lean-tos wherever space could be found or carved from the surrounding forest.

When *Santa Ana* failed to show up in November or December, the authorities must have been concerned but not overly. Winds were unpredictable, currents flowed contrarily, and perhaps departure from Manila had been delayed. There was no way to know.

Back in Cabo San Lucas, *Santa Ana* had been left for dead. All her cargo had either been removed or destroyed beyond hope of salvation. The only "property" left were two wounded Africans, Françisco and Diego, the former toeless from the fighting, the latter's amputated leg stump crawling with worms. Both were so badly injured that Cavendish had declined to take them.

The marooned survivors waited twelve days bivouacked under sailcloth in the scrubby backdrop to the beach before approaching the ship's carcass. When they did, things were not as dire as they had at first seemed. The desperate castaways decided to try to get her afloat again.

Santa Ana was still their best shot at survival, even if hope was meager.

Half of the 190 castaways worked in teams without rest for four days to empty the debris and ballast that had kept the remains submerged. As the wreck's condition improved, hope spurred a renewed energy and verve.

Slowly as the charred keel emptied, buoyancy returned, and the hulk began to float.

Meanwhile the remaining castaways felled some palm trees for makeshift masts, and the sailcloth that Cavendish had left reverted to its original vocation.

Santa Ana was now a viable vessel again, more of a low-slung cobbled-together raft than a royal galleon, but afloat and with propulsion of sorts.

On December 21, 1587, she left the fateful cape with the refugees aboard.

The improvised vessel somehow made a crossing of the Sea of Cortez and limped south for a dozen days and nights to the settlement of Santiago, just a few days' north of Acapulco Bay. There the hapless survivors received food and water and were permitted to put ashore the most seriously injured.

A fast launch was sent south under the command of Juan

Zorrilla de la Concha to spread the awful tidings to Acapulco, reaching the port on January 7, 1588.

The survivors arrived a day later, and immediately the local authorities appointed Father Marios Tello to open an investigation. A culprit had to be found for the loss of the king's property.

One by one, the exhausted men and women were interrogated by the senior military authority, Diego de Molina. A picture of the sorry string of events began to emerge. Those sitting and standing to witness proceedings in the rough wooden hut that served for a court in the sleepy town were outraged.

How dare Lutheran pirates steal the fruits of their hard work?

How dare they venture into Spanish seas?

How could a ship with such a fortune on board have put to sea without adequate protection?

Father Tello realized that this matter was far beyond his remit. Proceedings would have to be moved to Guadalajara, the site of the nearest Royal Court to the crime scene.

Those whose testimony was deemed most important tramped inland to the rapidly growing regional hub. There in the shadow of the half-finished cathedral, the senior scribe of the court, Juan Salado, compiled an official report for Mexico City and Madrid.

The final testimonies, from Captain de Alzola and seaman António de Sierra, were taken on January 24.

The pilot, Michael Sancius, now conveniently far away, was found to be culpable for the whole sordid episode.

The enquiry and accounting continued for over a year.

In the end, King Philip received only 168 golden pesos from *Santa Ana*, the proceeds of the sale of the healed African, Francisco, minus medical fees, other expenses, and vendor commission at 4 percent.

Everyone else received nothing.

The second set of Spanish officials to hear about the disaster were those in Manila. The Spaniard who had been abducted by Cavendish, Lope de Arjoma, was rescued by a passing ship and taken to the capital. There he presented the Englishman's letter to Governor de Santiago de Vera.

The Spaniard would have paled as he read Cavendish's words, expressing deep regret that *Desire* had not been able to visit his city and pledging to return soon to destroy it.

Francisco Mangabay, escaped servant of the hanged pilot, de Ersola, was also taken to Manila and testified at the enquiry on April 16, 1588. The governor, High Sheriff Gabriel de Ribera, and other leading citizens listened in anger and fear, and debated whether chase should be given.

Given their highly limited resources and the only recently suppressed Tondo Rebellion, they elected to simply send out warning messages to other Spanish and Portuguese outposts in the region.

On June 27, 1588, as the Spanish invasion fleet was approaching England on the other side of the world, an outraged bishop of the Philippines, Domingo de Salazar, wrote to King Philip II:

> *The grief that afflicts me is not because this barbarian infidel has robbed us of the ship* Santa Ana, *and destroyed thereby the property of almost all the citizens; but because an English youth of about twenty-two years, with a wretched little vessel of a hundred tuns and forty or fifty companions, should dare to come to my own place of residence, defy us, and boast of the damage that he had wrought. As your Majesty has here an army of captains, who, as I understand, are certainly as many as the companions of the Lutheran, he went from our midst laughing, without anyone molesting or troubling him.*

Virtually all Manila's citizens had owned a share of *Santa Ana*'s cargo. It was, after all, the only official link to the wider empire. Indeed, the Galleon of China was the very reason for the colony's being. They were financially ruined.

Coming on top of the destruction wrought by the great fire,

the constant Asian pirate invasions, and the rebellious indigenes, this calamity further threatened the very existence of the pre-cariously positioned Spanish outpost.

The third part of King Philip's empire to hear the dread news would have been Portuguese Malacca, where the Java-based merchants had delivered Cavendish's letter to Bishop João Ribeiro Gaio.

His mischievous missive stated that he had visited those regions, particularly the approaches to the Spice Islands, for trade, exploration, and prizes.

The horrified bishop would have forwarded the news to Governor General Manuel de Sousa Coutinho in Goa (on the western coast of modern-day India), capital of the Portuguese Indies. From there, the news boarded a ship for Lisbon, probably *Santo António*, an overladen ship that was lost with all hands on its 1589 voyage. Madrid would have heard the Javan news sometime in 1590.

All of these outposts of the Spanish crown passed on the news as quickly as they could. However, as witnessed by the sinking of *Santo António*, communications in the late sixteenth century were not swift or sure. A message from the far side of the Americas or Asia could take years to reach Europe, if it ever arrived at all.

The implications of the taking of the *Santa Ana*, the coup of transporting Christopher and his colleagues to England, the threatened uprising in Manila, and Cavendish's diplomatic doings in Capul and Java were massive. The English could now navigate to the west coast of the Americas and Asia, where they might find ready allies among Spain's rebellion-ready vassals, including King Philip's Portuguese subjects.

King Philip suddenly found that his newly won and highly lucrative Asian territories and the treasure-bearing Pacific seaways from Peru and Manila to Acapulco were weak, vulnerable, and might conceivably fall at any moment. Furthermore, the Portuguese monopoly on trade with Japan via the Indian

Ocean, on which King Philip's Portuguese subjects depended to fund their less profitable colonial infrastructure, could be in immediate peril.

Drake's raid a decade before had been considered a one-off, a lucky fluke. However, Cavendish had now proved that other undesirables could, and would, seek to emulate and even to better the navigational and piratical feat.

The control-obsessed king of Spain would have immediately feared the worst and come to the same conclusion as Cavendish had. Should the flow of global wealth to his treasury be disrupted, the financial domino effect could spell disaster for his power in Europe.

He was livid.

It was not just the secular authorities of Catholic Europe who despaired of the evil tidings from Asia. In Rome, Madrid, Paris, and Lisbon, the news caused consternation among the Jesuits who had enjoyed a monopoly on European religious contact with Japan to date.

The Jesuits had carefully avoided informing the Japanese about schism and disunity in European religion, and certainly not about their persecution in England, presenting their beliefs as the undisputed teachings of Christ, and Roman Catholicism as a universally accepted creed.

They were already in a precarious position in the late 1580s, due in part to their unmitigated success, but also to their desecration of Japanese religious sites and involvement in slaving. Furthermore, the missionaries knew that if Protestants were to reach Japan and reveal that many of their teachings were disputed, that there was no universally acclaimed God as they had claimed, all hell could break loose.

The flimsy house of cards they had built at the other end of the world would come tumbling down. The most successful Jesuit mission outside Europe, with around one hundred thousand converts, seemed in dire risk of collapse.

Christopher and Cavendish could not be allowed to reach Japan.

Meanwhile in Japan itself, Christopher's exploits went entirely unremarked.

During the years of 1588–1590, when news of the *Santa Ana* Incident was spreading through the outposts of King Philip's empire and seeping sluggishly back to Europe, great things were happening in the Land of the Rising Sun.

One hundred twenty years of war—fire, death, disunity, and turmoil—looked very much like they were coming to an end.

The effective ruler, Imperial Regent Toyotomi Hideyoshi, a man who had risen from the bottom of society to its pinnacle, had seized the reins of power after his erstwhile master Oda Nobunaga's assassination in 1582. He quickly went about completing the process of reunification and pacification which Nobunaga had begun.

In 1585, Hideyoshi had conquered the southern island of Shikoku. In 1586, he launched the biggest army Japan had ever seen, over two hundred thousand samurai, to conquer Kyushu, the southwestern island where Christopher would have been born.

Finally, in 1590, he moved northward to destroy his one remaining foe, the Hojo clan, and extend his rule over the whole country. The siege of the Hojo stronghold at Odawara near modern-day Tokyo was a forgone conclusion, but they were no pushover and stubborn warrior pride kept them holding out for months.

Hideyoshi's men, camped around the besieged castle, felt they were due some relaxation after their exertions, and to torment their hungry, bottled-up Hojo foe, they engaged in wild feasting with courtesans, circus entertainers, and raucous music. The famished stomachs of the men sleeping in their armor within the castle grumbled all the louder.

In the end Hideyoshi threw up a formidable castle on a mountain above Odawara Castle. It was built in a forest, so that when the trees were felled, it seemed to have magically appeared overnight. The awed and demoralized Hojo clan could take no more and promptly surrendered.

To celebrate his rise to national hegemon, Hideyoshi built a series of magnificent castles and palaces, decorated lavishly with elaborate carvings, hung with lifelike artwork, and adorned with gold and silver.

Toyotomi Hideyoshi, Imperial Regent of Japan.

The imperial regent had no idea that on the other side of the planet, a nation called England desperately wanted to approach him.

Hideyoshi in fact had no idea that England existed. Despite his love for European-made maps and globes, they were often interpreted for him by Jesuits, and details were fudged to match their agenda.

He was, however, becoming very well aware of the growing and not necessarily beneficial Portuguese and Catholic influence in Japan. Some of his closest allies and retainers had embraced the foreign religion, and he had seen the stone walls of a new Catholic town called Nagasaki bristling with cannon. Recently he had even dined aboard the fastest boat in contemporary Japan, a Jesuit-owned European-style galley, crewed by three hundred Japanese Christian oarsmen.

It was this last that was to prove the tipping point.

In 1587, while being entertained aboard, he intimated to his hosts that he desired the galley.

Its Jesuit owners foolishly tried to bargain for it, as if Hideyoshi was a merchant in the marketplace rather than an all-powerful ruler who held their fate in his hands.

The imperial regent politely declined a trade, brushed the matter off as if it was of no consequence, and seemingly continued to enjoy the entertainment on offer.

Within days, he promulgated a ban on slavery, an expulsion order for Catholic missionaries, and forbade his retainers from adhering to the European faith.

The fact was that the missionaries were no immediate threat to him and his estimated half-million gun-toting, battle-hardened samurai. He had gently tolerated them until now, even seeming to support them in an offhanded fashion.

But if the padres were arrogant enough to try to take advantage of him, despite all the favors he had already shown them, they would experience his wrath.

He never seriously enforced his missionary expulsion edict; the trade that the Portuguese brought was too lucrative, and the Japanese feared that were the missionaries to leave, their valuable business would disappear with them.

Furthermore, the presence of people and offerings of tribute from such remote ends of the earth provided a powerful form of legitimacy to Hideyoshi's newly established rule. People were willing to traverse the globe to pay him obeisance.

The edicts were more of a warning shot across the bow, obey humbly and submit, or else.

However, news of the promulgation itself would have reached Europe around the same time as Christopher and his comrades, causing further tribulation and panic in circles that remained loyal to Rome.

Anti-Catholic feeling was already running high in the Japan of the late 1580s. Were an English mission offering suitable tribute, trade proposals, and a maritime military alliance, to have arrived at Hideyoshi's Jurakudai palace in Kyoto, they would have been more than welcome.

More so if they had a Japanese interpreter to smooth things along.

26

The Thames

Desire, repaired and polished to a sheen in Plymouth after the historic voyage, made the last leg of her odyssey, east and then north along the southern English coast, to come to halt in the lee of Tilbury Fort's formidable defenses, deep inside the vast Thames Estuary.

A cool, languid breeze from the North Sea snagged at the proud ensign raised aloft the mainmast.

It was November 1588, a year since Christopher had been plucked from *Santa Ana*.

He gazed back to the gray-blue river mouth, gliding yellow sands to one side and low, barely discernible, forbidding hills on the other.

The journey up the estuary had been accompanied by the shriek of sea birds and bark of seals as, guided by a local pilot, *Desire* proceeded cautiously through the treacherous channels which guarded the watery entrance to the English heartlands. Ever-narrowing salt marshes and green grassy banks, interspersed with lazy pockmarked mudflats, had accompanied them the last leagues to Tilbury where they now rested.

The tired vessel's maritime worth proved beyond dispute; she would tomorrow be towed upriver to Greenwich near London, to probe a new realm, that of court politics.

Now safely in the shadow of Tilbury's great guns, London's last line of defense against seaborne attack, Christopher helped cover the sturdy new white sails with fine marine-blue silken damask bolts. The delicate silk would have been ripped to shreds in even the slightest gust of wind had it actually been used for propulsion, but that was not its purpose. *Desire*'s captain knew he had to wow the populace, and most importantly Queen Elizabeth, if he was to take his place among the Tudor-era heroes, and silken sails truly lent the ship the aura of a semidivine chariot poised to soar to the heavens.

Topping it all, a giant standard of shining blue silk and cloth of gold, those being the Cavendish family colors, fluttered merrily in the gentle early winter breeze. It was a cold but cloudless, bright, early winter day and the lustrous cloth, further bounty of the voyage, shone gloriously in the pale weak sun.

The silken "sails" furled for the final stretch, the ship's boats were lowered gently into the choppy brown river, and finally the Tilbury boom, the great chain which prevented unauthorized waterborne access to London, was lowered to allow them passage. The crew began their last arduous task, the business of towing *Desire* toward the capital, just discernible in the form of a filthy smudge hanging dankly in the distant sky.

Christopher and his colleagues on board feasted their eyes on the verdant lands bordering the wide river, antipodean from the lands of their birth. This was the land of lush green pastures that they had heard of on their voyage.

Nothing could be allowed to spoil the grand spectacle, so as they approached Greenwich, despite heavy rain, the great blue "sails" were released from their protective confinement, and the sailors changed into the gaudy cerulean outfits and great chains of gold in which they would present themselves at their homecoming.

The ship's tailor's concoctions had been greeted with hoots and peals of laughter when they appeared during the voyage, but now as *Desire* passed a final tight bend in the river, the vessel came within sight of the grandest building Christopher had ever seen, Queen Elizabeth's palace, it felt right to be dressed for the occasion.

River traffic had become more constant and as the City's dingy gray halo grew larger and nearer, more and more craft buzzed around them. Their arrival was a cause for jubilation; Cavendish and his men had sailed around the earth and returned in glory. All London was floating downriver to Greenwich to celebrate with a raucous waterborne merrymaking.

Christopher and his colleagues, rain dripping from the brims of their hats, looked on with awe at the scene. England was truly welcoming her distinguished visitors in the way she knew best.

The Londoners, well used to the wet skies, ignored the rain.

Old Greenwich Palace in the early seventeenth century, shortly after Christopher saw it. Engraved by Newton (probably Francis Milner Newton), 1789.

Toiling watermen panned skiffs, and teams of oarsmen propelled pleasure barges humming happily with drinking and feasting under sheltered gazebos. Christopher's eyes would have been drawn to the ladies, costumed in sumptuous dresses inlaid with pearls, beads, and embroidery, their hair covered modestly.

The men would have been equally fascinating for him. They sported cloaks rakishly thrown over one shoulder, wide starched-lace collars, and wore feathers jauntily pointing from velvet caps. All toasted the triumphant arrival with fine wine, white bread, and cold meats skewered on ornate knives.

The commoner sort of people looked more like their Plymouth brethren, more dourly outfitted, both sexes alike in simple, drab brown or colorless black. Only the robe design seemed to differ by sex. But they hailed *Desire* with gusto, downing beer in long draughts from pewter tankards before cheering and munching on rough bread and cheese. The Spanish Armada's defeat had given London similar reason to celebrate and now Cavendish's homecoming and flashy plunder proved that England had not only survived but was flourishing.

Some English eyes would have picked up the presence of Christopher and his four companions on the poop deck.

News had traveled swiftly, and there was great excitement about their arrival and the coming royal audience. To the English it probably seemed like semimythical beings had arrived to acknowledge the might of their Queen and her people's resilience against their enemies.

On November 12, 1588, in a sorry deluge, *Desire* reached her anchorage outside the Queen's palace and fired a salvo in salute.

Courtiers stood at the palace windows, protected from the downpour, and cheered the silken ship, unlike any other vessel seen in England before. The bawdier among the men waved their ornate hats in the air as royal heralds blasted out a trumpet fanfare of welcome.

Awaiting the Queen's pleasure, "the Gentlemen of the East" remained on the gently rocking ship as the lights of the palace glowed and flickered, reflecting like fireflies in the softly lapping waves.

Daylight brought visitors to see the famous vessel and view its equally marvelous passengers, the cream of local society got up in their finery for the unique occasion. Christopher, feeling awkward, smiled, bowed, and greeted the guests as they were presented to him, before in his turn, introducing his fellow "nobles."

The English marveled at these "Gentlemen," jabbering excitedly about their exotic robes, their stature, their "innate nobility," and their facility in the English tongue, a feat few foreigners bothered to achieve, and such a boon to Cavendish's grand homecoming.

One lady in particular, her striking red hair fighting to escape a black veil of mourning, Lettice Dudley, widow of Cavendish's late patron Robert, Earl of Leicester, wondered out loud that it would be a fine thing to have an "Indian" to grace one's household.

Not all the visiting English natives were of the same shallow bent, however. A clergyman with a short neat beard and curly mustache called Hakluyt would have been most courteous and talked to each of the young men, enquiring intelligently about their homelands and lives. He was effusive about their English skills. An opportunity such as this had never presented itself before, and as he made clear, he sincerely desired a deeper understanding of all they could enlighten him with. He left promising to visit them properly soon.

27

The Audience with Her Majesty

In 1588, there was no Fleet Street press to scream the news that a national hero had arrived with exotic guests from the furthest reaches of the world and was being received by Her Majesty.

In news distribution via regular newssheet and gazette, as in so many other things, England lagged behind many of her continental neighbors such as the Holy Roman Empire, Venice, France, and the Dutch Republic. The English relied on a few irregular pamphlets, expensive translations of continental bulletins, proclamations in public places, most notably at Saint Magnus Corner by the entrance to London Bridge, and dissemination in church sermons.

Hence, whereas later in history we could happily have looked to newspapers and newssheets for stories of Christopher and his comrades having met the Queen, in this case we have to rely on different evidence. A Spanish letter for example revealed that "it was as if Cleopatra had been resuscitated... Cavendish must have brought great riches."

"A new ballad of the famous and honourable coming of Master

Cavendish's ship called The Desire before the Queen's Majesty at her court at Greenwich the 12 of November 1588," a ditty that was registered with the Royal Stationers but whose exact lyrics are now lost, tells us that Thomas Cavendish traveled down the Thames with his ship decked out in blue silk and cloth of gold, and that Elizabeth dined aboard in great pomp and ceremony five days after *Desire*'s arrival.

This is when Christopher is likely to have met the Queen.

As a pale sun struggled to disperse the autumn river mists, Elizabeth herself came aboard *Desire*. Fanfares pealed and a trumpeter dressed in the Royal Coat of Arms declaimed, "Her Majesty Queen of England, France and Ireland, Defender of the Faith," as the monarch stepped nimbly aboard from the ornate silk-draped chair in which she had been gently hoisted.

Cavendish welcomed her with a deep and gallant bow on the half deck and ushered her on a tour of the more accessible parts of the polished galleon.

Finally, in the cloth of gold–draped Great Cabin, where despite its grandeur the width was so narrow that the Queen's voluminous dresses brushed both cabin walls, he motioned to the far end, where his couch was, and bade her recline on cushions of red silk.

Cavendish, bowing incessantly, then presented her with choice examples of her portion of the plunder. Gold bars, thick bolts of shimmering silk cloth, twists of radiant raw white silk thread, and great shining pearls in every color imaginable.

The Queen's eyes lit up, but her face remained calm and hard until Cavendish revealed the portable Japanese desk, which had remained quietly hidden under a velvet cover. She gasped at the perfectly fused, intricately carved, light-colored woods, and the lacquer with inlaid scenes of nature in gold leaf and mother of pearl, seeming almost to blush behind her thick makeup.

Cavendish informed her of the provenance of this astonishing work of art, which he had confiscated from the Spanish captain personally. With a flourish, he opened the hinged lid to display two tightly rolled scrolls. These were unfurled to reveal an even greater, more priceless and fascinating treasure than all the others in that room, the Great Mappe of China, and Christopher's English translation, the key to future navigations and their attendant riches.

Elizabeth enquired with a sense of wonder how they had made sense of the strange but beautiful symbols on the original, and whether the astonishing figures were really true.

This was the moment.

Christopher made his entrance, the other "Gentlemen of the Indies" following their leader.

They were introduced as "Gentlemen of Japan and Manila," and as Cavendish announced their names, they bowed perfectly before the Queen.

The subsequent banquet spilled out onto the half deck and the poop to accommodate the numerous guests. The plate was of solid gold, the beakers of rare glass. The centerpiece was a peacock, its plume reaching the length of the table, cooked and reconstituted with the original feathers, replicating the hue of *Desire's* ornamental sails.

Accompanying the great bird were pies, cheeses, fruits, seafood, and piles of soft white light-as-a-feather manchet bread. In front of the Queen herself was a large cake of almonds, sugar, and rosewater. This was Cavendish marchpane, a luxurious gateau created by and for the commander's family, and fittingly adorned with the Cavendish coat of arms in blue and gold.

Christopher and his fellow "Gentlemen" were honored to be granted the right of serving Her Majesty as she partook of the delicate foods that Cavendish had laid on.

After the food came the speeches and more toasts. Laudatory praise for the Queen's beauty, wisdom, and her enlightened reign that had made Cavendish's feat possible, passed the lips of many a tipsy or outright drunken notable that afternoon.

Finally, Elizabeth herself stood slowly to speak, nearly dashing her elaborate coiffure on the low-beamed cabin ceiling. Her words were flowery, her praise for Cavendish effusive. Graciously, she had individual words for each of the young Asian gallants who had traveled so far to pay tribute to her. Finally, she laughed, a great trill, a peal of glee, ending in a snort, not quite manic, but definitely triumphant, exclaiming, "the king of Spain barks a good deal but he does not bite. We care nothing for Spaniards; their ships loaded with gold and silver from the Indies come hither after all."

As Christopher replenished the Queen's glass, she would have bestowed a sweet smile upon him.

28

Discovered

The Tensho Japanese ambassadors to Rome were well on their journey home when the malevolent rumors started in late 1588 or early 1589.

The allegation was that the young nobles were not aristocrats at all, but simply peasants who Valignano had dressed up to become mere tools in a Jesuit publicity stunt.

Queen Elizabeth, while probably delighted that the two popes had been fooled by this deception, was no doubt concerned for what it implied about the true status of the Japanese "Gentlemen" who had just arrived at her court.

Sometime after Christopher's audience aboard *Desire*, he and his colleagues were found out.

Although it is unclear exactly when their exposure occurred, it is likely that Cavendish's ruse was uncovered during one of the interviews-cum-interrogations that Christopher and his colleagues underwent in the first days and weeks after their arrival.

Despite being impossible to say for sure, the increased scrutiny that the allegations surrounding the Tensho legates generated probably ended Cavendish's very real fraud, and Christopher's pretended status as gentleman.

Ironically, the four Catholic Japanese ambassadors were most definitely genuinely highborn.

However, noble-blooded or not, Christopher is reported to have been as well-educated as many European aristocrats and was to become highly respected for his judgment and experience. He also seems to have enjoyed a measure of personal charm, and adapted easily to new circumstances, which no doubt smoothed his life in London thereafter.

Subsequent references to him and his colleagues do not call them "Gentlemen of the Indies"; instead we find descriptions like the one penned by Robert Parke, who had been commissioned by Hakluyt to translate a much-anticipated tome, *The Historie of the Great and Mightie Kingdome of China, and the Situation Thereof: Togither with the great riches, huge citties, politike governement, and rare inventions in the same*, from Spanish in 1588. Parke dedicated it to, "The right worshipfull and famous gentleman, M. Thomas Candish, Esquire, increase of honor and happie attemptes."

With the following words he celebrated Christopher and his colleagues' presence in England.

But since it is so (as wee understande) that your worshippe in your late voyage hath first of our nation in this age discovered the famous rich ilandes of the Lu Zones, or Philippinas, lying neare unto the coast of China, and have spent some time in taking good view of the same, having brought home three boyes borne in Manilla, the chiefe towne of the said Ilands, besides two other young fellowes of good capacitie, borne in the mightie Iland of Iapon, (which hereafter may serve as our interpretors in our first traficke thither).

Gentlemen or no, Parke's comments show it was still considered an honor to host travelers from such distant and powerful realms in England.

He also specifically mentioned intellect and went on to talk about the rich potential for trade and the economic boom which would surely result. Finally, he revealed that Cavendish was planning another voyage to Japan with Christopher as interpreter.

The triumphant return of the Japanese mariner to the land of his birth was already the talk of London at the end of 1588, only a month after his arrival.

Cavendish, however, fell from royal favor around this time, for reasons which probably go beyond his brazen attempt to deceive the Queen about the status of her visitors from Asia.

The timing of *Desire*'s return was bad. Not only was the nation's attention still on the attempted invasion and its aftermath, it was also clear by now that Elizabeth was not going to produce an heir. The chief ministers of state were already grooming the young James Stuart, king of Scotland, to succeed, and the last thing they needed was for a youthful dandy like Cavendish to waltz in and somehow charm Elizabeth into marriage. Elizabeth's advisors had a track record of putting these upstarts in their place and bringing them down if need be. Cavendish may have suffered from a whispering campaign to discredit him.

Furthermore, only days before Cavendish's return to Plymouth, the nearest the Queen ever had to a male soulmate, Robert Dudley, Earl of Leicester, died. She was deep in mourning and would have found it hard to maintain positivity even in the face of such an astonishing feat as Cavendish's.

Dudley's last letter remained by Elizabeth's bed for the rest of her life.

The fall from grace had serious consequences.

Firstly, Cavendish was not granted the knighthood he would have expected, despite his enormous contribution to national pride and the royal coffers.

Secondly, the huge fortune which Cavendish had amassed mysteriously disappeared. Even given the extensive expense of preparing for the return voyage, repaying the mortgage on his ancestral lands, and no doubt enjoying lengthy and pricey celebrations, he seems to have got through this vast fortune at an amazing rate. One wonders whether he tried to somehow buy his way out of disgrace.

Thirdly, before setting out in 1586, Cavendish had paid the customary £2000 bond against piracy. Despite the *Santa Ana* being a "legal" privateering prize, the surety was forfeited to the crown and never returned. The stated reasons why are lost to the mists of time, but perhaps there was a case of "true" piracy that was not made public.

Fourthly, although other visitors to Europe from Japan have gone down in history, and other "exotic" travelers to England such as the Americans Manteo and Wanchese have been relatively well recorded in writings and artwork, Christopher and his colleagues essentially disappear from the wider public view. All but one of the subsequent sources for their lives are in private diaries and letters, not in books or official records.

"Gentlemen of the Indies" was big news. "Slaves of the East," less so.

29

London

All of a sudden, the wet autumn which had welcomed Christopher and his colleagues fled to be replaced with bitter cold, and people wondered out loud whether the Thames would freeze over. If it did, Christopher, still at rural Greenwich, would be at London to see it, and all the festivities that attended such a rare event.

The great capital of the English, which he had heard so much about over the past year, beckoned.

As the lodeman guided *Desire* gently round the last bend in the river before London, Christopher gazed through the whirling flurries of snowflakes at the ever less rural vistas opening out before him, taking in the pungent ordure—sewage, rotting fish, and worse—complemented by a natural salty tang.

On both banks, the lush marshy green and gently sloping hills, now pure white with unfurrowed snow, became ever more pockmarked with shipyards and other riverside industries. London sailors approaching their home port named the places.

Deptford, Rotherhithe, Limehouse, Wapping.

As the snow faded and they approached the edge of London proper, the pale winter sun caught a gleaming white tower, the centerpiece of a massive castle, a redoubt the like of which Christopher had never seen before. The almost angelic-looking edifice amid the river's fecal fumes presented quite a contrast to those approaching the capital city for the first time.

Beyond the Tower, London and its suburbs spread out before them, a teeming mass of buildings and spires that reached out to the very heavens through the gray gloomy cloud which hung lazily in the bracing air.

On the northern riverbank great buildings of stone and wood crept right down to the water's edge, hanging precariously out over the river as if the weight of the city behind were nudging them slowly but surely, higgledy-piggledy into a riverine grave.

Below them, uncountable wooden quays jutted out into the river, bent downward parallel to the sloping riverbed. At low tide, they would be stranded above the mud, roads to nowhere, but now at the tide's highest, they were half devoured by the river.

Around the quays skulled heaving throngs of boats loading and unloading people and goods from large craft, *Desire*'s size and more, anchored in the middle of the stream.

In contrast to the heaving north, the south bank was an oasis of peace. Also built up, but in a more leisurely, less confined fashion. Between the buildings stood trees and small fields of vegetables, green tops poking through the snow on the ground. Cows meandered slowly as they nosed around the slushy streets.

Looking beyond the quays and anchored vessels, there was a huge edifice actually built over the river. Upon closer inspection, it was revealed to be an enormous stone bridge with the swift current flowing under the superstructure through great towering arches. It was covered along its full length with tall buildings and there were even waterwheels under the north-ernmost spans.

Behind that, the ground on the north bank rose and an immense church, Saint Paul's Cathedral, reached into the goose-gray clouds. Despite the stunted steeple, apparently damaged by lightning, the City's tallest building caused Christopher goose bumps. Even viewed at this distance, the church he had thought so grand in Plymouth clearly did not compare.

Desire found her well-deserved rest in the middle of the Thames, moored off Her Majesty's Custom House Quay. There were many legal quays to which cargo could be landed in London, but this was a special case, and even though the vessel had already cleared customs in Plymouth, Elizabeth desired that her officers pay special attention that nothing of note disappeared covertly into the bustling City.

Desire was relieved of her rich cargo by teams of lighter barges. A few days later, considerably lighter and buoyed in the water, she was maneuvered back downriver into a dry dock at Wapping. The small galleon needed a complete refit if, as planned, she was going to repeat her amazing feat.

Thomas Cavendish's house, where Christopher would have stayed, is thought to have been in Saint Katherine's, a stone's throw below the Tower of London and just adjacent to Wapping where *Desire* was being refitted.

Saint Katherine's was not technically part of London. As a "Royal Peculiar," a parish released from local jurisdiction and subject directly to the monarch, since 1147, London's laws did not apply, the forces of order could not make arrests, and guilds had no authority there. Saint Katherine's enjoyed an anarchic freedom in contrast to its strictly regulated and law-bound neighbor. By the time of the Japanese mariner's visit, it had become a melting pot of several thousand "foreigners, vagabonds, and prostitutes," possibly more akin to the diverse edginess of remote frontier outposts like Manila than neighboring London.

Why Cavendish had a house in Saint Katherine's is not clear; it was certainly not the normal haunt of a fashionable courtier.

Perhaps he had inherited it? Or maybe he rented it for its proximity to places where he had business.

Christopher was island, frontier, and pirate nest bred. Like most other visitors, he would without doubt have felt a sense of awe and perhaps trepidation at his first experience of a major metropolis.

London, and its surrounding conurbation, at this time was the largest it had ever been, and easily the biggest settlement Christopher had ever set foot in, approaching two hundred thousand, a figure equal to all the other urban areas of England put together. This multitude was crammed into the square mile of the ancient Roman walls and overflowed beyond to the seat of government at Westminster and across the bridge to Southwark.

The buildings lining the dark and muddy streets, alleys, and lanes of England's capital, while relatively diminutive seeming in the shadow of today's skyscrapers, would have been seen and felt as overbearing and magnificent. Besides the overhanging black and white wood-framed wattle and daub dwellings of the masses were the great brick- or stone-built and expensively glazed houses of merchants, nobles, and other dignitaries, England's first attempt at what we would recognize as a shop, the Royal Exchange, and the halls of the twelve great guilds. Around one hundred church spires, their bells constantly tolling, cast a musical religious umbra over every street.

Just to set foot in the vibrant, noisy, and vivacious rutted alleys was to risk life and limb. Crime, disease, and violence pervaded the metropolis where many citizens were simply engaged in a desperate fight for survival. Rich, poor, rosy with health and ashen with approaching death, people teemed through the sewage and animal sweat–tinged narrow ways and wide thoroughfares alike. Brim-fire preachers, quack doctors, food hawkers, blacksmiths, market traders, deformed beggars, rag pickers, and urchin pickpockets competed to make a swift fortune, or end up penniless in the ditch that served as a public dump, surrounding the walls.

A view of London ca 1600. The Tower of London is to the right, and ships similar to Desire *are clearly visible. From* Civitates Orbis Terrarum *by Georg Braun, Frans Hogenberg, and Joris Hoefnagel. Held in the British Library.*

To travel pretty much anywhere within the city walls from Saint Katherine's, Christopher would have had to first pass by the large gallows that permanently awaited victims at Tower Hill, mostly political or religious incarcerates brought from the Tower of London to their premature, painful, and very public deaths.

In fact, no place in the City was more than five hundred yards from a site of execution, and the resultant cadavers, spiked heads, and cleaved limbs decorated city gates and the entrances to London Bridge.

Tudor England may have preached salvation through Christ, but forgiveness for transgressions was very much something which had to wait for the afterlife.

Although the young Asian men would certainly have stood out, they were far from the only foreigners in London, and, despite a well-known xenophobia, the City was already beginning to take on the multicultural feeling which it retains to this day.

The largest groups of outsiders were Dutch and other northern Europeans due to England's close economic, religious, and military ties to Flanders.

The refugee pretender, or rightful claimant—depending upon your perspective—to the Portuguese throne, Dom António, had a sizable entourage in attendance, and therefore even what might have been thought of as "enemy" speech was frequently to be heard, along with the other languages of the British Isles, Gallic, Gaelic, Welsh, Cornish, and Manx.

Africans would have been the most visible minority. Many brought much-needed artisanal skills such as silk working, needle making, and brewing. Others were employed as domestic servants, sex workers, and beggars.

If Christopher was in London on January 12, 1589, he would also have witnessed the notable occasion when Ahmad Bilqasim, an ambassador from the Moroccan Sultan Ahmad al-Mansur, entered the capital by torchlight accompanied by an honor guard of horsemen.

Christopher and his colleagues were the only Asians, however. Although records are sparse, it seems that there were only a handful more over the course of the next three decades and none of those caused such excitement as the young men of 1588.

Perhaps surprisingly, there was no Jewish community.

Having been expelled by King Edward I in 1290, not until the 1650s would Lord Protector Oliver Cromwell permit Jews to reside in England again.

London in 1588, was not only a city of business, but also just setting out on its journey to becoming a culture hub.

Inevitably the craze for Asia and all things Asian found its way into England's popular culture, exploding into an explicit fashion for collecting art and gismos, particularly porcelain, as contact with Asia grew in the decades after Christopher's visit.

Traces of this intense fascination pepper early English literature; authors such as Shakespeare, Edmund Spenser, and Christopher Marlowe, both before and long after Christopher's encounter with England, promoted the image of a glamorous world of adventure, romance, and wealth.

For example, in *Twelfth Night*, Act II, Scene III, first performed in 1602 in London's Middle Temple where many voyages for the East were planned, Shakespeare describes a character as a "Catayan," meaning rich and blessed by social harmony like Cathay. Other playwrights such as Thomas Dekker (*The Honest Whore of Babylon*), William Davenant (*Love and Honor*) use similar words, "Cathayan," "Cataian," and "Catayne," as adjectives to describe European characters in a positive light. The 1604 performance of *Masque of the Knights of India and China* even featured a Chinese magician descending from a "celestial realm" to inform the watching English king, James I, and a visiting French ambassador, of his utopian country.

Elsewhere, Shakespeare repeatedly alludes to the wealth of and high regard which the English felt for "the Indies."

One example is in *Comedy of Errors*, Act III, Scene II where the character Dromio compares his rather rotund wife to a globe in terms which happily insult the world known to Elizabethans but praise the riches of the East and Americas.

Ireland is "in her buttocks," Scotland is found "by the barrenness, hard in the palm of the hand," France is described as protrusions "in her forehead," and the Netherlands are too low to even be compared with. Spain is in her bad breath but sends armadas of ships to take the "rubies, and sapphires" of America and the Indies that rest like carbuncles upon her nose.

Only the Americas and Asia come out well in this xenophobic parody, the sources of incomparable riches, and furthermore, as kindred victims of Spanish machinations, potential allies.

30

Hakluyt

With the cargo unloaded, it was time to divide the spoils, a huge but welcome headache for all concerned.

After the customs tax and the Lord High Admiral's cut were dealt with, the sailors, those who had done the real work, got one third of the voyage's booty to divide between themselves according to rank. The other two thirds went to Cavendish who then repaid his investors, suppliers, and creditors.

Whether Christopher and his Asian colleagues were granted a share of the booty is unknown.

Although the details of the next few years are patchy, it is known that in the immediate aftermath of the voyage, Cavendish had contact with Elizabeth's most senior advisor, William Cecil Baron Burghley, her spymaster secretary of state, Sir Francis Walsingham, the astronomer and naturalist Dr. William Gilbert, and the alchemist and scholar John Dee. While published accounts of feats of navigation like *Desire*'s were often heavily censored to prevent top-secret information leaking to enemies, these men would have been trusted with the inside

story, warts and all, of the voyage. It was their job to ensure
that lessons were learned, new policy determined, and of course
use Christopher and his colleagues to best effect. They would,
among other things, be able to help with logistical advice for
future voyages and share knowledge of many things of which
the English were as yet ignorant.

No one in London, however, was more delighted to meet
Christopher than the geographer and intelligencer Richard Hakluyt, newly returned from being chaplain and secretary to the
English ambassador in Paris, and recently married to Cavendish's cousin, Duglesse.

Although after marriage he had been appointed vicar of the
parish of Wetheringsett, in Suffolk, the newlyweds probably resided mainly in London, leaving, as often happened, Hakluyt's
spiritual role in the hands of a hired curate.

Hakluyt, one of the foremost proponents of John Dee's dreams
of imperium, had a far more important job to do on behalf of
the nation. He was chief propagandist, working tirelessly behind
the scenes on the collection and sharing of intelligence, an eclectic, some might say eccentric, mix of everything from traveler's
tales to useful vocabulary in exotic languages, commodity advice for distant ports, navigational instructions, and sea charts.

In 1582, he had published his first work, *Divers Voyages Touching the Discoverie of America, and the Ilands Adjacent*, and only two
years later, attempted to ram home his message of needing to
hit Spanish interests in the Americas through colony planting,
by personally presenting Queen Elizabeth with a *Discourse on
Western Planting*. It was timed carefully to amplify support for
the Roanoke project which needed royal assent.

In 1589, he was due to publish his most ambitious work yet,
*The Principall Navigations, Voiages and Discoveries of the English
Nation*, which, among many other chapters, included the full
translation of the text on Christopher's Large Mappe of China,
and an eyewitness account of Cavendish's circumnavigation.

The conversations in Cavendish's town house were long and detailed, and Hakluyt left satisfied, ready to pen a quick but essential addition to the introduction of his new work:

Is it not strange that the borne naturalles of Japan, and the Philippinaes are here to be seen, agreeing with our climate, speaking our language and informing us of the state of their Easterne habitations. For mine owne part I take it as a pledge of Gods further favour both unto us and to them: to them especially unto whose doors I doubt not in time shall be by us carried the incomparable treasure of the truth of Christianity and of the truth of the Gospell while we use and exercise common trade with their marchants.

Mammon was a powerful motivator even for devout Protestants.

31

Trimley

Thomas Cavendish was gladly gadding about London, but he knew that there was one visit he could not put off any longer. Without the support of the people of his ancestral estate at Trimley in the southeastern county of Suffolk, none of his adventures could have taken place.

Home beckoned.

Cavendish decided to make his grand homecoming at Christmas, and although it cannot be said for certain, Christopher and his comrades probably accompanied him.

They took ship from London in December, making the short voyage to the mouth of the River Orwell, just north of where the Thames Estuary drains into the North Sea.

Christopher's ship approached the modest cape called Landguard Point in another blizzard.

His eyes met with a snow-encrusted land, rising gently from the sea and continuing more or less flat inland for as far as the eye could see, a jumble of tall, thick, bare-leaved winter woodlands and seasonally barren brown fields.

They tacked and saw two wide rivers convulsing into one estuary mouth; ruined fortifications were just visible on the cape. It was clear they would not be much use for guarding the land anymore.

The ship headed for the northern river mouth, where a well-wrapped party was waiting with horses. Despite the rain, they greeted their long-lost squire with lusty cheers as he was rowed ashore. There were more than a few sideward glances at Christopher and his famous colleagues; all knew their story, but none of the locals had ever met an Asian person before.

The welcome party led their charges up the rough track to the Cavendish family seat of over two centuries, Grimston Hall, an unassuming old-fashioned manor house commanding excellent views of the estuary and land about.

It seemed an unimposing home for the dashing world-famous seafarer.

A solid brick chimney stack stood at one end of the timber mainframe, which was filled with whitewashed wattle and daub, and latticed lead-glazed windows. Numerous outhouses stretched off the main manor, and the whole complex was almost surrounded by what had once clearly been a moat but was now a collection of ponds.

That night, the wintery waters would have been raided for the feast that celebrated Cavendish's homecoming, and the Asian men's arrival. It was a relatively informal event in the Great Chamber, where great fire-blackened beams lent a timeless quality to smoke-yellowed walls, and reed-strewn floors.

The household sat down, and after speeches and toasts, brought out their own knives and spoons to dine on the pewter dishes. Being Advent, a strict fasting regime was in place, no meat, cheese, or eggs until Christmas Day, but fish and eels were perfectly acceptable, and the diners tucked in with gusto.

First came white manchet bread accompanying a pottage made from salt codfish, dried peas, onion, turnip, carrot, and herbs. Following that came roast fish and vegetables. Chasing everything were wrinkled autumn fruits, and dried nuts.

Warm and satisfied from the huge fire and plentiful meal, and bathing in the soft amber light of pricketed candles, Christopher began to enjoy himself.

The landscape around Trimley consisted of gently sloping hills covered with a mixture of deciduous forest, marshland, and fields. Through it ran the River Orwell, normally almost lakelike in its passiveness, but in strong winds, its lazy demeanor could roughen in moments.

Trimley village, near the manor, straddled two churches along a road to the sea. Christopher had seen nowhere like it before. It lacked the fresh, frontier-like vitality of Manila, the grubby old feeling of Saint Katherine's, the sleek modern-smelling wooden cleanliness of Nagasaki, and even the seasonal, temporary feeling of a pirate base. These old dwellings seemed rooted in the very ground in which they stood, as if they had grown, like the trees which surrounded them, slowly and organically from the earth.

The better-appointed homes, smaller versions of Grimston Hall, had neatly leaded windows of blown glass, exquisitely carved doorways, and brick chimney breasts. These homes burned a soft black stone called coal, which gave out an amazing heat along with a blood-like, metallic odor. The chimneys, a wonderful concept that Christopher had not come across before, left the air inside clearer, and the tang of smoke less pronounced. Japanese houses cooked with charcoal in *irori* hearths and in Manila cooking fires were located outside.

Rather than smoke, the inside of houses smelled of the rushes that were strewn liberally about. It was an inoffensive fresh herby aroma, mixed with "dry." If "dry" was a smell. The straw-like softness felt comfortable after the hardwood, or baked hard mud floors of his previous lives, but best not to think of what lay underneath—the constant presence of dogs probably gave a clue.

Poorer dwellings were a very different matter. They could boast nothing more than window-like openings covered with oilcloth, and small holes in the roof to allow cooking fire smoke to escape. The dampness of the kindling in this rainy climate meant that those who lived within dwelt in a constant fog. It was hard to breathe, and the odor of smoke and damp rot permeated the single-roomed hovels.

Christopher had lived with the English for more than a year now, but certain things probably never ceased to amaze him.

At first, he had assumed it was the logistical difficulties that prevented them washing while at sea. They certainly enjoyed shaving, shearing long wild hair, and splashing around on beaches during the stopovers in Capul, and Saint Helena.

But now he found the English weren't that different from the Spanish, despite their frequent denials to the contrary.

Like the Spanish, they never actually bathed their bodies if they could help it, and certainly not communally in hot water as in Japan.

Instead, they rolled up their sleeves to wash their hands, faces and teeth with cold water each morning, shifted their underwear once a week (if they had a change), and combed their hair constantly. If the whole body required attention, a "dry wash" with a linen cloth seemed to be the preference. The English depended on the freshness of the water or cleanliness of the linen for cleaning.

Peculiarly, the English didn't smell particularly bad. How and why this was remained a mystery to Christopher. Perhaps the rainy climate had a cleansing effect?

Living with animals likely threw him at first.

In Manila, animals lived outside, rooting and pecking around fenced compounds or in the streets. On board ship, they were kept in pens and cages. In Cavendish's London mansion, there were only dogs, cats, and rats. No beasts reared for meat, although pigs roamed the fetid alleys freely.

But here in Trimley, in the middle of winter, the animals were a living heat source. Unbutchered pigs contributed their body warmth even as their salted brethren, slaughtered in November at Martinmas, hung as bacon from the eaves. Chickens and other fowl came and went as they pleased, nesting in with the people, and pecking around outside, happily ignorant of their imminent Christmas fate.

To step inside an estate worker's low-ceilinged cottage was to experience an assault on the senses. In addition to the smoke, the rancid, yet surprisingly complex stench of pig sweat, urine, bird dung, and worse would knock you back.

Christopher was told that in the summer, Trimley was a world of bold blues and vivid yet gentle greens, pleasant breezes, long days, languid heat, and cool dips in the River Orwell. A soft sun warmed the young world and people worked the fields with a spring in their step.

But the winter countryside he found now around Trimley was colorless and fettered with cold and ice. The days lasted only a few short hours, and the sole sounds were the forlorn cries of water birds beating their wings lackadaisically in ashen skies.

Christopher had never known such chill. It got inside him, and he felt as if he could never be warm again. His hands lost feeling, becoming stiff and clumsy. His legs were leaden and could only clump slowly around on the frozen ground.

London had been bitter, and the wind biting, but there had always been a building to be in, a fire blazing, and a mass of warm humanity hurrying through the streets. Here, there was only a landscape devoid of people, a frozen river, icy marshes, snowbound forests, and bare fields.

But soon it was Christmas.

Relative sloth was replaced by frantic activity, games, singing, and tomfoolery.

Christmas Eve saw the manor decorated green, red, and white, with holly, ivy, mistletoe, box, laurel, yew, candles, and a huge yule log which had been dragged in from the forest to burn merrily in the Great Chamber's hearth for the full twelve days of the winter festival.

On Christmas Day itself, after the first service of worship, the feast was served. This year, as thanksgiving for victory over the Spanish, by special order of the Queen the main dish was to be goose. It was the first meal she had enjoyed after word of the deliverance had arrived, and therefore representative of the nation's continued independence.

The tables also groaned with a more traditional tusked boar's head, mutton, pork, hare, duck, wild fowl, bread, cheese, fruits, several Christmas pies, and the same Cavendish marchpane that had been served to the Queen herself aboard *Desire* only months before. The fasting of advent had truly come to an end with this plentiful spread.

Christ's birth and the rich fare were hailed with the wooden wassail bowl. Cavendish took the first great swig of the warm sugar-sweetened spiced ale, before passing it to Christopher and his comrades as guests of honor. They then handed it around the Great Chamber to return, near empty, to the squire, who had the right of enjoying the crust of bread—the toast—which lay at the bottom.

Throughout the twelve festive days which followed, the household also enjoyed minced pies, the thirteen ingredients of which represented Christ and his apostles. These little pockets of goodness included a heavy mixture of spice brought by Cavendish himself from *Santa Ana*, dried fruits, and minced mutton from the November slaughter.

Every day, the kitchens worked from dawn until dusk feeding not only the household and guests, but the estate's tenants and many of the villagers. Cavendish knew his duty as squire. He also knew that the workers needed to replenish their energy for when the year's agricultural activities officially began on Plough Monday, immediately after the ploughshares had been blessed on the first Sunday after Epiphany, at the end of Christmas.

Christopher's first Christmas in England had passed, and the festive glow had returned warmth to the world.

32

A New Status

Despite the Christmas cheer, things must have looked bleak to Christopher as 1589 dawned.

The young Japanese man was no longer being addressed as a gentleman, and his already precarious life was more uncertain than ever.

He had probably assumed that he, Cosmus, and the Filipino lads would return to London with Cavendish when duty called the commander back to the capital, but they likely remained in Trimley.

London was a cesspit of plague, and the good, sweet and wholesome countryside air was much better for them. Besides, the gentleman scandal would still be the talk of the town, and Cavendish probably thought it best to lie low.

The youngest Filipino boy, too young to possess any particularly useful knowledge, was sent to join the household of Cavendish's late patron's widow, Lettice Dudley.

Christopher and his remaining colleagues would be called when the time was ripe.

As it turned out, the summons was not long in coming; the buzz in London involving Christopher took a new twist.

Those who had met Christopher and his colleagues were impressed by what they had seen. In the words of Francis Pretty, a gentleman who shared Christopher's quarters on *Desire*, and probably referring at least in part to the only Asians who he had actually met, stated that Far Easterners:

> *are men of marvelous capacitie in devising and making all maner of things, especially in all hande crafts and sciences: and every one is so expert, perfect, and skilfull in this facultie, as fewe or no Christians are able to goe beyond them.*

On the back of opinions like these, Christopher's star did not tumble in flames. Rather, he acquired a new role, that of Asian sage.

From now on, Christopher is described as a "naturalist," a relatively new term which would later, in 1834, be replaced by its modern appellation, "scientist."

One thing that London was beginning to thrive on for the first time in the 1580s and '90s, as it still does today, was international networks of people and information. The movement which sprang from this post-Renaissance international network is known as the Republic of Letters, a group of corresponding scholars, and enquiring minds who fostered a new intellectual vigor in a continent which had long been bound by the limits of classical knowledge and the tenets of religious scripture.

Christopher was thrust to the fore of this, becoming a strand in London's exciting new web of knowledge.

The voyages to distant realms, which were becoming increasingly ambitious as Elizabeth's reign wore on, coupled with the ever-increasing numbers of Protestant refugees from the continent, brought a form of riches which receives little comment today, but at that time enjoyed support from the highest in the land, including Robert Cecil and the Queen herself.

Europe's first direct contact with worlds it had never experienced before brought not only trade commodities and precious metals, but also a plethora of unknown, and in some cases virtually incomprehensible, fauna, flora, fruits, seeds, and medicinal drugs.

Some of the new plants, such as potatoes, tomatoes, chilies, and Indian corn (sweet corn or maize), went on to delight taste buds and provide the calories and nutrition which fueled Europe's rise over the centuries to come. Others like tulips lightened hearts and delighted souls, and some, such as tobacco, kill to this day.

The key to this increased bio-mobility was fast-developing maritime technology. It is difficult to carry a living plant on camel, horse, or foot. Travelers tended to choose higher-value, lower-weight items to maximize profits. A large vessel, however, is quite a different prospect. It is perfectly possible and logical to transport plants and fruits by boat.

Ships, in fact, sometimes bore more than a passing resemblance to floating farms, with tubs of vegetables and herbs, not to mention clucking chickens in cages, and milk cows tethered belowdecks.

While the animals rarely made it to the vessel's destination, plants and their seeds often did. At the end of a voyage, when they were no longer needed as food, the exotic specimens were then sold, or given away, to excited friends and patrons to experiment with.

In this fashion, myriad plant species we now take for granted joined the as yet barely classified contents of the continent's own forests', fields, and mountains, in being explored by well-connected naturalists, apothecaries, noble ladies, court officials, and university scholars. These "botanographers," as they were known, included some of Europe's greatest enquiring minds, including Marie de Brimeu, princess of Chimay; Ulisse Aldrovandi and his wife Francesca Fontana; Conrad Gessner; and Charles de l'écluse.

To friends, colleagues, and patrons, they reported their discoveries and accompanied the written word with pictures, diagrams, seed specimens, fruits, insects, books, antiques, animals, maps, minerals, and fossils to catalog, process, and advance knowledge of the natural world.

In the peaceful herb gardens of Europe, a botanical revolution was taking place that would eventually form the foundations of modern science.

It is through these eager scientific correspondents that we learn something of what Christopher was up to on his return to London in mid-1589.

James, or Jacques, Garet Jr. was one of the increasingly numerous Dutch-speaking diaspora to base themselves in London. Refugees from the terrible post–Reformation conflicts, they brought knowledge, skills, cosmopolitanism, international connections, and wealth to England's capital. Most importantly they transmitted intellectual vigor, becoming some of England's first active naturalists, and inspiring locals to follow in their footsteps.

One of Europe's leading apothecaries, Garet was at the forefront of trying to understand the biodiverse new specimens that arrived at his pharmacy to establish their decorative, medicinal, and nutritional uses. He became particularly famous for his tulips, a flower that had been introduced to Europe only a few years before from the Ottoman Empire. He was also said to purvey the best opium in town.

Garet's home was a little more than half a mile from Saint Katherine's, on a relatively clean, well-to-do, winding thoroughfare called Lime Street. The road was blessed with numerous gardens, and home to a particularly enquiring and organized group of naturalists. Conveniently the Dutch postmaster was also a resident, making for easy communication with the Continent.

Lime Street was London's acknowledged center for those interested in the natural world, and home to Mathias de L'Obel, Thomas Moffett, James Cole (born Jacob Coels in Antwerp), Thomas Penny, and others. The little community fed off each other's energy, using their fertile gardens and full-to-bursting "cabinets of curiosity" for mutual intellectual and scientific stimulation.

On the evening of July 28, 1589, James Garet Jr. sat comfortably at his large wooden desk. The bright candles cast their warm light on the paper before him, beside which lay a freshly sharpened quill. But he hesitated to grasp it; a little more reflection was called for.

The day had been momentous, in so many ways, and would surely lead to myriad fruitful discoveries.

Thomas Cavendish's success had inspired a lot of other would-be adventurers to dream of their own circumnavigations, and John Chidley's looked like it would be the first to actually depart for the Strait of Magellan, and thence the west coast of South America and East Asia. Today's meeting had been arranged to help prepare the voyage in which Garet was investing a considerable sum of money, and an even larger dose of hope.

Chidley and his second in command, Captain Polvohele, had been staying with the apothecary for months while they completed the final preparations. In return, Chidley had consented to install specially made soil tubs on one of the ships to collect plants. Garet's manservant was to accompany the voyage and be responsible for specimens which would be acquired from everywhere the ship landed. It was to be England's first attempt at a naturalist voyage of discovery, inspired and part funded by a Dutch immigrant, as well as a traditional English privateering mission of destruction and plunder.

Chidley was desperate for Cavendish's intelligence, and so it was that the famed circumnavigator himself had been invited to dine in Lime Street. *Desire*'s commander brought two of the famous Asian naturalists, the Japanese man Christopher and the Manilan Alphonso, the French pilot Sancius, who had more experience of the Americas than any man in England, and the ship's doctor. They carried some of the weird and wonderful botanical specimens that they had brought back the year before.

It had been an edifying day. The highlight for the plant-obsessed naturalist had been the testing of a brown-colored star-shaped dried fruit from China which had been taken from *Santa Ana*. It was beautiful in its aesthetic and near-symmetrical perfectness.

Garet had stroked its rough surface lightly, taken it in the palm of his hand, then raised it gingerly to his nose, and finally touched it to his tongue.

The licorice-like aroma was intense, but strangely the antici-pated flavor burst did not occur. Following Christopher's guid-ance, Garet then added it to hot water, and after a few minutes the brew had a pleasant, light, aniseed flavor. When he licked the fruit, its taste had also been enhanced.

It would make an extremely flavorful addition to food, and there must surely be a medicinal benefit too. Unfortunately, Christopher and Alphonso had been unable to inform him of any known apothecarial usage. Further testing would have to wait.

Fascinatingly, they could not agree on what it was called, the naturalists and Sancius seemed to think it was named "damor," but the doctor was convinced that it was called "cinchi."

To Garet, it seemed more likely that the Asians and Sancius were correct, though the thing that nagged at the back of his mind was that the three men were primarily known for marine science, not as botanographers.

Next, the ship's doctor produced an American fruit, seem-ingly of the cocoa family which he named "oregioella." This was also consumed as a beverage, and when they tested it, the resultant brew was bitter but invigorating.

Finally, Garet asked the Japanese naturalist, who was well

known in London's scholarly circles for his writing skill, to render the Chinese fruit's name in his native script. The man used a brush and black ink to paint the characters exquisitely onto a piece of the apothecary's finest paper, writing top to bottom, in graceful flowing characters.

This was the first time Garet, and most others present, had ever seen a script other than the Roman one written, and he was mesmerized by the experience. Once it had been sanded, he held the paper up and they all studied it from every angle. It was an almost magical moment.

Garet himself was intrigued by the day's events. Over the course of his career, he had acquired and subsequently grown seeds and plants from all over Europe, Anatolia, the East Coast of the New World and the West Indies. Plants from the western parts of the Americas or Asia, however, rarely crossed his threshold. Garet hoped Chidley and Polvohele had been satisfied and inspired to bring him back more specimens.

This voyage was the most ambitious investment in exotic plant collecting that he, and probably England, had ever embarked upon, and was bound to increase his fame in naturalist circles. He hoped for a speedy return so that he could furnish his colleagues and friends with any number of rare specimens. Having real natives of the Far East, naturalists at that, present in his house to help plan his grand scheme had been quite something. A unique and special occasion.

It had been an unforgettable day.

Garet raised the quill and started to write in French to one of Europe's most eminent scholars, his friend the Flemish naturalist Charles de l'écluse, better known by his Latin name, Carolus Clusius.

Monsieur Clusius Jay receu toutes les vostres finees and cell du XI maij 1589...

I had the Indians that Cavendish brought with him here in my house and showed them [the star anise,] asking what it was. One who came from the Philippines called it "damor." I also asked, separately the other Indian who also came from those whereabouts, and he too called it "damor"...it is drunk with water, as we do here with anise and water.

I also send you the word Damor written in the Indian's own hand in his own language, he wrote starting from the top and then going down, as you will see from this handwriting.

Mr. Cavendish's doctor called it Cinchi, but I am inclined to believe the Indians above the doctor.

Finally, the events of the day imparted to his eminent friend, he signed his name, *Jacques Garet le Jeusne*, folded the paper, addressed the back, and sealed it with fine red wax. His man would take it to the postmaster, along with a boxed sample of the *damor* or *cinchi*, three oregioella fruits, and the unique example of Japanese writing. Soon, it would board a ship to the Dutch Republic, and make its way slowly to Clusius in the Holy Roman Empire city of Frankfurt, where he had established a famous experimental garden.

Along with the significant contribution to contemporary botanical knowledge, Garet's letter recounts with fascination the first-ever instance of an East Asian language being written in England.

If it was Japanese, as the observers thought, it is likely to have been the phonetic *kana* script, but there is also every possibility that it was in fact the Chinese characters 八角, bā jiǎo, that were written for Garet and the other amazed onlookers. Christopher is likely to have spent more time in communication with literate Chinese people such as ships' pilots during his seafaring days, and he may have chosen to write in that language instead.

Ironically, the unnamed ship's doctor's word, "cinchi," is close to the modern Japanese name, *shikimi*, which refers to a very similar plant called Japanese star anise. This plant though is highly poisonous, and used only in incense, and as the doctor did not point this out, it is highly likely that the similarity is a coincidence.

The botanical information resulting from Christopher and Garet's meeting contributed to Clusius's great work, *Exoticorum libri decem,* "Ten books of exotic life forms" of 1605, a Renaissance botany masterpiece which is still consulted by historians and scientists today.

Without the groundbreaking work of people like Clusius, Garet, and their informants like Christopher, Alphonso, and Sancius, Europe, and the world, would be a far different place.

Garet was to be sadly disappointed in his hopes for exotic souvenirs from Chidley's voyage. Although the small fleet reached the Strait of Magellan, they could not prevail against the shocking weather. Fights over ever-dwindling food supplies ensued, and some men were abandoned to their fates before the survivors turned for home.

The voyage ended in utter disaster, running aground on the coast of Normandy where the locals took everything they had plundered in South America and put the survivors on a small ship home.

Only six of Chidley's men returned to England. The commander himself and Garet's manservant were not among them.

33

Compasses

The properties of lodestones, naturally occurring pieces of the mineral magnetite, to lend their magic to iron and naturally point toward the north (or to the south if you choose to read the opposite end of the magnetized object), had been documented in China since around the beginning of the Common Era, and in Europe around the turn of the twelfth century.

Cultures all over the world initially seem to have used these stones, or objects magnetized by them, for spiritual rather than maritime navigation purposes. Christians needed to know where Jerusalem lay, Muslims sought Mecca's direction, and East Asians primarily needed to determine the northeast, as from that direction came evil spirits, demons, and misfortune. Cities, buildings, and graves needed to be carefully designed to have the appropriate geomantic spiritual defenses.

Compasses of the type developed over time in China and used in East Asia were highly intricate, and included information about constellations, lunar stations, and the eight trigrams from the ancient divination work, *Yi Ching* (*Book of Changes*).

They were hugely complicated magic-seeming machines, operable only by those inducted into the secret and semimystical ways of geomancy and horoscope casting.

A Chinese geomantic compass with a dry-pivot needle.

Asian sea rovers, however, were not normally geomantic scholars, and relied on a much simpler form of the instrument for navigation. From around the eleventh century, magnetized metal, normally forged into the shape of a fish, floating in a bowl was surrounded by twenty-four concentric circles, containing not only directional lore, but information on myriad elements, divisions, winds, and constellations.

In Europe's ships, the compass was a simple device pivoted on a needle without the extra computations available on Eastern instruments. These primitive devices were often inaccurate, and sailors could not maintain their magnetism for long because of the extreme rarity and huge expense of the crucial lodestones. The highly risky nature of maritime travel would have meant that only the very richest of mariners would have risked such a valuable object on a ship.

Further from home, especially in unfamiliar hemispheres when cartographical and astronomical knowledge could not act as a backup, navigational accuracy deteriorated swiftly. These deficiencies resulted in the loss of thousands of lives, and countless valuable cargoes globally.

The Reverend William Barlowe was one of England's foremost scholars of magnetism and more specifically in its application to oceangoing navigation. He had heard tales of the astonishing feats of Portuguese ships, navigated mainly by Asian and African pilots, and was determined to discover just how they achieved so much in the vast seas and oceans on the far side of the globe.

He came to believe that the cause was superior navigation equipment, and therefore he was now in the process of designing a revolutionary new compass to aid English mariners in their seaborne endeavors.

William Barlowe was lucky enough to be able to consult Christopher and Alphonso, the only two men in England that knew anything about East Asian compasses.

It was a great relief that they could speak English.

His questioning, probably in the company of his friend and collaborator William Gilbert, was prescient and wide-ranging. He enquired into everything and anything to do with Eastern shipping, sailing methods, seaborne technology, maritime culture, and of course navigation. Christopher and Alphonso answered him as best they could and offered to demonstrate the construction and use of the compass commonly used in the seas around China, Japan, and Luzon.

Barlowe had a lodestone, so they simply needed to assemble the tools to recreate the Chinese instrument. Cavendish's staff, although they could not supply authentic porcelain as would have been used in Asia, gladly provided a flat clay dish to hold water, and a small pin to use as a pivot. All that was lacking was the needle, but Barlowe had one made to the naturalist's specifications.

It was thin, around six inches long, and shaped like a fish. In the center on the lower side, it had a small dimple for the pinhead.

A sketch of the Chinese mariner's compass, with a fish-shaped needle floating in water, similar to the one that Christopher demonstrated to William Barlowe.

Christopher drew lines in the dish to divide it into four. These represented the protective directional deities: the Azure Dragon of the East, the Vermilion Bird of the South, the White Tiger of the West, and the Black Turtle of the North. The vicar had a good think about these and decided they must be similar to the Greek wind gods, Boreas, Zephyrus, Notus, and Eurus.

Christopher then carefully stuck the pin into the center of the dish with a piece of wax, poured in water until the pinhead was nearly covered, and demonstrated how to tenderly stroke the lodestone four times from the center of the fish-shaped needle to its tail. The wizardry was performed, and the fish was now magnetized.

He explained to the vicar that his simple compass would normally be used in conjunction with the additional local skills and knowledge of a pilot, just as in England.

Gently, the needle was placed on top of the pin where it would be able to move freely in the water.

The fish head pointed south!

Barlowe laughed out loud. It was the opposite way to an English compass, which always pointed north. Because Christopher had magnetized the tail, it was that which pointed north. Not the head.

Barlowe was well satisfied by the experiment, staying at Saint Katherine's for a few more days continuing his discussions, before reluctantly bidding Christopher and Alphonso a fond farewell.

Barlowe's book of 1597, *The Navigator's Supply*, recounted how fascinated he was by his experience of talking to the two young Asian men,

Some fewe yeeres since it so fell out, that I had severall conference with two East Indians which were brought into England by Master [Cavendish,] and had learned our language: The one of them was of Manillia, in the Isle of Luzon, the other of Miaco in Japan. I questioned with them concerning their shipping, and manner of sailing. They described all things farre different from ours, and shewed, that in steade of our Compas, they use a Magneticall Needle of sixe ynches long, and longer, upon a pinne in a dish of white china earth filled with water: In the bottome whereof they have two crosse lines, for the foure principall windes: the rest of the dicisions being referued to the skill of their Pilots. Upon which report of theirs, I made a present trial howe a Magneticall Needle would stand in water, and found it to prove excellently well; not doubting but that many conclusions of importance in Marine affaires will thereby more readily be performed.

Strangely, Japanese pirate ships at Christopher's time are recorded as using a dry compass, somewhat like the European ones, and probably introduced through contact with the Portuguese in the latter half of the sixteenth century. They appear to have found them easier to use, as they required less expert training, but they were also less precise and durable than the water compass that Christopher described. This probably means that although he was Japan-born, he had more experience of sailing in the Chinese fashion, another clue in Christopher's fascinatingly multicultural tale.

Barlowe was unable to incorporate the Asian technology into his newly improved compass. Unlike the seas where Christopher had sailed before Spanish capture, English machines needed to operate in extremes of cold, in the freezing waters to England's north, in the cold southern escapes from the Atlantic, and hypothetically in the long sought-after Northwest Passage. A wet compass would have frozen solid and been useless for large parts of the year.

Modern compasses solve this issue by adding industrial alcohol to lower the temperature at which the liquid turns to ice. It was not until the nineteenth century, when English mariners were still complaining that Chinese compasses were superior, that British ships managed to adopt Asian-style liquid compasses.

Barlowe's instrument, incorporating gimbals to ensure that it remained horizontal in rough waters, and more durable steel needles, allowed the true north, as opposed to the magnetic north, to be calculated, and perhaps following Christopher's instruction, Barlowe also advocated stroking the needle three or four times to ensure it remained magnetic for longer.

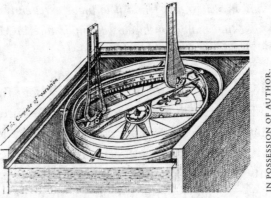

William Barlowe's compass of variation. This engraving was first published in The Navigators Supply *by William Barlowe, 1597.*

Despite its limitations, Barlowe's compass was a huge improvement, and for the next two centuries it ensured that cargos of people and supplies could be transported to little-charted lands more safely and with improved efficiency. Large-scale settlement and viable commercialization of the North American colonies would have probably been far harder, or even impossible, without Barlowe's compass.

One navigator in particular, William Adams, a friend of *Desire*'s pilot Timothy Schotten, and almost definitely one of the first people to use a Barlowe compass, not to mention a Molyneux globe, was to put these new navigational aids to excellent effect. He may also have met Christopher and was certainly in London at the same time as the Japanese mariner as he married Mary Hyn in Stepney, only a mile or so from Christopher's abode in Saint Katherine's, in 1589.

Eleven years later, he would achieve what Englishmen had been trying to do for over a century, and actually set foot in Japan.

His career there was to be meteoric. Becoming a trusted member of the shogun's inner circle, building the first Japanese ship to navigate the Pacific to North America, establishing himself as a successful merchant, and assisting in the construction of the city that we now know as Tokyo, were just a few of his many accomplishments.

He is remembered and honored in Japan, England, and elsewhere to this day.

Books often talk of technology and cultures such as gunpowder, paper, Islam, and Buddhism spreading gradually along trade routes such as the Silk Roads over decades or centuries, but this meeting between East and West shows that process in the flesh. There are likely to have been many more such conversations between Christopher and people like him and London's intelligentsia, lost to time, but crucial in European maritime technology, and the nascent scientific revolution. Fascinating but forgotten footnotes to history.

These interactions between Christopher and his comrades, and the great and good of London, are the first documented intellectual exchanges between English speakers and East Asians.

34

English Triumph to English Despair

The euphoria of the deliverance from the Armada quickly evaporated as it became clear that what could have been a decisive
blow to the enemy had been utterly wasted.

The Queen's government would venture no more funds than
the bare minimum, and lack of basic provisions meant that an
attack could not be pressed home. After the battle at Gravelines,
English bellicosity swiftly petered out, and the crews simply
drifted, starving, back into ports along the Channel coast. Some
men even reported drinking their own urine. Henry White, an
officer on one of the ships, wrote that "our parsimony at home
hath bereaved us of the famousest victory that ever our navy
might have had at sea."

The following year, under the dual command of Francis Drake
and John Norreys, the English belatedly tried to push home
their advantage by sending their own armada to attack the Iberian Peninsula.

The mission's aims were to finish off any surviving ships from
the previous year's invasion attempt, plunder the treasure fleet

from Spanish America, capture the Portuguese-held Azores to establish a first permanent Atlantic colony, and foster rebellion in Portugal.

Due to lack of state funds, the huge force of one hundred fifty ships and twenty-four thousand men was privately funded via a joint stock company, and largely because of the wider commercial rather than purely military focus, it was an unmitigated disaster.

None of the stated aims were achieved, and only 102 ships and 3,722 men staggered home. Destitute and desperate, the survivors formed "disordered assemblies," and mutinied to demand their unpaid wages.

England was now weaker than ever. Her economy was battered further through the massive loss of private investment that had been sunk into the attack, her fighting men's morale and willingness to do battle decimated, and her weapons of war lost to the sea and the Spanish.

Spain on the other hand was left free to rearm and equip for further invasions in the knowledge that England's recovery would be far slower.

Christopher's last year in England, 1591, was another difficult one. Extreme drought caused crop failure, and the Thames was so low at times that people could walk across from London to Southwark. In the terrific heat, the plague reared its head, schools were closed, and citizens went in fear of their lives.

Meanwhile in Catholic Europe, plans were put in place to minimize the threat from an English mission arriving in Japan with a Japanese interpreter.

Christopher and Cavendish had to be stopped.

35

Farewell

Leicester, a large and well-maintained veteran vessel of four hundred tuns named for Cavendish's late patron, Robert Dudley, Earl of Leicester, lolled comfortably in the Orwell's slow current. Small boats swarmed around her, loading victuals and chandlery supplies.

This year's drought had pushed prices to wild heights, so Cavendish decided as far as possible to use resources local to Trimley rather than purchase materials on the London or Plymouth markets where greedy merchants would inevitably take advantage. In Trimley he could rely on his estate and local suppliers such as Henry Seckford in Woodbridge. Nearby Ipswich was, furthermore, one of the greatest shipbuilding centers of England, second only to London, so sailcloth and suitable timber were cheap and plentiful. *Leicester* would be well prepared for the arduous mission before her.

Cavendish had secured salted mutton and pork, hardtack of barley and rye, dried peas, herring from the North Sea, butter, and hard cheese. Many tuns of hoppy beer would mean that

sailors could drink safely for months until the first likely landfall in Brazil.

There was no need for trade goods, or gifts to offer as tribute to the rulers of the Japanese; these would be plundered from
Portuguese and Spanish settlers along the way.

Christopher's was not the only mission to depart for Asia that
year. England had already waved farewell to two other trans-
oceanic missions, that of James Lancaster to the Indian Ocean
in April, and the Earl of Cumberland's fleet bound for the Spice
Islands on June 18.

Cavendish's royal warrant was kept vague, as was customary,
so that the Queen could deny that she had condoned piracy. It
cryptically tasked him:

> to take in hand a voyage by sea, for the service of the realm, and
> to the increase of his own knowledge, whereby he shall be the bet-
> ter able hereafter to do service.

The mission's target was top secret, but no one was fooled.
Why else would Cavendish take his two Japanese advisors, both
Christopher and Cosmus, and leave the three Filipino ones if
he were not aiming for an audience with the Japanese court?

In Plymouth, *Leicester* rendezvoused with the four other ships
of the fleet. *Roebuck*, two hundred forty tuns, a ship owned
by Cavendish since 1589, and rumored to have been used extensively for clandestine piracy, the much smaller *Daintie*, and
Black Pinnace, and finally a fully refitted *Desire*. They topped up
supplies and replaced the several men who had already jumped
ship when they guessed the immensity of the perilous task before them.

The lesser ships were rumored to be under orders to use their
diminutive size to discover the Strait of Anian and nose out the
Northwest Passage from the Pacific side. *Content*, *Desire*'s companion on Cavendish's circumnavigation, had attempted this

path, but had never been heard of again. Perhaps they would discover her fate as well as England's salvation in the icy wastes.

Black Pinnace *on an earlier voyage to repatriate the body of Sir Philip Sidney after his death in the Netherlands in 1586. Thomas Lant, 1588. It is the only one of Cavendish's ships of which a portrait remains.*

This mission within a mission was under the command of John Davis, a man whose heart burned to reach the Far East, and whose book, *The Worldes Hydrographical Description* includes a passage stating that it was composed from the "aucthoritie of writters, and experience of travelers."

Whether Christopher himself was one of these travelers or not is sadly left unsaid.

John Davis was far from the only interesting character among the three hundred fifty men who sailed with Christopher.

Thomas Lodge was perhaps the most enigmatic of those hot bedding in *Leicester*'s Great Cabin. A dreamy drifter of about thirty-three, born to money and educated at Oxford, he had rejected the legal career that his social-climbing parents desired for him, and chose instead the uncertain life of a playwright.

By 1591, he was established as a writer, and just prior to this voyage, he had published what was to become his most famous work, *Rosalynde or, Euphues' Golden Legacie* whose storyline Shakespeare dramatized in *As You Like It*.

It seems puzzling that such a man should be part of a potentially deadly voyage of plunder to the farthest parts of the world, but Lodge is believed to have spent time in prison for suspected Catholic sympathies and was likely fleeing debt and destitution when he signed up for the mission. He needed to get filthy rich, quickly, and in a socially acceptable, patriotic way. Privateering likely seemed the best option.

Also aboard was Robert Hues, a mathematician and geographer who had met Cavendish a decade before while training in the art of navigation under Walter Raleigh.

Hues was the resident naturalist, and his mission was of great national importance. He was to gather intelligence on the stars of the southern hemisphere, a task never before undertaken systematically by an English speaker, and as future voyagers would rely upon his observations, research, and conclusions, he had the lives of both his current colleagues, and even sailors as yet unborn, in his delicate long-fingered hands.

By far the most important character for Christopher himself was thirty-two-year-old Anthony Knyvett, the illegitimate son of Sir Henry Knyvett, and nephew of Thomas Knyvett (who later became a baron). Both senior Knyvetts were patrons of London naturalists and involved in the wider blue-blooded court circle which Cavendish inhabited. Christopher and Anthony had probably become familiar with each other through the Lime Street connection. Their close personal friendship is the first-ever documented between Japanese and English-speaking people.

Christopher would have wondered about the composition of this crew. There were too many "adventurers," and not enough sailors. As a mariner himself, he knew that the gentlemen adventurers would not be much help in a ferocious tempest, nor when a ship was becalmed for weeks on end. They would fight with great gusto and bravado as they had been raised from birth to do, but would they take their turn at the bilge pumps in the pitch black as the hull filled with icy water around them? Would they subsist on foul and crumbled biscuit crawling with wee-vils for months on end without grumbling? He had his doubts.

The Plymouth sojourn was brief.

Due to the drought and general scarcity of food in 1591, the mission was already long past its planned departure date. If they were to be safely through the Strait of Magellan before the next southern hemisphere winter set in, they would need to proceed with all haste. Failure to arrive in time would mean unendurable weather and freezing winter quarters, or skulking for months in Portuguese-controlled waters around Brazil until the conditions became clement enough to attempt a passage. Either was likely to result in many deaths and the probable failure of the mission.

The fleet was anchored once more outside Plymouth's walled harbor beneath the fort's great guns. It was August and the days were long. Christopher again heard the sounds of laugh-ter, cavorting, and merrymaking carrying clearly over the gen-tly swishing waves. The men were making the most of their last nights on land.

Christopher would have gazed out to sea from Plymouth Hoe contemplating tempests, hunger, disease, and the violence of the long voyage ahead.

He was supposedly homeward bound, although in actual fact he had not been in Japan for nearly half his life, nor been among other Japanese people, save Cosmus, for more than five years.

He wore an oil-worked sailors' smock and leather jerkin, had his hair cropped short, and a sea dirk hung at his left side. He looked more English than Japanese, but he probably no longer noticed.

The clouds floated by in mountain-like mauve-tinged jum-bles. *Leicester* seemed to lie directly in a sunray, pointing her down a shining path out of the bay and toward the open sea.

Christopher may have wondered if it was the goddess of his youth, Mazu, flickering in the flaming sunset to mark their way.

He had left his homeland as an enslaved child on a pirate ship, but Christopher would be returning with a noble representative of a foreign country to be rich, famous, and respected. It must have been a strange feeling for the young man who had seen and suffered so much.

The squadron of five ships weighed anchor and headed for Brazil on August 26, 1591. The great and good of Plymouth gathered to wish them Godspeed. The two chalk giants on Plymouth Hoe added a silent farewell.

36

Spy

Christopher had known that the early part of the voyage would be tedious; the days dragged on forever. Life slowed down and stretched out.

After two weeks, they passed the Canary Islands, specks of black rock and sand poking their heads out of the blue sea. This was often a prime location to find Spanish or Portuguese prizes, but no easy prey revealed itself, and the fleet continued south to the point where the trade winds would head them west across the Atlantic to Brazil.

Every day, the crew members offered up exhortations to their God for a safe crossing. Christopher would have followed the motions but may well in truth have been more worried about his Lady Mazu's warm blessings. A voyage unblessed by her light and love could only have one outcome.

At least he had a new friend. Anthony Knyvett. The two of them became inseparable, whiling their time away as best they could with the other gentlemen adventurers on music, story-telling, writing, and card games. The mid-ocean sun beat down upon them, and everyone's skin became tanned and leathery.

As the fleet continued slowly south, rations were cut.

Vegetables were long gone. Only a little salt pork, rancid butter, and the powdery dregs of crumbled ship biscuit remained to form a kind of vile soupy stew. All Christopher's external senses would have screamed against this nauseating concoction, but he could not resist his empty and howling stomach.

Then the heat and bad air of the equator brought *mal de Luanda*. Men started to die.

Worst of all, one day the wind simply ceased to blow. This was the dreaded doldrums, and the ships could do nothing but allow themselves to drift on the ocean currents until the breeze got up again.

Fights broke out over the smallest thing. Anxiety infused every activity. The mission was at risk of failure before they had even crossed the Atlantic. Only prayer and the dwindling beer ration remained to take the edge off the tedium and worry.

A Portuguese crew member, perhaps lonely among the English, befriended both Christopher and Cosmus. He had voyaged to Brazil before, and so they eagerly listened to his tales of their next landfall.

It was a hot forested land, inhabited by both Portuguese settlers and Indigenous peoples. These Natives went nearly naked in war, painted only in fearsome patterns, but fought bravely with club and bow. It was said that they roasted their defeated foe over fires and devoured them to inherit their strength.

The towns of São Vicente and Santos, where they were now headed, were the most important settlements. These small settlements had grown rich on Europe's insatiable appetite for exotic and expensive sugar.

To grow the sugarcane, a slaving industry had developed, many of the once-ferocious Indigenous people, their numbers much reduced by epidemics, were pacified, baptized, and reduced to plantation workers. Yet the population dwindled still, so an alternative source of expendable labor had been tapped in Africa. Black-skinned war captives from Kongo were ripped from their homes and transported to Brazil instead.

Christopher would have felt a huge conflict well up within him. His childhood had not been idyllic or peaceful; he and Cosmus had also been taken, terrorized, and trafficked like the Africans and Brazilians who the sailor had described.

Sitting on a ship on the other side of the world, he likely tried to recall the teeming streets of ports where he had run wild as a small boy, and the beaches of Fukabori where he had roasted wriggling fish over sweet-smelling fires while watching the layered mauve clouds drift over Nagasaki Bay.

Christopher realized he wanted to return to the place of his birth, if only to check that the memories were real, and not flights of his childhood imagination.

The English plan was likely for Christopher and Cosmus to represent them in Japan, as Manteo had in America. A wealthy life awaited him, and he knew that he was Cavendish's, nay England's, man now.

So, when the Portuguese sailor casually suggested that it might be faster to return to Japan overland…rather than risking the Strait of Magellan, where death stalked all who dared enter… Christopher blinked and said nothing at first. Perhaps the heavy sun was getting to the mariner, giving him delusions.

The man continued, explaining that the land route across South America to the Pacific was quicker and safer by far.

Christopher laughed. The idea was surely a joke. Plainly ludicrous. They were with Cavendish…and even if the land route was shorter, which he seriously doubted, the English commander would never give up his ships and venture over land.

The sailor read his mood and dropped the subject.

One becalmed and idle afternoon, the Portuguese man brought up the subject of jumping ship again. This time, he specifically suggested that after they got to Brazil, Christopher, Cosmus, and he should set off to find a Spanish ship bound for Manila and get to Japan that way. The Spanish who lived on the Pacific side of the continent would reward them well for abandoning Cavendish.

The man grinned nervously; he knew he was playing with fire.

The two Japanese men smiled back and bade him good night.

It had been a long time since they had conversed in their own language, but now it seemed imperative that they did. They both knew that this man had been sent to sabotage the voyage, to deprive Cavendish of their services. Without them, even if he reached Japan, the English would have a difficult time of it.

What should they do? Should they try to forget the whole episode? Keep it secret in case it rebounded upon them?

They debated long and hard. Around them, the clump and scrape of spoons on wooden bowls rang out as the hungry men held their noses while trying to keep down their revolting gruel and foul beverage.

The animated conversation in Japanese would have attracted funny glances. It was clear that something important was being discussed, and on a ship where no one had anything better to do, the two foreigners babbling in their incomprehensible tongue would have become the evening's entertainment.

There was only one possible conclusion to the deliberations. Their loyalties lay with Cavendish. He had freed them, treated them well, and supported them for three years in England. Now he was taking them home where they would be set up as men of substance. They were important and trusted members of his crew; not to tell him of this plot would be betrayal.

In the swiftly approaching equatorial sunset, the two Japanese men approached Cavendish's cabin.

His servant refused them entrance as the commander was at dinner and not to be disturbed in any circumstances.

Christopher tried again. They had found a traitor and must speak with the commander. The servant shook his head again. It was simply against his orders, and to disobey would provoke a furious reaction from the increasingly short-tempered Cavendish.

There was nothing for it. Christopher shouted out so Cavendish could hear through the closed door. "The Portugal is a traitor who wants us to run away with him in Brazil." The whole crew could hear, but he did not care. The door burst open, Cavendish, looking pale and weak, leaned on the door frame for support.

Christopher, with Cosmus nodding along, told the whole story from scratch again.

"Get the sorry swine here," Cavendish bellowed to his man outside.

The trial by lamplight was brief. The verdict was swift.

Within moments the Portuguese sailor was breathing his last, grabbing helplessly at the noose as his lungs struggled for air and his face turned purple. The weak lantern light barely pierced the now pitch-black night.

When fluid started dripping, forming a puddle on the polished deck, it was clear the would-be saboteur was gone.

Knyvett recorded this encounter in his account of the voyage:

The general being at dinner, these two Japoners came to his Cabbin, telling their tale so loud that every one might heare the report (which was thus) that the Portugall of the ship was a Traytor, and that he had often given them counsel to run away with him at Brasil: moreover (quoth he) if it had pleased God wee had taken the Towne of Santos, as our General had pretended, from thence that hee would guide them to the South Sea, where they should be well rewarded for their intelligence; upon the which accusations, the poore Portugall was hanged. And as for his going from Santos by land through America, to the South Sea, has been a thing impossible, for the Countrie is all Wildernesse, and full of Savages.

With the excitement over, the corpse was cut down and flung overboard without ceremony.

Cavendish turned and staggered back to his cabin.

Christopher felt relief but was also overwhelmed.

He thought back to when the Spanish pilot had been hanged on Capul three or four years before. That time it had been a Spaniard hanged on the word of a Portuguese. This time a Portuguese on his word.

Cavendish had again acted decisively. Made his decision swiftly. Enacted it immediately.

The mission had rid itself of a serious threat, and Christopher found refuge from emotional tumult in sleep.

37

Celestial Adventures

While the sailors saw to the becalmed ship, most of the gentlemen adventurers whiled away their time in idle pursuits.

One man, however, was busy with a very different type of activity.

Robert Hues dozed away his days in the armory and spent his nights observing the stars.

At nightfall, he leaped off the mat where he had been sleeping, eagerly arranged his instruments and took careful notes of all he observed while continually referring to several volumes that he had brought with him.

Among them, Christopher would have seen one called *Geographia*. It was written by the great Egyptian scholar Ptolemy only shortly after Christ's time and held all the secrets of the universe as passed down by the ancients.

Today, it is common knowledge that Nicolaus Copernicus had theorized and written about the nongeocentric nature of the solar system and universe in 1543, but his work was virtually unread at this time, and even scholars like Hues were skeptical about its worth.

Most people, Hues included, continued to follow the ancient Ptolemaic theories intertwined with more recent Christian religious dogma, firmly believing that the Earth was not only the center of God's creation, but that it was the most corrupt part of it. They thought that humanity occupied a midground between savage animals and angels, God's helpers in the heavens. The "fixed stars" (what we know as *stars*), and the "wandering stars" (our solar system's *planets*) inhabited a more brilliant realm between mankind and the pure and eternal divine, located somewhere behind them.

There were estimated to be around 72 constellations formed from 1022 "fixed stars," which transmitted God's light to earth.

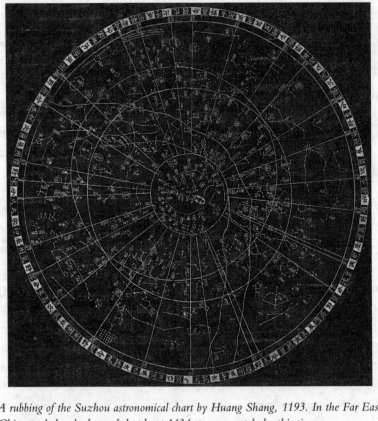

A rubbing of the Suzhou astronomical chart by Huang Shang, 1193. In the Far East, Chinese scholars had recorded at least 1434 stars accurately by this time.

For Hues, his endeavors were therefore religious, scientific, and patriotic. He was seeking a more practical knowledge of the heavens for navigation, but also to reveal and understand the realm of his creator on behalf of his Queen and nation.

In the Far East, Chinese scholars had recorded at least 1434 stars accurately by 1193, and to that was added southern hemisphere knowledge from Arab and Persian explorations as well as that of Chinese seafarers who are thought to have ventured as far south as the Australian continent. As a sailor, Christopher's knowledge would have encompassed much of this, even if it was more practical than scholarly focused.

Hues and Christopher were in close proximity; even sharing the same sleeping quarters, they could not very well have ignored each other, and for Hues like his London naturalist colleagues, Christopher would have provided an interesting foil on which to test his developing theories.

As they crossed the equator, Christopher observed the changing night sky. The stars of the north, the divine guides, had gone, to be replaced by the great cross constellation of the south that the English called the "Crusiers." *Leicester* seemed to be heading right into the deep, dark blue center where two small stars cast their light to lead Christopher and his colleagues onward.

38

Manna from Heaven

It took a whole month for the wind to fill the sails once more. The already tardy mission had been delayed further. Sickness continued unabated. Food and drink rations dwindled further, and starvation was added to scurvy's scourge. Men's skin started to tighten around their jowls and take on a colorless hue beneath the sunburn.

The most serious cases simply lay prone in corners, while others stumbled about their jobs, working to the extent of their fading energy.

Every few days, the whistle blew, prayers were briefly said, and another bundle that had once been human slid into the deep. Then the listless survivors returned to their duties, wondering when their turn would come.

After twenty days of following winds, an endless low gray-green shadow melting lazily into the clouds on the horizon appeared.

Brazil.

The men's spirits suddenly spiked. Final bites of food, saved for the very end, were devoured. Last ounces of energy were found. Half-dead men reanimated.

Closer in, they could see steep green hillsides with golden beaches stretched out below them. It was not very unlike the stunning scenery of the Philippine islands, but the navigator in Christopher knew this was no island, it was the edge of a massive continental landmass of unimaginable proportions.

Leicester continued her approach and then veered south following the coast. They needed a landmark.

Two small ships appeared, and Cavendish's fleet gave chase. One got clean away, but the other was taken without a fight.

The ship's pilot, Gaspar Jorge, came reluctantly aboard the English flagship and informed them that they were at Cabo Frio. There was no settlement there, but there was one a day further south on Ilha Grande.

Christopher and his friend Knyvett, skin tight and eyes bright with desperation, joined the rest of *Leicester*'s men in ransacking the ship. But even their deep hunger disappeared when they saw this ship's grim cargo.

On the dark decks below, Christopher found dozens of starving Africans, chained to each other and to the ship, lying in their own filth. Numerous cadavers, released from the torture of this world, lay among the listless survivors. The smell of death, feces, urine, sweat, and fear was nauseating.

Compared even with the walking-skeleton–like English, pallid skin clinging to bony faces, and teeth loose in bloody gums, these people's condition was beyond belief.

Despite the shock of this human tragedy, the sailors' desperate hunt for food continued. One flour chest was revealed to contain a hidden priest. He was mercilessly cast overboard, and the food was transferred to *Leicester*.

Aside from the Africans, the main cargo was sugar, a rare and expensive luxury. The English devoured it as if it were the cheapest of vittles. Some were instantly sick. Others sat back in stupefied gluttony, satisfied looks playing across their thinned-out faces. Their hunger was, at least temporarily, well sated.

The pilot, Jorge, did not return to his ship. It was standard practice to abduct navigators, and they were always well treated as long as they behaved themselves. Their art was semisacred—without them a ship could not proceed.

As promised, a day later they reached the small settlement on Ilha Grande. It was just a few rough huts. But there was food!

All order broke down. Normally, shore leave was granted in shifts to ensure that ships remained defended and supplies were distributed fairly. Not this day.

Led by the eager gentlemen adventurers, the crews of the five ships rowed past the rocky entrance to the cove and as they approached the beach, many dived in, eager to be the first ashore.

There, they raced to the store houses of the settlement, captured the surprised inhabitants, and left them trussed on the beach.

The first arrivals banded together with friends and grabbed the best supplies. Fat pigs, squawking hens, cassava, vegetables of all shapes and sizes, bananas and casks of *cachaça* spirit. They then headed for the woods to devour them, keeping their ill-gotten gains from other groups who roamed the forests and beaches trying to pilfer what others had already stolen.

Christopher and Knyvett were not among the first to land and would have found only a few lonely provisions remaining, so they took their guns into the steep forested hills to find game, roots, or anything else to wolf down.

It was night by now, and the sweet aroma of roasting pork attracted them to a divot on the hillside where eight mariners were hammering at each other in a massive fistfight over who should have which part of the spitted hog.

With the fire burning brightly, the forest behind was plunged into a deep darkness, as if a curtain had been closed tight. Christopher, with Knyvett behind him, sneaked silently up, dodged

276　　　　　　THOMAS LOCKLEY

between the flying fists unnoticed and grasped a red-hot hind leg. His hands were screaming at him to drop the scorching meat, but his stomach spurred him on.

It came away so easily, that Christopher almost fell head over heels into the firepit. Knyvett saved him by shoving at the small of his back to keep him upright, and they ran headlong through the twisted undergrowth, batting at vines and ducking under low-hanging branches to get as far from the brawl as possible. Howls of rage pursued them into the darkness.

When all was quiet, the two friends stopped and attacked the huge joint from both sides. They had pilfered a good eighth of the beast, and the juicy, fatty meat filled their famished bellies. A pleasant porky greasiness played across the dry skin of their wind-blistered faces.

Christopher and his friend wrapped the remainder in leaves and lay back satiated and comfortable.

For the first time in weeks, they passed a merry evening, laughing, exclaiming at funny episodes, and occasionally gorging again at the remains of the joint.

The roaring thunder of the ocean, amplified by the steep slope on which they lay, formed a backdrop to the forest soundscape of chirping insects, the snap of falling twigs, and the occasional shrill cry of a sleepy bird.

Replete and warm in the warm night, they bivouacked under the stars and found refuge in sleep.

Awaking at first light, they immediately started to scavenge for likely looking plants. The potato-like roots they found looked hard, but plump and juicy, and reminded Christopher of those that he had first eaten on the voyage to England four years before. Now, using their bare hands and broken branches, the two friends dug as many fat tubers as they could, took off their shirts, and wrapped them tight and safe within.

As they descended the mountain in the direction of the ravaged settlement, many of the three hundred plus Englishmen could still be seen spread out among the trees sleeping off their gluttony. Others were setting out to see what more they could find. All cohesion and discipline had disappeared.

Had an enemy attempted an attack, the whole sorry force would have been massacred in moments.

Christopher and Knyvett came upon *Leicester*'s musicians who had raided a litter in one of the outhouses. They pooled their supplies for breakfast. Suckling-puppy and root stew, an exquisite meal not to be forgotten in a long time.

The ravaged hamlet and wild mountainside were never going to be enough. With their immediate hunger satisfied and no prospect of much more food, groups of Englishmen slowly congregated on the beach. Cavendish seemed in a mood to ignore the indiscipline, understanding that extreme hunger trumps all, and that his men had needed their release.

He gave orders to torch the settlement and sink the captured Portuguese ship.

The now unchained Africans were left to wreak revenge on their erstwhile captors. Christopher suspected that the near-white beach would soon be tinged with blood. Jorge, the pilot, would be glad to have been abducted by the English.

Forgotten in all the excitement, Christopher had clocked up another momentous first.

He became the first documented Asian to set foot in South America.

39

Santos

Now that Jorge had revealed their precise location, they knew that their target Santos was mere days away. Real action was imminent.

Christopher, too important to risk in an operation like this, was not permitted to join the assault, but Knyvett would have gleefully revealed all afterward.

Daintie headed up the attack with a covert mission. Pretending to be a trading vessel blown off course in need of supplies, she cruised into the Bay of Santos to be welcomed with open arms. This remote European outpost was desperate for trade goods.

Little did the good burghers suspect the true intention of this small and unthreatening craft, and she was readily given permission to trade before sailing off again.

They reported that the town was utterly undefended and as it was Christmas, the people were in a festive mood. Their guard was down.

Leicester and *Roebuck* were too large to approach unnoticed, so Cavendish appointed his cousin, Captain Cocke, to lead the main attack speedily by rowboat from *Desire* and *Black Pinnace* while he remained out of sight nearby.

At 10:00 p.m. on Christmas Eve, the order to man the boats for a surprise attack was given softly.

Cocke might as well have shouted it, because pandemonium ensued as men fought tooth and nail in the pitch black, punching, kicking and butting to be the first to get to the boats. One would-be attacker fell into the sea and sank swiftly in his heavy armor, which should have given the others food for thought, but it didn't. The uproar echoed around the bay.

It could only be a matter of time before the alarm was raised, and the Santos militia mustered.

All need for silence long forgotten, Captain Cocke roared the order for everyone to return to the ships where he gave them a tongue lashing they would not forget. Discipline was restored, and around midnight, Cocke ordered a boat with twenty-four chosen men to form the vanguard. They pushed off, and an hour or so later another three heavily laden rowboats set off from the two small ships.

Jorge had informed them of the exact time when the Christmas mass would be at its height, and as the church bells rang out, the now near-silent attackers crept softly into town. It was pitch-black, and steadfast in their devotions, no one noticed the soft clank of muffled weaponry in the streets.

Enjoying utter surprise, the twenty-four men rushed the church, and confiscated the shocked population's weapons. Then they stood back, waiting for the reinforcements to arrive.

The small English corps could do nothing more. It was an awkward moment.

Had the three hundred shocked worshipers charged the English, they could only have got off one volley before the fighting became hand-to-hand. The raiders would have been easily overwhelmed, but with a high butcher's bill for the townsfolk. All knew it.

The jittery jailers waited with guns loaded and slow matches at the ready.

Hours later, the reinforcement boats, overmanned and clumsily rowed by amateur gentlemen adventurers, landed and the town was secured. While the population cowered under English guard in the church, the raiders ran riot, looting and pillaging to their hearts' content.

It was only the European townsfolk who had been at prayer, the resident Brazilians were still at large and watched on with interest. Captain Cocke thought that these sparsely clothed people might prove useful allies, and ordered that they be left unmolested, allowed to come and go freely.

The Portuguese population remained hungrily confined to the church as their livelihoods were ruined, and their homes ransacked. That evening they were unceremoniously expelled from their own town and left to fend for themselves in the countryside.

The natives continued passing in and out of town quietly as the English gorged themselves on uneaten Christmas feasts. As well as meat, they purloined sugar, pastries, fresh cassava bread, saltfish, cheeses, milk, eggs, fruits, and vegetables.

This was so far from the rancid shipboard gruel that battle-hardened men cried at the sight and smell of the delicious Christmas fare in Santos' empty homes.

Cavendish's arrival two days later was not as triumphant as planned, however.

The day before the commander made landfall, Captain Cocke had discovered the stupidity of his dismissing the Brazilians.

Fully aware that the English marauders would steal the town's winter supplies, a far from rare occurrence in the previous decade, they had naturally decided to put their own survival first by carrying out vast quantities of food to hide in the surrounding forests.

By the time Christopher and the remaining two hundred

members of the mission arrived, the town's storehouses were near empty. In a rage, Cavendish put a stop to the free movement, raving about his cousin's stupidity.

The commander ordered the outskirts of the town razed, and the center turned into an English fortress.

40

A Misunderstanding

Christopher and Knyvett were assigned quarters in the town's finest building, the Jesuit residence.

Cavendish took the grandest of the cells, the one occupied by the mission superior only days before, and the other three hundred odd Englishmen spread out across the little town, dossing down in beds still warm from their owners' bodies.

Cavendish, like Cooke, was slapdash in his organization, setting no real watch, and the men were unleashed to plunder at will. Christopher joined in the spirit-fueled looting with gusto. Bottles and barrels accompanied the men as they went from house to house, storeroom to storeroom, grabbing whatever took their fancy. This wealth had been created by the sweat and blood of enslaved people, and Christopher had no qualms about "liberating" it.

Earthen floors were cleaved open to reveal gold, silver, pearls, and other stones. Jewel-encrusted golden boxes containing holy relics were smashed and slivers of holy bones and fragments of the true cross were tossed onto filthy floors for passing feet to grind down, or dogs to gnaw at.

Days later, when there was nothing more left to filch, Cavendish tried to restore some order.

Teams were ordered out foraging. Others set to building a new pinnace boat of twenty tuns to be called *Crow*. She would be able to do the inshore and river work, tapping the wealth of Chile, Peru, and New Spain. A crew of twelve was assigned to her.

What few victuals there were to be had were loaded for the coming attempt at the Strait of Magellan.

It was not enough, and they all knew it.

Christopher had noticed that Thomas Lodge was a lot gentler than his peers. His plundering had a polite veneer to it, undertaken almost reluctantly with as little violence as possible.

Lodge's father had been Lord Mayor of London, one of the most important men in England, but his son just wanted to write stories. Knyvett said that he had apparently been cut out of his father's will, he was clearly a dreamer who had been forced into a military life.

One day, he approached Christopher with a book. Evidently proud of his find, he wanted to show it to someone who he thought might appreciate it as much as he. It was a Jesuit language manual to aid in the conversion of the local people which all the other looters had scorned as it had no monetary worth. Christopher tried out a few of the words with Lodge, and they both laughed at the strange sounds.

Over a long afternoon of drinking, Lodge may have told Christopher of a story he had in mind now he had at last set foot in the fabled Americas. He would call it *A Margarite of America*, and it would be a love story between an American prince of Cusco, and Margarita, the daughter of Muscovy's king. A story of New World and Old finding peace in unlikely romance.

London would go wild for this legend, fairy tale, and travel narrative, actually penned near the place where it was set. It would be both informative and entertaining. Maybe it would even be made into a play.

When Santos and its surrounding farmsteads had been bled of absolutely anything of value, Cavendish commanded an attack on the nearby settlement of São Vicente, the oldest Portuguese town in Brazil.

Christopher probably joined the raid, sauntering the few miles along the flawless beach, but he would have felt a little anxiety about the assault. The undisciplined column of two hundred was a sitting duck for the Portuguese and their local warrior allies who lurked nearby in the hills and forests.

The English, weapons clinking happily at their sides, jaunted casually along the beach swigging from flagons of wine and snacking on cold meat and fresh cassava bread. Not a soul was to be seen. Even the oxen that powered the mills were gone.

The stroll was only interrupted to torch five sugar mills. The cane burned merrily, forming a sweet-smelling smoky backdrop to the golden sands.

Upon reaching São Vicente, they found it equally deserted. What was portable was speedily removed, and all else put to the torch. The dry thatch burned swiftly as the satisfied soldiers sauntered back along the beach, joking about their exploits.

Fears of surprise attack had been real and justified, but happily for Christopher they proved to be unfounded.

Unbeknownst to Christopher, an English Jesuit called John Yates, who had recently been resident in the very mission house in which they were now staying, later wrote a letter to the prominent English Catholic exile, Francis Englefield. The missive, which was captured and handed to English intelligence, described how Cavendish's men "misused and violated the churches and relics," including the miraculously preserved head of Saint Katherine, one of the eleven thousand virgins of England, a deeply revered host of maidens who had met their martyrdoms at the hands of Hunnish warriors more than one thousand years before.

Yates and Englefield were Spanish informers, and it is thanks to this letter that we can confirm that Spanish intelligence was following Christopher's participation in Cavendish's Japan-bound voyage.

> *Cavendish, [...] took a great ship laden with gold, silks, and much riches, and also three [sic] boys of Japan, and returned rich to England, upon the words of the Japanese boys, to lade there, and come back [to Asia].*

Christopher and Knyvett had come to trust each other like brothers, and they decided to pool their plunder, splitting whatever they found two ways, to form a kind of communal insurance policy. Christopher, for his part, would have rejoiced that he had been so accepted among the English.

It was getting perilously close to the southern hemisphere winter, and while the gentlemen adventurers drank insouciantly, the sailors grumbled disconsolately. Many of the sailors had been on the previous circumnavigation, and they knew what was coming in the Strait.

In desperation, a petition was raised to persuade Cavendish to either leave immediately or winter in this warm and pleasant spot. The danger from the Portuguese be damned.

Cavendish, however, dismayed at the lack of food supplies, dallied indecisively. It was the last real chance to lade the ships' holds, and he was uncertain what to do. After another four weeks of indecision, he made up his mind and gave orders to sail southward.

Christopher likely agreed with the sailors. Even if only half their tales of the Strait were true, he knew it was not going to be passable during winter. They would likely be coming back here soon, tails between their legs.

He devised a plan and put it to Knyvett, who after some thought agreed. They would bury their communal treasure here and come back for it if, as expected, the passage was impossible.

The two men got together early on the morning of departure. Knyvett produced a chest which he had found hidden under a bed in the Jesuit house, and Christopher added his own considerable loot to the seventeen hundred golden pieces of eight it already contained. He took a captured dugout, saying he would be back in two hours.

As he paddled off into the estuary upon which Santos lay, tendrils of thick smoke drifted over from the fires that were even now being set by the departing English. Flames hurtled through the small town, catching on the thatch and creeping down wooden frames. There would be little left besides ash for the Portuguese when they returned.

With smoke pervading his nostrils, Christopher paddled his little craft for an hour, but started to feel increasingly anxious. Leaving the treasure here was only sensible if they were actually returning.

But how likely was it? If they passed through the Strait, they would never be back, and thinking on Cavendish's character, Christopher knew he would push the men to the brink of death to achieve his goal.

Many would perish to satisfy that iron will.

Even if they did not reach the other side, and were forced to return to Brazil, would Cavendish not seek out some unburned settlement? Santos would not be thriving again for many years, and there were plenty of other plum locations to maraud.

Reluctantly, but with increasing determination, he paddled the canoe around and returned to Santos. They had not agreed where to meet, so he beached the canoe and hopped on one of the last rowboats heading out to *Leicester*. Knyvett was nowhere to be seen, but Christopher was not overly worried; he had probably been assigned another duty.

Three hours later, the boats were ready to start the laborious process of getting the galleon underway, but Knyvett was still not aboard. Suddenly, from out of the river mouth burst the canoe that Christopher had so recently abandoned. Inside was Knyvett, paddling for all he was worth. What was he doing!? He was going to be left behind!

It took Knyvett ten minutes, head down and paddling for all the world like the beasts of the apocalypse were behind him.

He left the canoe to the tide and clambered up the side. Veins almost popping out of his forehead, he screamed for his money again and again as he paced the length of the ship.

Christopher did not know what to say. He proffered the chest, which only seemed to make Knyvett angrier.

Words failed Christopher. He now realized he had made a dreadful mistake. It looked like he had stolen the treasure and left Knyvett to certain death in Santos. The returning Portuguese would have taken out their vengeance on him alone, and it would no doubt have been a long drawn out and brutal end.

He understood Knyvett's rage, but he was speechless. Helpless to express himself in the face of his friend's savage animosity.

And that was that. Their former friendship was over. The first-ever recorded Anglo-Japanese friendship and the first-ever Anglo-Japanese breakup.

Knyvett's account of this tragic episode is thus:

From our first setting forth from England, till we came to Santos, I had a great love to Christopher the Japon, because I found his experience to bee good in many things. This Indian and I grew into such friendship one with another, that wee had nothing betwixt us unknown together. I a long time having found him true, I told him of the money I had found under the Friers bed; with that hee told mee of some money that hee had got, and wee swore to part halfe from thenceforth whatsoever God should permit us to obtaine: some foure dayes after that, when we were ready to depart, he told me that that time of the yeare was past wherefore it was best to hide our money in the ground, and remaine in the Countrey. I believing his perswasions, agreed to doe what he thought best; thus we determined both, that the same day we were to goe a shipboard, that then he should take all the money in a Canoa, and hide it by a River side; in the morning I delivered all the money into his hands, and he swore than in lesse then two houres he would returne, but I staied above five houres, and might have tarried all my life, for he was gone aboord Ship, afterward by good meanes I got mine own againe and so our former friendship was parted.

It was January 22, 1592.

41

To the Strait

Santos's fires dwindled into a gray-green haze behind them.

The town had singularly failed to render the expected bounty, and it was with heavy hearts and not a little disappointment that the men of *Leicester* and her companion vessels continued their voyage. The small fleet, grown by one with the addition of *Crow*, was headed south toward Río de la Plata, the River of Silver.

The bright wide-open summer vistas of Brazil gave way to threatening clouds and ash-gray skies, and the demoralized sailors went about their daily tasks sullenly, their energy sapped by meager rations, low morale, and a deep foreboding.

Two weeks later, Christopher would have done anything to return to that placid, half-hungry monotony.

Off Río de la Plata a mighty storm blew up.

Sheet-like rain swept in without warning, pummeling the wooden superstructure, knocking men from their feet in a trice and sweeping unsecured equipment into the depths.

Heaving waves rose up like great cliffs, and pausing at their peak, crashed down. Within minutes, tattered shards were all that were left of the sails.

Every crash threatened to be the last the wooden vessel could endure.

Leicester was left helpless, drifting wherever the sea took her. Her tightly secured boat was ripped from the deck, never to be seen again, and horrifyingly, the new boat, *Crow*, keeled over, sinking with all hands.

Cavendish, in a manic fever, ran around belowdecks encouraging the crew who were cowered in corners, clinging to barrels, chests, and guns.

The pumps continued, never stopping. Every man took his turn, there was no class difference anymore, death would embrace them all equally.

Suddenly, like a phantom from the waves, sprang an out-of-control *Roebuck*, ramming *Leicester* to crush the poop deck like an eggshell under foot. Then *Roebuck* was gone, swallowed by the storm.

Everything that had been in the armory and Cavendish's cabin behind it simply disappeared. All that was left to Christopher and those who had lodged there were the clothes on their backs.

For three days the blasting winds and rain continued. Earlier tempests, however bad they had seemed at the time, paled in comparison with this torrid monster.

When the seas finally calmed, there was not a ship in sight.

Whether the other vessels had sunk, or still survived to fight another day, *Leicester*'s survivors could not know.

Cavendish's men were shaken to their very core, and perhaps something within them died that day.

They had come for easy money, a crack at the enemy, and the chance to return home as heroes. Their lack of far-faring experience, in the main, had not prepared them for any of these hardships. That many of them had lost their warm clothing and plunder in the crash with *Roebuck* only reinforced their despair. The weather was getting colder. They were going to freeze.

There were murmurs of mutiny, and the atmosphere on board turned ever uglier until the commander could ignore it no longer.

Cavendish assembled the men on the half deck, and, with the splintered stumps of the poop as his backdrop, ordered that all talk of returning to Brazil was to cease. They were to rendez-vous with the other ships at Port Desire (modern-day Puerto Deseado) in Patagonia, a place he himself had discovered and named on his previous voyage, where there was plenty of game and fresh water in addition to the possibility of a little respite.

He offered a handsome £20 reward to the first man who spotted another ship.

Hope of rejoining their lost comrades soothed the men, and the mutiny was calmed.

Leicester set a course for Port Desire. Essential repairs and the construction of a makeshift rowboat to replace the one which had been lost started immediately.

Ten days later, *Black Pinnace* hove into view and a lucky sailor found himself a handsome £20 richer.

They were no longer alone.

Port Desire on Cavendish's first visit there in 1586. The ships are revictualling, and the hunting of penguins and seals, and even a temporary furnace, can be clearly made out. H. Palthenius, 1626.

Port Desire was at the mouth of a shallow and rocky river. Brown cliffs marked the gateway to a barren, treeless land of rock and scrubby green vegetation that stretched as far as the eye could see. It was one of the most forlorn landscapes that Christopher had ever seen.

The southernmost of the distinctive cliffs looked like a watchtower, and perhaps if anyone else had threatened to visit them there, it might have performed well as one. But visitors were unlikely. Few attempted this harsh passage, especially not in this season.

Their arrival was greeted by the wraithlike screams of sea birds, and a pod of darting dolphins. The tired crewmen, sore pressed and ready to collapse, were delighted. Dolphins, King of Fish, were considered superb omens.

Roebuck and *Desire* had been there for some time bobbing happily in the river mouth, and had stocked up on tons of fatty, fish-like penguin meat for the next leg of the journey. There was a good supply of an herb called scurvy grass too, known to be effective against the sickness, and the men were in good health.

Leicester was too large to risk in the narrow river mouth, but Cavendish was rowed over to consult with his captains and to hear that *Daintie*, the small ship that had been filled with Santos and São Vicente's meager plunder, had fled back to England.

Having appraised the situation, he sent orders that *Leicester*'s crew should take as many penguins as they could from the craggy, almost colorless islands at the mouth of the river. They had just two days to do this, as a speedy departure was imperative.

Christopher would have gone about butchering with gusto. These funny birds were easy prey. They could not fly, seemed trusting of humans, and a bang on the head was all that was needed. The plucking and salting teams then did their jobs, and the unpalatable but nutritious meat was packed into barrels and stowed. The eggs made for a delicious snack while they hunted.

Cavendish, evidently shaken by the loss of his cabin, *Daintie*'s flight, and *Leicester*'s attempt at mutiny, announced that he would continue the voyage on *Desire*. Christopher and Cosmus likely accompanied him back aboard the ship that had taken them to England.

Three months after leaving Santos, a voyage which should have taken a month, on April 8, 1592, *Desire*, accompanied by the three remaining ships, rounded Cape Joy and approached the Strait of Magellan.

The gateway that eventually led to the Pacific was anything but joyful and welcomed them with a savageness to take the breath away.

Each time they thought the voyage could only get better, it somehow plumbed new depths of despair and suffering.

42

Hell Froze

Slow progress was made for the first ten days. The seaways narrowed slightly then widened, then narrowed again. When there was any visibility, Christopher could see colossal snow-covered mountains, glaciers that looked like rivers of ice frozen in the act of tumbling toward the sea, and great floating icebergs.

Pinpoints of fire in the dark night added a ghoulish air of mystery and fear. Did they bubble up from a hell beneath the earth, or were they acts of men? Snow and sea spray turned the world into a densely layered, rushing white, and it was impossible to tell.

Charles Darwin later called the Strait of Magellan a "savage magnificence."

Lungs heaved to breathe the icy air, and the intense, penetrating, benumbing rawness, made men's minds and bodies sluggish. Even in a tarred linen smock, leather jerkin, and woolen clothing, Christopher was numb.

Many of the mariners had little with which to fight against the cold besides a daily ration of Brazilian *cachaça*, and men literally froze to death, one blackened frostbitten limb at a time.

After several weeks, they reached Port Famine (modern-day

Puerto del Hambre in Chile) an ice-sheathed, windswept bay
where lichen-covered rocks cowered under snowy blankets, and
the storm-beaten trees sported a kind of frosted wispy growth
that looked like a beard tumbling downward in fantastic frozen waterfalls.

None of it was edible, despite the crew's desperate attempts to
make it so, and the starving men resorted to mollusks and sea-
weed from iced-over rock pools. The scurvy cleared, but it was
little comfort to those who succumbed to the weather instead.

Then something amazing happened. One day hundreds upon
hundreds of naked men, women, and children clutching bundles of downy feathers in their hands walked out of the snow.

The people at the world's end had come to trade.

These people would have been the Yaghan, Selk'nam, or the
Kawesqar. All three were nomadic seafarers eking out a hunter-
gatherer living in one of the most inhospitable climates on earth.
Before extensive contact with Europeans in the nineteenth century, these three peoples used animal grease instead of clothing,
and stayed warm by squatting to reduce body area exposed to
the elements, sheltering in caves and rock formations, and by
lighting extensive fires. Tierra del Fuego (Land of Fire), the archipelago to the south of the Strait, was so named for the numerous fires that outsiders traveling through observed.

Charles Darwin, nearly two hundred fifty years later, was
not complimentary:

> But I have seen nothing which more completely astonished me than
> the first sight of a savage. It was a naked Fuegian, his long hair
> blowing about, his face besmeared with paint. There is in their
> countenances an expression which I believe, to those who have not
> seen it, must be inconceivably wild.

Cavendish's starving sailors desperately tried to barter for
food, but these people had none to spare, and tried to exchange

goods for feathers instead. Christopher and his colleagues had little need of birds' plumage and attempts at trade foundered.

After a week, progress again became possible, but not for long. On April 18, not halfway through the Strait, the four ships could go no further against the extreme elements. Shelter of sorts presented itself in a secure bay, but even as some of the stronger men foraged for shellfish and the gigantic pearls they contained, scores of others simply lay down to die.

Had Christopher had the energy, he may have idly wondered, as he prized a jewel from its shell to devour the meat below, what the Queen would do with these gems. Would these strings of pearls, paid for with so much death, decorate her hair or perhaps adorn a long flowing gown of ice-white silk?

Knyvett took off his socks one day to inspect his benumbed feet. To his horror, his toes remained inside. Where they should have been were black stumps, and the dead flesh was alive with burrowing lice taking refuge in the relative warmth.

Another man named Harris, a goldsmith, brought along especially to handle the plundered loot, attempted to blow his nose, only for it to fall into the fire around which he and his colleagues were trying to warm their frozen limbs. The dead organ roasted quickly in the embers.

Despair pervaded every man.

Cavendish wrote, "our shippes not to be handeled in such extremitie of winde, no nor canvass to holde the furie of the wynd."

John Davis recorded conditions of "bitter and most merciless fury."

Deriving a perverse literary inspiration from these events, Thomas Lodge later used the imagery of this experience in his *Margarite of America*:

And as the ship far scattered from the port, All well-nigh spent and wrecked with wretched blast, From East to West, midst surg-

ing seas is tossed, So I, whose soul by fierce delay's effort Is over-come in heart and looks defaced, Run here, run there, sigh, die, by sorrow crossed.

An indication of the mental toll these hardships took on Cavendish's men can perhaps be ascertained from the fact that after narrowly surviving the Strait, Lodge's work took a new course a few years afterward. No longer was he a lighthearted dreamer poet and satirist writing of romance and adventure; instead he mainly published socially critical moral tracts like *Wits Miserie and the World's Madnesse*, trained to be a medical doctor, and publicly converted to Catholicism for which he later spent time in exile.

The nightmare-inducing experience of the Strait of Magellan profoundly changed his and no doubt other survivors' lives forever.

The cycle of harrowing misery and grisly death continued unabated. Stuck at the end of the world, starving without shelter amidst ever-worsening conditions, each day saw eight or nine more deaths.

In this living nightmare, we have no news of Christopher, but he must have been equally mentally scarred and probably despaired, both of ever reaching Japan, and of even seeing the next dawn.

43

Escape

With only four months of the barest rations left, and little prospect of finding more, even the rats, near-last resort of starving seamen, were in danger of shipboard extinction.

Spare parts for the four flailing vessels were in even shorter supply, while of the seventy-five survivors on *Desire*, only fourteen were sailors.

Would it be the near-shattered ships or near-broken men who gave up first?

Cavendish debated long and hard with John Davis who was adamant that the weather would soon clear, and they must press on. The crew of *Desire*, better fed than *Leicester*'s, were of the same opinion.

Davis's mission to discover the navigable passage back to Europe at the northern end of the Americas, the twin of this southern one, depended upon pressing through, whatever the cost.

But Cavendish had had enough. He returned to *Leicester* from *Desire* in a foul temper, his every move threatening violence.

As snow fell in flurries around them, his remaining crew assembled on deck and huddled together for warmth.

Perhaps with Christopher standing beside him as living proof of civilization on the other side of this vicious, wild passage, Cavendish reaffirmed his commitment to reaching the riches of the East.

To disbelieving grumbles, he raised his voice to a motivational roar, reminding them that this was not the only route. There were two known ways out of the Atlantic, and he had traversed both.

They would leave this realm of snow and ice, and head east, to the Cape of Good Hope and approach Asia via Africa instead.

His battered and frozen listeners hesitated, not quite believing what the leader was saying. They were going to escape this hell, and they might yet live to return home as wealthy heroes.

They cheered with renewed hope and Cavendish immediately ordered the ships eastward out of the Strait.

Davis very, very reluctantly followed his commander's new orders.

With Cavendish back on *Leicester*, and settled in a makeshift cabin belowdecks, the men got to talking among themselves. Many also had experience of Africa's stormy cape from the circumnavigation. Christopher remembered as well as any that plans to land there had been thwarted due to the currents and winds. It was no sailor's paradise.

The men reminisced about the warm climate in Santos, the weakness of the Portuguese, and the relatively friendly natives. Why could they not just take a Brazilian town, live off the land, perhaps find some gold?

Then *Leicester*'s men did what Elizabethans did when they could take no more.

They appointed leaders and went en masse to demand an audience with the commander. They were polite but firm in their humble supplication, putting it in terms of concern for his well-being, claiming that they were most willing to lay down their lives for him, but there were not enough provisions to reach Africa. The mission should, they implored him, return to refit and revictual in Brazil, then return here at a seasonable time to complete the mission that they were pledged to.

It was a mutiny. A polite and deferential mutiny, but still a mutiny.

The battered and decimated crews, led by gentlemen adventurers, some of higher social rank than Cavendish himself, used to social deference and having their authority respected, had effectively taken control.

Cavendish remonstrated with them, flew into rages, threatened violence, and appealed to individuals by name, trying to divide and rule with sugarcoated promises.

But this time the men would not be swayed.

Defeated and outmaneuvered, Cavendish acceded to the petition, but at the same time, citing the lack of food, he ordered eight of the sickest men abandoned to save essential supplies that could keep others alive.

Icy waves washed what remained of the castaways' frostbitten, blackened feet as they breathed their sorry last on a lonely beach at the end of the world.

Within five days the fleet was free of the Strait's frozen grip and back in the Atlantic. It was May 18, 1592.

They headed back north, but this time into the jaws of a baited trap.

44

Resurrection

The ships veered north together, their few remaining graying sheets billowing while the forlorn shreds of tattered sails flapped impotently.

During the night of May 20, *Desire* and *Black Pinnace* simply disappeared.

The men of *Leicester* and *Roebuck* were now left alone in the wide ocean with no knowledge of what had happened to their comrades.

Christopher's tiny floating world had shrunk further, and it was to get smaller still. Off Río de la Plata once more, day turned to night, thunder and lightning rent the sky, and a deluge fell like a mighty waterfall. Shattered souls, almost unrecognizable as men, staggered back to the bilge pumps.

The last *Leicester* saw of *Roebuck* was in a fork of lightning, her main mast snapped like a dead twig. Then she was lost to view among the mountainous waves.

In his haste to escape the Strait, Cavendish had set no rendezvous, so there was nothing to be done except continue north and pray they bumped into their comrades.

Despite the victory over their commander in the Strait, mutiny remained a threat. The crew were loath to return to unquestionably obeying the orders of a man who seemed increasingly unrealistic, perhaps unhinged even.

As the waves calmed, the exhausted men descended to the gun deck and collapsed, to sleep where they lay.

Cavendish descended belowdecks wielding a length of rope the thickness of a man's arm. In a fury, he lay about him, shouting curses and whipping at the spent men. To escape the flail, one man grabbed the near-comatose Knyvett to use as a human shield. It proved effective for the mutinous sailor, but Knyvett himself suffered a bloody lash to the head and lolled insensate.

Cavendish had not meant to kill, simply to frighten, and suddenly his rage was spent. He departed the gun deck in repentance, leaving Knyvett for dead.

As passions calmed, the will to survive triumphed over sleep, and the crew returned to work. Knyvett's corpse was taken on deck to commit to the depths.

Christopher stood to pay last respects to his former friend. It had been a beautiful and unique relationship while it lasted.

The plank was laid over the side, and Knyvett's blanket-wrapped body placed upon it. The cadaver suddenly buckled, struggled, and screamed "NOOOOOOOOOOOO."

Knyvett's frost-blackened body and rope-mangled scalp were hauled back on board, and he lived to fight another day. The crew staggered back to work. The ship continued north.

45

Slaughter

Fifteen days it took them, but the floating wreck that was *Leicester* arrived back where she had put out from half a year before, in Santos.

It was June 1592.

If they had been hungry last time they made landfall here, the crew were now walking skeletons.

Christopher's body had likely weakened considerably, with teeth ready to tumble from his gums at any moment. He was not alone, and it was easy to see why most men preferred to stay in their ancestral villages and die young from plague, bloody flux, or even from hunger and poverty, rather than risk everything for fame and fortune, only to die in long-drawn-out agony in some accursed corner of the world.

The end result was the same, but the landlubber probably suffered a little less.

Cavendish swore blind that the mission was still on, but no one else seriously believed it. All the men wanted was an end to this hell, and preferably to survive.

That was the most any of them could hope for now.

Leicester approached Santos's calm golden beach, so peaceful and warm-looking after the interminable violence of the voyage.

Much of the damage they had wrought was already repaired, and there were signs of renewed industry and agriculture.

The plan was to loot, send food back to the ship, and then to spread out, but not too far, in search of further supplies.

One of the more remote sugar mills, perched atop the beach midway between Santos and São Vicente, looked ripe for the taking, but with the rowboat lost and the rest of the squadron dispersed, *Leicester* had no way of landing men or bringing supplies aboard.

The best the crew could muddle together was a ramshackle raft of empty barrels and sugar chests trussed together with frayed rope. In the absence of oars, planks served as paddles. Despite the hazardous prospects, everyone wanted to go first, and this time social rank prevailed.

The noblest of the surviving gentlemen adventurers tooled up with their last resources of energy and before the galleon even came to anchor, they were lowering their ramshackle craft into the water.

Christopher climbed giddily on and held fast.

The waves lapped gently as the exuberant squad paddled through shoals of silver-colored fish to reach the shore. Immediately, they jumped into the surf and staggered off pell-mell, swords drawn, toward the mill, all weakness temporarily forgotten in the hunt for food.

For the first time in months, something went right. The enslaved mill workers and gang masters had fled, and the only sign of life was a lowing ox harnessed to the wooden frame that turned the mill. Christopher threw open a door, saw a barrel of sugarcane juice and fell upon it. Ignoring his long, dank hair dripping down into the liquid, he lapped up the juice like a dog.

It was heaven, and he felt immediately rejuvenated, and light-headed with the sugar rush.

All around him, his comrades were doing the same. Instant gratification was the order of the day.

In the outhouses behind the mill, they found great bacons and hams hanging from the eaves, and golden cheeses piled high on wooden shelves. Pecking hens, ignorant of their imminent fate, watched them indifferently.

The starving mariners ran around whooping and stuffing themselves with whatever they could get their hands on. It was a moment of pure elation and raw bestial gluttony. All thought of the famished men remaining aboard *Leicester* was forgotten.

The scene that confronted Christopher would have been comical had it not been so desperate.

One emaciated gentleman sat in the corner cradling a huge cheese in his arms and sobbing like a baby while he stuffed his mouth with handfuls of soft yellow flesh. A toothless sailor broke raw eggs down his throat, swallowing like they were manna from heaven. A bald fellow lay prostrate below the butchered ox letting the still-pumping blood fall directly into his mouth. Another delirious mariner juggled a range of small fruits with great skill and dropped them into his mouth. Sticky juices washed down his chin to soak his jerkin, but he paid them no heed.

Weapons and armor, family heirlooms of great value, lay, discarded like trash, on the floor.

Had the inhabitants attacked at that moment, there would not have been a man left alive, but all would have died in ecstasy.

Once the English raiders had returned to earth from their gastronomic heaven, they remembered their stricken crewmates and, feeling guilty at their excesses, loaded supplies upon a small abandoned Portuguese barque.

A team sailed it back to *Leicester* where the men rejoiced as if the cargo were pure gold. Cavendish might have restricted their consumption and tried to ensure that rationing was observed, but he did not.

Many a joyous jig was danced that day by men who at dawn had felt like they might never stand again.

In the evening, the barque was sent back ashore to reload and return the next day. That night, those on shore insouciantly feasted again, this time tapping casks of harsh red wine and roasting the chickens and pigs which had been pecking and rooting happily only a few hours before.

As the setting sun cast its majestic glow over the hinterland to the west, Christopher, soaking in the warmth of the beach's residual heat, wondered if he would ever be this happy again. His belly felt like it would explode several times over, there was a pleasant greasy feeling to his skin, his gums and teeth were already feeling tighter, and a warm vitamin glow rose within him. To believe one minute that death was at hand, only to be delivered in such a magnificent, and sensorially gratifying manner, brought a welling sensation of satisfaction. Another deep swig of tannic red wine only added to his euphoria.

The next day, a hungover landing party accompanied another load of sugar and maize back to the galleon.

With a modicum of supplies ensured. Cavendish dispatched the barque to seek out the fleet's lost ships, wondering perhaps if they were sheltering somewhere along the coast. It was imperative that the squadron be reunited if the mission was to continue.

Cavendish could ill afford to lose more men, and the shore party were ordered to stay aboard to safeguard against the possibility of revenge attack. They protested vehemently, convinced that there were no Portuguese around, and there was still plenty more loot to be had. Cavendish relented and reluctantly permitted them to go, as long as they did not stray more than a mile from the raft.

The new war band left *Leicester* at 4:00 a.m. to be on the beach at sunrise. In high spirits, they were starting to feel less like loose bags of bones, and more like fighters again.

Later that morning, Christopher, with several unplucked hens hanging by the feet from his fists, returned to the raft.

The young Japanese mariner and two other paddlers transferred the meager cargo of fowl, one bleeding pig, and a few paltry baskets of maize to those waiting on deck and prepared to report to Cavendish that the raiding party had ignored orders and plunged further inland.

Cavendish's usual wrath was not long in coming.

Despite the fast-encroaching night, he sent the three men straight back ashore to order an immediate withdrawal. When they arrived, it was too late to go any further, so they curled up on the dusty floor of the mill and slept until dawn.

The next morning, they headed inland searching for the missing raiders.

While hiding in bushes, they saw the mangled bodies lying neatly in rows as hundreds of armored Portuguese militiamen and Native warriors with longbows and great clubs milled around laughing and joking.

The small corps of drunken gentlemen adventurers would have stood no chance against this army. Furthermore, there was no sign of any enemy casualties, and Christopher had to assume they had been taken by surprise and offered no quarter. The deed must have been swift and bloody.

Suddenly, he heard the jingle of weaponry behind him and willed himself invisible against the light jungle, not moving a muscle. Luckily, the Portuguese militiamen did not seem to be taking their search awfully seriously and passed him by. As soon as they were gone, he and his two comrades moved slowly out of the foliage and cautiously started toward the sea. When they thought they were clear, they got their heads down and raced for the shore.

A hail of arrows soon buzzed around them, but the survivors managed to dive onto the raft and, bellies to the floor, paddled for all they were worth. After a hundred yards or so, the missiles started to fall short, and then ceased altogether.

The three fugitives reached *Leicester* shaken, the only survivors of yesterday's boisterous band.

The English Jesuit Yates described it thus in his letter to Spain: "Only two or three survived, of whome one is a Japan boye."

Cavendish was devastated. These raiders had brought about this tragedy through their own indiscipline, disobedience, and reckless greed. However, they were not mere common sailors. They sprang from England's most illustrious families, and he would have to personally break the tragic news to their parents upon his return.

Despite the catastrophe, they could not leave. The barque's return was imminent, and *Leicester*'s men were still hoping against hope that at least one of the dispersed squadron would find them.

On the eighth day, the barque returned, but her scouting mission had been to no avail. The crew dolefully made ready to leave.

Then suddenly without warning, something astonishing happened. From far out to sea, came a cannon salute.

Roebuck.

The two ships were reunited, and *Roebuck*'s men gladly pounced upon the stores that *Leicester*'s reluctantly shared with them.

One glance was enough to see why she had taken so long to navigate north on the Atlantic currents. She was an abject ruin. Only her rear mast remained, and she was almost sail-less. But at least she still had her boat, so before scuttling off to hide and refit, Cavendish decided to conduct a lightning raid on Santos.

Eighty men landed on the familiar beach and proceeded to run amok. The ruins of Santos itself rendered little, but the farms inland, which had suffered less English attention last year, had recovered somewhat, and the war band managed to carry off a large quantity of fresh produce, including cassava, bananas, and pineapples.

As they rowed and paddled steadily toward the two galleons, six canoes bristling with muskets shot out from the river mouth. Their speedy approach threatened to quickly overwhelm the overloaded English boat and raft.

On board *Leicester*, Christopher knew that Cavendish could not afford another disaster. The commander's face hardened, and he ordered the cannon loaded with chain shot. Despite the risk to *Roebuck*'s boat, the gun crews let off a broadside.

This was the first time that *Leicester*'s ordnance had been fired in anger, and Christopher had forgotten how much the recoil would affect the ship.

The shots did not touch the canoes, but they got the message. As the guns were swabbed and reloaded, the attacking craft turned swiftly around, their crews' heads down, paddling for their lives.

Another salvo rang out.

The range was better this time, and a line of splashes indicated the missiles had fallen just short of the fleeing enemy.

Cavendish beamed, the first time Christopher had seen him smile for weeks.

Soon the new supplies were being hauled up the sides by eager hands and stowed below.

Cavendish then ordered a strategic retreat north to the island of São Sebastião to rest, refit, and live off nature's bounty for a while.

The damage to both ships, however, was more than nature alone could repair. They needed good strong sailcloth, thick rope, and a myriad of other stores that could only be gotten— paid for or plundered—in a proper ship's chandlery.

The Portuguese pilot, Gaspar Jorge, now suggested a new approach. Why not go where nobody would be expecting them?

He suggested Vitória, a well-established island town with an easily navigable approach through a wide river estuary.

São Sebastião was forgotten. The two galleons and their new barque set a course for Vitória—Victory!

46

Defeat in Vitória

The voyage northeast up the mountainous Brazilian coast took eight days, and Jorge piloted them with the skill of a man intimately familiar with every inch of this wild green coast.

Vitória itself was a small settlement on an estuary, accessed through an island-speckled bay in the shadow of towering mountains where three small ships, potentially laden with supplies, lay temptingly at anchor, just crying out to be taken.

Jorge had sworn that there would be adequate water depth for both large ships to get inshore for their raid, but the plumb line only indicated fifteen feet. *Leicester* and *Roebuck* needed double that.

Cavendish swiftly descended into his familiar rage, and the Portuguese pilot, a man who had done his best by the English, was strung up without trial or ceremony. He was still gasping his last in the gathering dusk as Cavendish turned away to order an immediate attack on the boats.

But the gentlemen adventurers would not be swayed. They much preferred to wait until morning and fight in the light.

Cavendish was apoplectic.

He stormed into his rough-got-up cabin and slammed the door.

Silence reigned until one of the men laughed. Then they got on with their evening. Cavendish had lost any authority he ever possessed.

In the morning the attackers awoke to drifting clouds of thick, noxious smoke. The fields had been fired.

The locals had been far from idle in the night, and rough bastions had appeared on both sides of the channel that the English would need to attack down. Tripod-mounted muskets could clearly be seen atop the earthworks and razor-sharp pike heads reflected the morning sun's beams through chinks in the smoke.

Had they followed their commander's orders the night before, Cavendish's men might have escaped swiftly without a shot being fired. Now they would need to struggle every inch of the way past fortified positions and impassioned defenders fighting to protect their families and livelihoods.

The raiders were not going to be gifted fat hogs and winter-ready storehouses this time around.

Under the gaze of lifeless Jorge's hideous, toothy grin, two boats bursting with one hundred twenty fervidly excited attackers pushed off to launch a maritime assault through a drifting miasma in near-zero visibility.

The dead pilot's eyes seemed to play on the high-spirited raiders, cursing their day's work from the afterlife.

The stakes were high, and Cavendish's new plan of attack was cautious; he could ill afford to lose more men and he knew it. Captain Morgan, the most senior surviving officer, was tasked with a recce mission. Only if he judged that they were able to proceed through the smoke screen and take one of the ships swiftly without serious threat from the waterside fortifications were they to attack.

If not, he was not to launch a land assault, but to return for reinforcements and new orders.

Christopher and his comrades skulled slowly through the lingering smog, hoping that they could simply sneak by the swiftly built fortifications undetected to grab an enemy ship. For once, the men obeyed orders and remained quiet.

Suddenly from the fog came a burst of flame. Musket fire from close range. A spooked and trigger-happy defender had accidently given away his position.

Morgan thought swiftly. Cavendish had expressly ordered him to avoid a frontal attack on a defended position, but the men in his boat were raring to go. Pent-up fear, frustration, and rage were eating away at their souls. They needed action.

With gestures, Morgan ordered the larger rowboat to go a short way further up the channel, land, and then support his attack from the rear. He and his men would mount an immediate assault.

Christopher tensed. They could easily be rowing into a wall of lead, darts, and arrows, not to mention sharp pikes and great war clubs. He remembered the twenty-two comrades whose bodies he had seen laid out. The smallest details of caved-in skulls and mangled armor came back to him. Those beautifully carved Brazilian bludgeons had done that.

The final moments before the attack were the worst—he could do nothing except await the beaching of the boat. He held his gun over his chest; it was loaded, tapped down, and the match was smoldering. Ready.

Closer and closer they rowed. His mariner's bones could feel the seabed coming up to meet them. How many times in his life had he approached a beach? Hundreds? Thousands?

But never had he done it in thick smoke, charging into enemy fire.

The crunch of the keel on sand was the sign. Morgan pointed his sword, giving the order to attack. Christopher paused to fire

his gun at the vague fortifications, paused a second for the recoil, slung it over his shoulder, then drew his sword.

Forty warriors. One goal. The mortal fear and consequent
self-loathing evaporated to be replaced with overwhelming
adrenaline. Cavendish's men went straight at the enemy as one
through the spray.

The hazy armored shapes appearing out of the smoke must
have terrified the defenders and having returned the English
fire with a ragged and ineffective salvo, they fled.

The attackers vaulted over the ramparts and cheered. The
bastion had been taken in less than a minute with no casualties.
It looked like Captain Morgan had made the right decision.

But what now? They had won an empty fort, and they still
could not see more than a few yards in any direction.

The man next to Christopher suddenly fell, an arrow judder-
ing just under the brim of his steel helmet.

After a moment of near silence, the whooping screams of
hundreds of unseen warriors ululated through the air. A drum
started to beat, slowly at first, then faster and faster.

Suddenly it stopped. A single male voice rang out, rising to a
crescendo; a great conch shell blasted its long note.

Then the earth shook with an invisible legion of charging
Brazilian warriors.

Christopher's heart must have frozen.

From nowhere, with unbelievable force, a wooden dart struck
him in the left shoulder. It spun him around and threw him to
the ground.

He pulled the lethal spike out of his shoulder and bound the
wound with his ragged shirt to stem the gushing blood.

Christopher staggered up, held on to the ramparts, reloaded
his gun with difficulty and rested the musket on the hard-packed
earth. The pain from the wound was sharp, but not immobiliz-
ing. If the dart was poisoned, the effects were slow.

The gun stock fit neatly into his unhurt right shoulder. He
waited.

As the smoke cleared, he could see that his comrades, on the defensive now, had done the same. A wall of muzzles faced the enemy.

The earthquake of charging feet got more intense, and the first indistinct warrior shapes appeared sprinting and hurdling through the lifting smog. All along the rampart guns spat, and the smoke thickened again as discharge drifted above the bastion.

There seemed to be a brief pause, but the human wave quickly regained momentum.

Rank upon rank of tattooed club-wielding warriors, their cheeks pierced with bones and their heads crowned with feather headdresses, broke into their final sprint a few yards from the fort.

Soul-curdling battle cries rang loud.

A couple of the faster-loading Englishmen got off another shot at point blank range, but then the tattooed foe were scaling the rampart and jumping down among them, kicking, screaming, and clubbing with unbridled bloodlust.

All knew of the vicious English marauding. All wanted to exterminate this threat to their communities.

It was a matter of strength and numbers now. Clearly the natives, stronger, better fed, and numbering in their hundreds, held the upper hand.

The forty men huddled together in a circle as they were surrounded and corralled, English gun stocks clashing desperately with Indigenous bludgeons. Several fell, including Captain Morgan.

Then suddenly, leaving only a small party of skirmishers to harass Cavendish's men with darts, the bulk of the Brazilians faded back into the smoke.

Leicester's thirty odd survivors, leaderless now, just ran.

The other English boat, which had not engaged yet, could be seen a hundred yards away approaching a similar bastion. The enemy must have pulled back from Christopher's small squad to concentrate on stopping this larger one from landing.

Without the benefit of smoke to cover their approach, the men on the boat were under heavy fire. Then it jarred to a halt, stuck on a rock just off the beach, and Christopher looked on in horror as several men toppled backward into their waiting comrades.

But worse was to come. Thinking that they had struck the beach, screaming their war cries as one, the English leaped over the side.

It was not the beach.

In seconds, seventy or more fully armored men simply disappeared beneath the softly lapping waves. An eruption of bubbles on the surface was all that betrayed their watery graves.

Lightened of its human load, the boat lifted itself from the rock and drifted away. One helmeted corpse hung over the stern, his face gazing downward into the water as if searching in vain for his lost comrades.

The Brazilians now refocused on Christopher's squad.

Just managing to run despite the pain in his shoulder, he abandoned his gun and reached the boat with ever more missiles falling around him. As he was hauling himself over the side, another arrow struck him in the leg, and he collapsed into the hull.

A wave lifted the boat off the beach, and, unpowered, the boat drifted off slowly. But men were still on the beach.

It was a hopelessly unequal fight, hundreds against a handful. The abandoned English waded up to their necks as arrows fell around them and cried for the boat to come back. But not one man on board made to turn around. It would have been suicide.

The small vessel drifted out of missile range, and the subdued men bent to the oars. All were wounded.

It had been a terrible morning, and all for nothing. Not a single barrel or chest of supplies had been won for the death of more than eighty men.

47

End of the Road

Barely a hundred crew remained in the two ships, and most lay prone on the gun decks, ravaged by wounds, hunger, and disease. The few dozen who could stand faced an unrelenting grind.

Shortly after the Vitória debacle, *Roebuck*, despite her abject condition, somehow slipped away in the night, taking most of the remaining victuals, and both of the doctors.

Leicester was alone again.

Cavendish still refused to give up.

Again, and again over the next few weeks, he tried to bully and cajole the survivors into following orders.

Firstly, the commander attempted to have them return to the Strait of Magellan, then when the whole crew rebelled, he asked them to at least try for Saint Helena where there would be food, and they might catch a Portuguese Indiaman returning to Europe.

He reminded them of the lush vegetation and bounteous hunting that his crew had enjoyed four years before.

They refused.

★ ★ ★

With every rebellion, the commander's already extremely fragile grip on his men slipped further and further away. On one occasion he had to truss up the chief mutineer and threaten to throttle him.

While repairing the worst of *Leicester*'s damage on the island of São Sebastião, Cavendish abandoned the sickest of the men, among them Christopher's former friend Knyvett, to conserve food.

Of the remaining crew, not a few jumped ship. The wild jungle seemed a better bet for survival than remaining with Cavendish.

But the island sojourn ended with a bang.

Pirate hunters, determined to avenge the terror and immense hardship that English ravaging had caused them and their families, kept a close eye on their enemy.

When a deserter was caught and revealed the sorry situation, the local men stalked through the jungle to unleash a surprise night attack.

No quarter was given. Twenty-eight sick men were massacred on the beach, clubbed about the head like baby seals.

Knyvett, who had, by his own account, astonishingly nursed himself back to health by eating the blubber of a rotting whale, and one colleague, Henry Barrawell, were spared, thanks to their relative strength, and the ability to speak Portuguese.

They were immediately enslaved.

As the Jesuit priest Yates put it in his letter, Cavendish was being "well whipped with the scourge of God, for the irreverence he committed against His Divine Majesty and His saints, especially against a holy head of one of the 11,000 virgins of England."

Leicester's crew, observing the aftereffects of the massacre the next morning from their ship, immediately weighed anchor and left Brazil behind them for good, charting a course for Saint Helena. The tiny speck of land in the southern Atlantic was missed through a navigation error, and at some point, shortly after this, Cavendish sat down to write his will, witnessed by, among others, Robert Hues. He added as an aside a venom-filled account of the voyage. Addressed to his friend and executor Tristram Gorges, it begins,

> *Moste loving frinde, there is nothinge in this worlde that makes a truer trial of frindeshippe then at deathe to shew myndefullnes of love and frindshippe which nowe you shall make a perfect experience of, desiring you to holde my love as deare dyeing poore, as if I had bynn moste infinitelye riche.*

Cavendish's words make it abundantly clear that he did not expect to be alive when Gorges read it. He blamed the failure of the voyage squarely on the shoulders of John Davis, who he believed had deserted him when the ships were separated in the night.

It cannot be said for certain, but Cavendish most likely took his own life.

In Tudor times, "self-murder" was a crime against God and punishable by forfeiture of all earthly goods and chattels to the crown if proven. His sister would have been forbidden from claiming her inheritance.

If it was suicide, it was hushed up to allow her to inherit, and the true facts remain a mystery to this day.

Leicester and *Roebuck* did make it back to England to deliver Cavendish's last will and testament; however, there is no record of when they arrived, or exactly how many men lived. The only survivors who can definitely be confirmed are men like Lodge and Hues whose later achievements attest to it.

Knyvett made it back to England in 1601 after years of slavery and a series of harrowing adventures to publish his story as *The Admirable Adventures and Strange Fortunes of Master Antonie*

Knivet, which went with Master Thomas Candish in his Second Voyage to the South Sea, 1591.

Thanks to family connections, he gained employment at the Royal Mint and enjoyed a long life, dying in 1649.

Desire under the command of John Davis managed to recover somewhat, and Davis, believing that Cavendish would have tried for the Pacific again, headed to the entrance to the Strait of Magellan to look for him. When *Leicester* failed to appear, Davis successfully traversed the strait into the Pacific, only to be blown back into the Atlantic by terrible contrary winds.

Realizing that there was no hope left for this mission, Davis headed to Port Desire, loaded fourteen thousand dried penguins to supplement *Desire*'s scarce rations, and headed for home.

After a skirmish in Brazil which left half the surviving crew dead, John Jane, an officer on *Desire*, reported what must have seemed like the end of days:

> *our dried Penguins began to corrupt, and there bred in them a most lothsome and noisome kind ugly worme of an inch long. This worme did so mightily increase, and devoure our victuals, that there was in reason no hope how we should avoide famine, but be devoured of these wicked creatures: there was nothing that they did not devour, only iron excepted: our clothes, boots, shooes, hats, shirts, stockings: and for the ship they did so eat the timbers, as that we greatly feared they would undoe us, by gnawing through the ships side. Great was the care and diligence of our captaine, master, and company to consume these vermine, but the more we laboured to kill them, the more they increased; so that at the last we could not sleepe for them, but they would eate our flesh, and bite like Mosquitos.*

Desire just made it to Ireland in June 1593. Sixteen of the seventy-six men who had departed England survived. The terrors of the voyage meant that only five, including Davis, were well enough to move.

As far as is known, *Desire* never sailed again.

Black Pinnace accompanied *Desire* through the Strait, but disappeared one night, and is believed lost with all hands.

So, what happened to Christopher?

There is one mention of "two east Indians [...] of Mr. Candish" on a voyage of Robert Dudley, his brother-in-law (and son of Cavendish's patron of the same name), in 1595. But these were the older Filipinos, Alphonso and Antonio, who had not accompanied Cavendish in 1591. The youngest unnamed Filipino boy continued in service to Lettice Dudley, or possibly her daughter-in-law, Frances Walsingham, daughter of the old spymaster, the reference is ambiguous. His life story beyond this is unknown.

After Yates's mention of a "Japan boye," there is no more record of either Christopher, or Cosmus either.

This sadly means that Christopher almost definitely succumbed to the perils of the voyage, to die a horrific death far from the distant home he was trying to reach.

Although there was a steady stream of deaths throughout this failed voyage to Japan, there were six main points where Christopher, and indeed his colleague Cosmus, could have perished.

Firstly, during the ill-fated attempt at the Strait of Magellan when dozens died from exposure. However, Christopher was strong, and it is hard to believe that the English commander would not have protected his "key to Japan." It seems likely, therefore, that he survived the icebound hell at the bottom of the Americas.

Knyvett narrowly avoided being buried alive at sea, but many other men did die on the voyage north, in the fearsome storms, and from complications like extreme frostbite that they had contracted in the Strait.

Christopher could have succumbed in the second São Vicente raid. We do not know if it was he, or perhaps Cosmus,
who Yates reported surviving the massacre by the understand-
ably vengeful local inhabitants.

A few weeks later at Vitória, every single one of the assault
corps either perished in the battle, was abandoned to certain
extermination on the beach, or experienced severe wounds in
the retreat. Some survivors were said to look like pincushions,
with as many as five arrows piercing their flesh.

Christopher might have died here or shortly afterward from
his injuries, and although it may be a coincidence, it is at this
point that Cavendish seems to have given up on reaching Japan
and settled for the scant hope of capturing a Portuguese ship in
the seas off Saint Helena instead.

The penultimate candidate for place of death is the pirate
hunter's ambush at São Sebastião. Most of the sick and helpless
sailors were dispatched with a blow to the head, and two were
enslaved, but none were reported as Japanese.

The final option for Christopher's demise is somewhere on
the return to England after the hopeless attempt to locate Saint
Helena in October or November 1592.

Wherever it was, it is highly unlikely to have been a natural
or painless death.

48

Mazu's flame

Japan, in 1592, was focused on its largest military project yet. Invasion of China via the Korean peninsula.

The now undisputed hegemon Hideyoshi had sent diplomats to Korea, Ryukyu (modern-day Okinawa Prefecture, Japan), aboriginal peoples in Taiwan, and the Spanish in Manila, demanding fealty and military support.

None of them had replied properly, and even the normally sycophantic Japan-based Jesuits had politely declined to loan two Portuguese galleons for the assault.

The imperial regent was white with rage. His will would not be thwarted, he would punish these impudent foreigners and fulfill his destiny, which was, he believed, to occupy China's Dragon Throne. They would all rue the day they refused Hideyoshi's generous offer of vassalship.

The would-be conqueror gathered one hundred sixty thousand samurai, twenty-four thousand muskets, seven hundred transport vessels, and three hundred warships for the assault on Korea that would secure the flanks before the warriors pushed on to Beijing.

Hideyoshi and his advisors commanded proceedings from Na-goya Castle in northern Kyushu, surrounded by another eighty thousand reserves and all the logistical support workers and camp followers that go with a project of this enormity. In all, perhaps half a million people were involved.

It is thought that England managed to mobilize around six-teen thousand to fend off the Spanish Armada, which probably itself comprised a little over sixty thousand sailors and soldiers. The extreme difference in available manpower and resources between Europe and Japan (and for that matter, China, as evi-denced by Christopher's translated map), which Spain at least was highly aware of, underlines one of the reasons for the awe in which Europeans held East Asia at this time.

Hideyoshi's immense treasury was already depleted in 1592 and continued to bleed gold and silver at an alarming rate as the war dragged on in the face of an unexpectedly effective Korean naval defense, and a Chinese counterattack.

This is the moment that Christopher and Cavendish would have waltzed onto the stage.

They could have offered *Leicester* and *Roebuck*'s strength against the fearsome Korean turtle ships, brought looted Span-ish riches to fill depleted coffers, and concluded an alliance to conquer a highly vulnerable Manila.

Cavendish, who almost definitely bore a letter from Queen Elizabeth addressed to "The Emperor of Japan," would have become the first ambassador to be sent directly by a European monarch (Valignano in 1591 had been sent by the Viceroy of Portuguese India, not the court in Lisbon). Christopher would have been the legation's interpreter.

It would have been a truly momentous occasion. One of those with the potential to change the course of history thereafter.

Anglo-Japanese relations would have exploded into life.

It was not to be.

The lives of most Japanese people during *The Age of the Coun-try at War* and Elizabethan England were short, hard, and brutal.

Christopher's was no exception, but he made his years count, accomplishing almost unbelievable things in the quarter of a century he sailed the Earth's oceans. Quite by accident, he became a pioneer in global travel, technology transfer, international relations, and cross-cultural communication. Prime among his feats was establishing human contact between the two archipelagos that lie at each end of the Eurasian landmass—Japan and the British Isles.

Wherever it was that he perished, at around the age of twenty-five, he likely died in hunger and agony. A heart-wrenching end to a momentous, inspiring, and legendary life.

But his existence exemplifies the fact that it is not only those who were born to rule that make history. This man who endured slavery, abduction, and at times horrific conditions, left a unique legacy in the worlds of science, culture, international relations, and politics.

The fact that Christopher was the first documented Asian person to learn English, engage in intellectual exchange with English speakers, and to set foot in North America, South America, and Britain, is in itself astonishing. However, his part in enabling and inspiring the English to up their game through improved nautical technology and intelligence played a key part in ever more confident and competent maritime activity.

Two centuries later it would result in the founding of the USA, and later the other English-speaking nations of North America.

Christopher's contribution to human history is as a representative of tens, probably hundreds of millions of people, for whom no written record remains. These people have always been in the shadows, but now can shine in the light of day.

If Christopher's life demonstrates anything, it is that oppressed, trafficked, and marginalized peoples have contributed far more than mere sweat, blood, and tears to human progress.

Christopher, Mazu's flame shines for you.

ご機嫌よう、バンザイ!

Epilogue

Japan, England, USA, the World

News of Christopher and Cavendish's demise diffused slowly around the world via letter, word of mouth, and intelligence dispatches.

There would have been quiet jubilation and relief in Madrid, Manila, Mexico, Lisbon, Goa, and Macau. The Portuguese and Spanish monopoly on East Asian contact with Europe was secure, and the Catholic authorities must have hoped that this failure would deter other interloper Protestant pirates from attempting what Cavendish had.

In fact, the opposite was true.

Interest in Japan and China, but especially Japan, exploded in England.

A 1593 document held in the Calendar of State Papers (government archives), about Japanese pirate activity in the Philippines, reveals that the English were not only bothering to keep tabs on Japanese-Spanish issues, but also rooting for the Japanese. The intercepted dispatch describes how the Spanish employed two hundred fifty Japanese mariners as galley oarsmen, *without chaining them, smoothing them with fair speech, and allowing them weapons, [such as] pikes and swords of Japon.*

The report then gleefully continues:

these good fellows...spying the Spaniards asleep, fell upon them, and cut their throats. The Governor awoke with the noise, and the captain..., perceiving it, entreated him to come out of his cabin, which he had no sooner done, than they slew him

before escaping with the Spanish ship.

Music to English ears! As they read and discussed the report, the Queen and her advisors must have thought back to the only Japanese people they had ever met in person, Christopher and his friend Cosmus.

In the initial years after Christopher disappeared from history, it would have been the personal legacy—memories and information retained by those whom he had met in England—which counted most. The scholars who had contact with him, both directly and indirectly, such as Hakluyt, Barlowe, Molyneux, Garet, and Clusius all released their ground-breaking, revolutionary books, globes, maps, and compasses in the years after Christopher's departure.

Colonization of North America had taken a back seat after the Roanoke disaster, and although piratical voyages to loot Spanish galleons continued, England remained focused on reaching Japan and the Far East.

Mariners like John Davis and Timothy Schotten who met him in person planned ever more daring voyages into the Asian unknown. Around 1593, Schotten even somehow got hold of a Portuguese "rutter" or navigation manual, thought to have included detailed knowledge of the seas around Japan. Such things were closely guarded secrets, and immense skullduggery must have been involved in its procurement.

Queen Elizabeth also seems to have had up-to-date information on contemporary Japanese affairs, probably through intercepted Portuguese intelligence reports.

In 1596, she wrote a personal letter to Hideyoshi, the imperial regent who was even then engaged in the attempted domination of Korea and China.

In Cavendish and Christopher's time, Elizabeth had not been sure who the ruler of Japan was, but this time she knew exactly who to address. The problem was, what title should she use? Had Hideyoshi been successful in his invasion? Was he even now the emperor of China as well as king of Korea and imperial regent of Japan?

There was no way to know, so when addressing the letter, which would have been scheduled for arrival a year or two later, she hedged her bets as to the title she should use.

Emperor and Great Lord over all the famous kingdoms of China and the territories and islands adjoining unto the same; Dayri or Great King of Coray, Tambano, Bungo, Giamaco, Xumoto, Ciazzura, Mino, Voari, &c. Taicosama

She addresses him not only by his Japanese rank, *Taicosama*, i.e., Imperial Regent, but as lord of a number of Japanese domains, as King of Coray (Korea) and Emperor of China.

The man who was supposed to deliver the letter, Benjamin Wood, perished on the way, and Hideyoshi failed once more to receive Elizabeth's letter.

The Queen also penned personal letters to the Emperor of China, which she entrusted to voyagers who were attempting to navigate the Northwest Passage,

A 1602 version, carried by George Weymouth, began:

ELIZABETH BY THE GRACE OF GOD QUEEN of England, France and Ireland Defendor of the faith etc. To the great, mighty, and Invincible Emperour of Cathaia, greeting. Wee haue receaued dyvers, and sondry relacions both by our owne Subjects, and by others, whoe have visited some partes of your Majesties Empire and Dominions, wherby they have reported unto vs aswell your Inuincible greatnes, as your kynd usage of Strangers, that resorte unto your Kingdomes with trade of merchandize, which hath wrought in us a desire, to fynd oute some neerer waye of passage by Seas from us, into your cuntrey...

The letter refers to "our owne Subjects, and by others, whoe haue visited some partes of your Majesties Empire and Dominions," which may be an indirect reference to Christopher.

The letters never made it to the emperor of course, but in a fascinating historical footnote, were actually presented to the director of the State Archive in Beijing in 1984, four centuries late.

Success continued to elude the haphazardly organized, badly supplied, and underfunded English. Unlike their Spanish, Portuguese, and Dutch competitors, they did not always enjoy unequivocal state backing. Nor did they have any guiding strategy, royal or otherwise, beyond hurting the Spanish, amassing glory, and getting rich quick. Their actions depended more on the personal whims of amateur aristocrats like Cavendish rather than coordinated long-term objectives.

The key players in Elizabethan England realized this, and eventually decided to organize.

In 1599, a select group of investors raised more than £30,000 to form a startup joint stock company called the English East India Company (EIC), which systematized voyage funding and routes, worked on wider strategy, and after the 1604 peace with Spain, was able to slowly grow and thrive, reflecting England's more secure place in the world.

As the EIC initially enjoyed only modest Asian success, the English gaze once more started to shift toward North America, and in 1607, Jamestown was established by the Virginia Company of London. Its early years were fraught with danger and starvation; but it survived, and even saw the first disembarkation of enslaved Africans, captured from a Portuguese vessel in 1619.

English-speaking settlement of the northeastern part of what is now the USA continued slowly, in fits and starts, from then on.

The EIC plodded on, but later, in what would have been a severe shock to the founder shareholders, actually came to rule a large portion of the planet and dominate much of world trade.

It led to a British Empire in Asia and later became one of the root causes of the independence of some of the North American colonies. The Boston Tea Party of 1773 was originally a protest against the EIC being granted trading privileges outside Asia to the detriment of the American colonists. The Bostonians were only too aware of the rapacious and malignant reputation it had won on the Indian subcontinent and were determined to prevent EIC tentacles reaching them.

Brytanici Imperii had become more than the pipe dream of courtly aristocrats like Thomas Cavendish and alchemists like John Dee. It was a growing global reality.

But in the 1590s, even Dee's finest magical instruments, the famous shew-stone, spirit mirror, and rock crystal ball, could never have predicted such an outcome.

Some Englishmen could not wait for their compatriots to become more organized and sold their services, and some might say England's hard-won maritime secrets, to the better organized Dutch. Two of these men were William Adams, a possible acquaintance of Christopher, and Timothy Schotten (likely a Dutchman or Flemming long in the service of the English), who had sailed extensively with the Japanese mariner.

Around eight years after Christopher's death, Adams set foot in Japan, the first Englishman to do so. He staggered ashore in a shocking state of health from his Dutch ship, *de Liefde*, the lone survivor of five companion vessels.

★ ★ ★

Schotten never made it.

The vessel he had piloted, *Hoop*, had made it across the Pacific Ocean, and repeated *Desire*'s revictualing-on-the-move stunt in the Marianas, only to be parted from *de Liefde*, and never heard of again.

In 1604, a few years after Adams's arrival—a fact his compatriots were not to know about for some years—the explorer, and sometime acquaintance of Christopher, John Davis, was once more engaged as pilot "to discover and trade with Cathia and Japan."

On Christmas Eve 1605 after leaving Java, Davis's ship *Tiger* met a small Japanese vessel that was so overladen as to be in danger of capsizing. It transpired that the crew's original ship had sunk, and they had pirated a local craft transporting rice to get them home.

The English offered aid, and the two ships took refuge in the lee of a small island close to modern-day Singapore. The Japanese were invited to join the Christmas festivities and responded by also hosting the English sailors aboard their vessel. This carried on for two days, everybody apparently friendly.

Then the atmosphere changed from amity to suspicion, however, and for reasons that remain unclear—perhaps overconsumption of alcohol played its part—the English decided to search the Japanese cargo for hidden treasure to steal. The crew were held prisoner in a cabin, but Davis, trying to diffuse the atmosphere a little, allowed them to keep their weapons despite the captain ordering them disarmed.

Shortly before sunset, the captive pirates suddenly charged out of their jail.

Davis was the first Englishman they saw. They grabbed him, pulled him back into the cabin, inflicted mortal wounds, and then charged out holding the dying seaman before them as a shield.

The fight on both ships was a wild hand-to-hand affair. It

is not hard to imagine the desperate clash of Japanese and English blades as darkness embraced the tiny floating battlefields.

All the Englishmen who had been on the Japanese ship were killed or thrown overboard, but the Japanese sailors failed to take control of *Tiger*. The outnumbered mariners retreated back to the cabin where it had all started and held out for four hours trying repeatedly to set the ship ablaze.

The end only came when the English loaded two cannons and literally blew the last holdouts away.

Having survived the battle but too shaken to continue without Davis's expertise, the English ship turned pirate itself, seized two Chinese ships, and set a course for home.

While Davis was being butchered, William Adams had become a trusted retainer of Shogun Tokugawa Ieyasu, instructing his men in gunnery and sharing knowledge of mathematics, geography, and shipbuilding. Later, he interpreted for European dignitaries at court. Adams's utility to Ieyasu was recognized through promotion to the senior samurai rank of *hatamoto*, and a medium-sized fief. He also married the adoptive daughter of a business associate, Oyuki, a wife of some social standing.

The new Japanese lord was however forbidden to leave Japan. He had become indispensable to Ieyasu.

An English ship, *Clove*, eventually reached Japan in April 1613, exactly twenty years after Christopher's planned arrival.

Thanks to Adams, the EIC were welcomed and granted trading privileges by the now-retired shogun, Ieyasu, and his son Hidetada, the new ruler. As part of the elaborate exchange of gifts that this entailed, a letter of greeting and friendship was presented from King James I, Elizabeth's successor. Gifted to Ieyasu by the EIC, as beautifully revealed by Timon Screech in his excellent book, *The Shogun's Silver Telescope*, was a cutting-edge telescope, being the first such technology to reach Japan, and the first to have ever left Europe, in return for which James received two ornate ceremonial suits of armor.

Was the choice of presents simply coincidence? The technical excellence of the telescope was a testament to how far England had progressed technologically during the past decades, and perhaps the militarily weak nation was trying to prove it had something to offer the partnership. The Japanese gifts, from a newly unified and unspeakably wealthy realm, underlined both military might and highly sophisticated artistic prowess.

Either way, Anglo-Japanese relations had gotten off to an auspicious start.

When *Clove* eventually set sail to return home with the gifts, letters, and glad tidings of contact having at last being established, a group of fifteen Japanese mariners numbered among the crew and became the first Japanese people since Christopher and Cosmus to reach London.

True to form, the lack of a noble title, unusual talent, or high level of education meant that these men were not made a fuss of. The only mention of their stay is that they were granted warm clothes to help them deal with the ice and snow that winter.

Eleven of these men survived to arrive back in Japan in 1617. They were not happy, and the head EIC merchant, Richard Cocks, recorded that, one of them *"took Capt. Adams by the throte in his owne lodging,"* demanding that he support their claim for underpaid wages and also compensation for their trading losses of 350 *taels* on the voyage.

The local authorities ordered the EIC to settle with them to the tune of 402 *taels*.

The EIC merchants established their main trading post on the small western island of Hirado. Dreams and expectations of trade and alliances, sky-high since before Christopher's time, were at last realized. A bountiful future seemed within grasp!

The English recorded their Japanese experience in great detail and disseminated the information to compatriots through letters and diaries. These men were not the arrogant mustachioed nineteenth-century Imperial British grandees of popular imagination. They approached Japan in a generally respectful manner, trying their best to integrate, often dressing in "Japon fation," and following many Indigenous customs which they professed to admire greatly.

One letter from Richard Cocks was shown to King James I. It was accompanied by a record, akin to the map of China which Christopher had translated in 1588, of the estates and incomes of Japanese lords "most of them equal or exceeding the revenues of the greatest princes of Christendom."

Despite the extensive hypothesizing about the wealth of Japan over the previous century and more, Sir Thomas Wilson, who showed it to the king, noted that "neither our cosmographers nor other writers have given us true relation of the greatness of the princes of those parts."

It was shocking to find out just how powerful the rulers of "the most remote part of the world" actually were.

The letter from Cocks included detailed and highly accurate descriptions of Japanese cities, including Edo (which would later become Tokyo), Kamakura, and Kyoto. James was flabbergasted, dismissing the letter as: "the loudest lies that ever [he] heard of."

As the trading post stuttered through its first few years, Japanese mercenaries increasingly fought for the English. Battle-hardened samurai, out of work now Japan was at peace, had been in demand as hired muscle all over East Asia for some time, and Europeans saw an easy solution to their lack of local muscle.

The Shogun's government was appalled by the constant complaints it received from Asian monarchs about its citizens overseas raping and plundering innocent locals and attacking Chinese merchants. By the 1630s, the answer had become simple yet brutal and all-encompassing in its scope. Along with a prohibition on Christian missionary work in Japan, the expulsion of Iberian

merchants, and a range of strict immigration and trade restrictions, came an absolute injunction on Japanese subjects traveling overseas under pain of banishment and death.

The ban was to last two hundred thirty years.

However, by the 1630s there had ceased to be any Englishmen in Japan. Adams had passed away in 1620, and the EIC had
failed to reap the vast profits expected.

A century or more of dreaming had led to wildly inflated
and inaccurate expectations of a market which, as John Davis
had stated with great certainty in *The Worldes Hydrographical Description*, was ready to devour English woolen products with a
voracious appetite.

In reality, Japan had virtually no need of wool except to manufacture a few pieces of specialist military equipment which
were no longer in great demand due to the breakout of peace.
Nor could England provide other in-demand products such as
Chinese silk, and therefore the English had little to trade with.

The EIC resorted to sailing locally purchased Japanese-style
ships to engage in inter-Asian trade, exchanging Asian-made
cloth and Japanese weapons in Southeast Asia for luxury goods
such as sappan wood, which sold well in Japan. However, it was
never enough to cover the high costs of the trading post, and
time and again huge losses were posted.

The reasons for the failure were more than just inadequate
products, however.

Mismanagement of funds, corruption, Dutch aggression, weak
logistics, insufficient planning, a flimsy supply chain, and wan-
ing Japanese interest also played their roles.

The EIC applied for, and eventually received, the shogun's permission to leave temporarily, departing Japan on Christmas Eve
1623. This "temporary" departure was to last a very long time.

No one could have fully foreseen the strict restrictions which
Japan would enforce in the 1630s. It had always been an open

country, happy to share its secrets and welcome to foreign trade and know-how.

This failure, along with the extreme distances and danger involved in voyaging outside the Atlantic was a reality check which provided further impetus for British concentration on what would later become the United States, the Caribbean nations, and Canada.

North American colonies, worked by both willing immigrants and enslaved Indigenous, Irish, and African people, could provide what England herself could not, ample trade goods to strengthen the mother country. Sugar, tobacco, lumber, and a whole host of crucial commodities that allowed England to escape the penury of Elizabethan times and grow powerful enough to rival, and eventually better, the larger and richer states on the European continent.

The Americas made England, and it was dreams of China and Japan which lit the fuse to start it all off.

This shift in focus did not mean, however, that the English had entirely given up on the Japanese dream.

In 1673, the EIC sent a ship, optimistically named *Return*, to renew the old trading rights.

The Japanese officials in Nagasaki—now restricted to Dutch, Chinese, and a handful of other Asian traders—were not happy to have this unsolicited incursion from a long-forgotten trade partner to deal with. In fact, one of the last such unwelcome incursions, by a Portuguese mission from Macao in 1647, had resulted in nearly the entire crew being decapitated. Only a skeleton corps had been spared to deliver the message that once-expelled peoples were unequivocally not welcome in the Land of the Rising Sun.

The English had not been expelled however; officially they had simply taken a leave of absence, and so their petition was forwarded to the shogun's government for consideration.

In the end, it was denied for several reasons, but the main

sticking point turned out to be that the Dutch had, as part of their customary annual report on European affairs, informed the Japanese that King Charles II of England had married Catherine of Braganza, great-granddaughter of the lady of the same name who had welcomed the Japanese Tensho Embassy legates to Portugal in Christopher's time, and a princess of Japan's long-term enemy, Portugal.

(The Portuguese sent the deeds to seven small islands called Bombay as part of the Queen's dowry, but unfortunately no map to say where it was; it was presumed to be somewhere near Brazil.)

Return left empty-handed, but at least her crew kept their heads.

Japan had always been more important to England than England had been to Japan and during the eighteenth century the Japanese largely forgot about the country where Christopher had caused such a stir.

As a consequence of the union with Scotland, England became part of the Kingdom of Great Britain in 1707, and later the United Kingdom when Ireland was incorporated in 1801. The idea of Japan carried on in fits and bursts. Most famously in the story of *Gulliver's Travels*, Jonathan Swift's classic tale in which the hero visits Japan and has an audience with the shogun.

East Asia in general also continued to enjoy a wide popularity in Europe and the Americas during the seventeenth century. Confucian philosophy was particularly in vogue among the literati who saw it as a model for stable and peaceful government. Some intellectuals such as the philosopher and politician Sir Francis Bacon even went as far as proposing that Chinese characters be adopted in England. He probably would have been less keen on this had he understood just how many centuries of effort it had taken the Japanese to adopt this complicated writing system to the vagaries of their own language effectively.

During the eighteenth century, Japanese commodities such as porcelain, tea, and furniture, as well as curios like pornographic *shunga* artwork, continued to arrive in the European and American worlds through the Dutch, and kept the idea of wealthy and civilized but mysterious realms on the other side of the world alive.

Then, right at the end of the century, a newly birthed English-speaking nation, the United States of America, made first contact with Japan amid circumstances of subterfuge and skullduggery.

The Napoleonic Wars were one of the first truly global conflicts, with battle sites on virtually every continent. Even distant Japan did not escape.

When the Dutch Republic capitulated to France in 1795, the trading post in Nagasaki, and all ships which supplied it, became a legitimate target of the British war machine.

Fearing expulsion from Japan, the Dutch had neglected to report the demise of their nation, and tried to carry on relations as normal; Nagasaki was the only place left on earth where the old Dutch Republican flag remained flying.

To maintain the ruse, and avoid attack by the British, the Dutch hired neutral, mainly American, ships to handle their Asian trade. When nearing Japanese waters, the Stars and Stripes would be lowered, and the Dutch ensign would be hoisted; thus the ships entered Japan under false flags.

The Japanese, though, sensed something fishy was up when *Eliza of New York* arrived in Nagasaki in 1798. A number of the crew were African American, and there having been virtually no people of African heritage in Japan since around 1640, these men drew Japanese attention.

Intentionally or otherwise, Captain William Robert Stewart benefitted from the confusion to launch an audacious fraud. Having embarked a rich cargo on behalf of his Dutch employers, the ship encountered extremely rough weather after leaving Japan, but managed to find safety on a peninsula south of Nagasaki.

What happened after the repairs had been carried out is unclear, but in the confusion Stewart seems to have absconded with the ship.

IN POSSESSION OF AUTHOR. NAGASAKI MEISHOZUE

Eliza of New York, the first American ship to attempt trade in Japan, goes down. Except it was a fraud—the ship reappeared again three years later as the Emperor of Japan. *Print from* Nagasaki Meishozue *(Pictures of Famous Places in Nagasaki), 1930 edition, p.364.*

Two years later, Stewart, presumed lost at sea, miraculously appeared in a ship named *The Emperor of Japan*, which it transpired, was none other than *Eliza of New York*, renamed and back in service.

The Dutch confiscated his cargo, bought with the proceeds of their stolen goods, and Stewart was sent in chains to the Dutch East Indies (modern-day Indonesia). Incredibly, he escaped and again attempted to trade with Japan in 1803.

Although his Japanese career was a total failure, it shows the enduring idea of Japan as a wealthy realm of endless opportunity for adventurers daring enough to brave the challenges.

With the exception of the occasional Russian border incursion, this was the first time for hundreds of years that Japan had been sucked into geopolitical tides emanating from Europe. The government was not amused, even less so when in 1811, HMS *Phaeton*, a British ship of the line, entered Nagasaki harbor threatening violence against the Dutch.

The Japanese were utterly unprepared, and their defenses were shown to be hopelessly inadequate in the face of the threat that the British Empire now presented. The aftermath was to prove of long-term consequence.

To atone for the humiliating incident, the Nagasaki magistrate Matsudaira Yasuhide performed *seppuku*, ritual suicide. Local domains who had let the country down were heavily penalized. Research into European technology, weaponry, and customs were greatly increased. New defense strategies, including an armament drive, and eventually a shoot-unknown-ships-on-sight policy, were implemented.

Perhaps most forward-thinking, however, was the initiation of English and French language studies. The language of the potential British enemy, and French, the contemporary language of international diplomacy, were gradually added to the long-established study of Chinese, Dutch, and Portuguese.

Japan had taken its first tiny steps away from an Asia-centric world into a new and growing Eurocentric international order.

It was also around this time, in 1792, that the first Japanese people arrived in what is now the territory of the USA.

As Japanese citizens were still forbidden from foreign travel, they were all castaways whose ships had drifted after being caught in storms.

The first recorded were Daikokuya Kodayu and his crew who were castaway on Amchitka, now one of the westernmost islands of Alaska, but then a part of the Russian Empire. He traveled more than five thousand miles, across Russia to the capital, Saint Petersburg, and was granted an audience with Queen Catherine II before being permitted to return to Japan.

Of the many other accidental travelers in this era, the most notable was a man called Otokichi, who was castaway in what is now Washington State, but was then part of the Hudson Bay Company's territory (encompassing much of modern-day Canada). He later worked actively for the Americans and British who were attempting to open relations with Japan. Among his many accomplishments was the first translation of parts of the Bible into Japanese. He never returned permanently to Japan and died a rich man in Singapore in 1867.

During the nineteenth century, Japan became increasingly important to a USA expanding eastward overland and engaging in ever more Pacific maritime activity. The islands were a potential source of supplies for the long-ranging American whalers and traders who could be at sea for years on end. The problem was that Japan fired upon unexpected foreign shipping, resolutely refused trade, and declined to even consider speaking with the representatives of foreign countries with which it had no traditional ties.

Then came the huge shock of China's 1842 defeat in the First Opium War. The cataclysmic event, in which the British Empire asserted with overwhelming force its right to deal illegal narcotics to China, turned the world on its head. European military might had easily prevailed, alerting the previously untouchably powerful East Asian realms to their contemporary military and technological weakness in spectacular fashion.

Japan was no exception. Alarm bells rang and further attempts to update military technology, particularly in relation to the manufacture of large guns, stronger fortifications, and oceangoing shipping were set in motion. Although research and development progressed slowly, it would stand Japan in good stead during the next decade when pressure to open the country to diplomacy and trade on the European model could no longer be easily resisted.

In 1854, after eight months of wrangling, reflection, debate, and infighting, with the threat of gunboat bombardment looming overhead, the Japanese government signed the Treaty of Kanagawa with the USA. It provided for American ships to be supplied in two Japanese ports, and a consul to be stationed in the shadow of Mount Fuji at the tiny and remote coastal town of Shimoda.

Shortly afterward, Japan signed similar treaties with Great

Britain and Russia, who happened to be in the middle of fighting on opposite sides in the Crimean War (1853–1856) and needed naval supply stations in Japan to counter each other in the Pacific. Yet again, a European conflict impacted Japan.

American and European dreams of trade were still unrealized, however. Supplies for ships was one thing; access to Japanese goods and more importantly to the Japanese market were something the shogun's government was still unwilling to contemplate.

That is, until 1858, when under intense pressure, and what was construed as another implicit threat of bombardment, Japan signed the first of what are known as the unequal treaties with the United States, Great Britain, Russia, the Netherlands, and France.

These agreements, akin to those imposed upon China after the Opium Wars, permitted trade (besides opium) in select Japanese ports, the right for foreign citizens to reside in those ports, extraterritoriality (the rule of foreign law over foreign residents), and the right for foreign countries to impose import and export duties without regard to Japanese national interest. On the positive side, they also provided for diplomatic exchange, and opened the doors to technology transfer should Japan choose to go down that path.

For the first time in more than two centuries, ships from English-speaking countries were permitted trade in Japan.

This book is fundamentally about a world that oriented toward what we now think of as "The East." Christopher and his colleagues were brought to England to help English sailors achieve their dreams of navigating, *orienting*, to the Orient—the very word we use for direction finding was coined to describe every serious European mariner's goal.

In that age, Europeans expended vast sums and died in their droves to reach the Indian subcontinent, China, Japan, and the Spice Isles in anticipation of huge financial, technological, and political rewards. The profits they made, the technologies they adopted, and the political capital they eventually accrued through colonization, changed the balance of power in Europe, underpinning wealth and empire in previously weak and peripheral countries and regions.

While many states initially welcomed their new European trade partners, others, particularly China, saw the Europeans as disruptors who were unwilling to conform to East Asian legal and behavioral norms. Executions without recourse to local law, slaving, and piracy only reinforced the view that they were unruly pests rather than potential allies or reliable partners in trade. They hence saw little value in communication and trade, which puzzled and angered the Europeans who had never really considered that East Asia might not desire contact with them.

Prester John, and the Great Khan, had been expected to welcome them as allies with open arms.

Initially, smaller countries like Japan, embroiled in war and division, found reasons to maintain these new links, that is until it became too much trouble and they decided to copy China by forcibly ceasing almost all European contact.

Other states, such as those of the places we know of today as India and Indonesia were swallowed violently or by legal trickery.

As colonies, they became sources of enslaved or cheap labor, and endlessly productive money trees for European imperialists.

European nations became rich.

Where unimpressive, disease-ridden settlements had previously lain, rose grand cities with wide boulevards and sewage systems.

The sumptuous country houses of England, the canaled elegance of Amsterdam, Madrid's great palaces and churches were built not only on the profits of Elizabethan-style looting (although plenty of that went on too), but also on regulated and legalized tribute, tax, and customs revenues collected from sovereigns, merchants, and peasants at the far ends of the planet.

Where only privateers and semivolunteer, medieval-like military structures had existed, formidable, professional military machines rose to project brute power and deadly political force. Where magic, cosmology, and alchemy had ruled, research and technology exploded into industrial and scientific, not to mention cultural, revolutions.

None of this could have happened without Europe stealing resources that by rights belonged elsewhere.

On the back of the colonial plunder of human lives, resources, and strategic advantage, global tides changed. Over the next two centuries, the world's geopolitical power axis tilted from East to West. Global power—military, economic, legal, cultural, and political—became concentrated in Europe and began to hover over the Atlantic to include North America.

The East Asian ruling classes' attitude to Europeans had proven to be prescient. China and Japan were eventually forced into relations and semicolonial status at the end of a gun.

After the unequal treaties were concluded, Asian elites traveled to the new centers of power to shore up their domestic political positions, buy the latest weapons, study, and obtain loans to prosecute revolutions and counterrevolutions.

Asian workers increasingly made the journey westward (or eastward over the Pacific Ocean) to find their fortunes in the goldfields of California or earn a few dollars building American railroads. That is until immigration from China, and later Japan, was legally restricted by people of mainly European origin, who feared the land they had taken from others would in turn be taken from them.

Time was reverting to an era of greater contact, only in an astonishing role reversal, this time it was the Japanese ruling class, and eventually the Chinese elites also, who felt the need to emulate the mighty power of America and Europe. Not the Europeans who prostrated themselves before Asian rulers and bureaucrats in the hope of acquiring wealth, preferment, patronage, the secrets of alchemy, and the keys to the cosmos.

In what was an unprecedented occurrence in world history, with reverberations that last until this day, the tables had turned.

The world's fulcrum had moved westward and despite a tumultuous twentieth century it has largely remained that way until the twenty-first.

The major exception of course was Japan, which managed to avoid becoming a colony, and joined the exploitative, extractive, manipulative, and racially laden imperialist game by colonizing its own neighbors to emerge as a world power in the early twentieth century. It lost that status through defeat in war but regained it again through aligning unquestioningly with the USA to become a peaceful economic and cultural Soft Power in the latter half of the century.

At the beginning of the second millennium, global tides have seen a major "reorientation."

China has joined Japan at the top again and is being closely followed by an Indian nation which largely achieved the long-sought unification of the subcontinent at the same time as independence from the British Empire in 1947.

The countries and regions which were the fantasy of early-modern European navigators, the dream which in the end drove Europe to colonization of all the other continents, are now the second, third, and fifth largest economies in the world. Writing in 2023, the People's Republic of China is forecast to overtake the USA as the world's largest economy in the near future. Economists are divided on when this will happen, but nobody seriously disputes that it will.

It is not only economic power. Culture and technology too are sweeping the world. As in the sixteenth century, Japan and China have become models for others to aspire to and emulate. From sushi and ramen to Sichuan spice and delicate dim sum, industrial policy, disaster management, poverty alleviation, infrastructural magic, and space exploration.

Few people remember, however, that we have seen this before—this is nothing new. We are simply returning to a form of the world Christopher and Cavendish knew.

Some readers will be wondering what this diatribe about European imperialism and colonialism has to do with Christopher's story.

Well, the history that flowed from his encounter with Tudor England, both directly and indirectly, is at the core of the modern world whether we like it or not.

It is tempting to assume that Europe, the continent of my birth which I have a deep fondness for, has always been top dog. The racial, linguistic, social, cultural, and economic capital accrued from this "fact" is deeply entrenched and has vast global ramifications today.

I myself am a good example of this acquired capital privilege. The fact that I was born in London and have English as my mother tongue has made it far easier to carve out a career as a teacher and researcher in Japan than had I, for example, been born in Athens.

As Christopher's story shows, the "fact" of continued "top dog" civilizational superiority is far from truth, and in almost every case the Europeans of a few centuries ago approached distant Asian states in awed respect, bearing tribute, and ready to kowtow just as any other supplicant from a "barbarian/uncivilized" tribute nation would.

Although this book only concentrates on the cases of Japan and China, it was also true of the larger states of the Indian subcontinent, Persia, the Ottoman Empire (a major destination for enslaved Europeans throughout much of history), and to some extent of African empires and kingdoms such as Mali, Abyssinia, Kongo, and Morocco.

It took hundreds of years for Western Europe to effectively come to dominate these places and create the foundation of the world in which we live in today.

This is the hard conclusion.

While it is far more comfortable to pretend that brutal events like the Opium Wars, the enslavement of millions of people,

the majority from Africa, or the genocide and theft of Indigenous lands around the world that happened centuries ago has
no connection to our modern-day lives, the opposite is quite
blatantly true.

It is no coincidence that the contemporary world's most powerful and richest societies, and especially their elites, were generally the colonial exploiters, and in many cases are still in effect
the beneficiaries of those historical wrongs.

Furthermore, the peoples who were the victims, if they did
not succumb to genocide, have not forgotten, and their historical experience informs how they deal with inter-ethnic communication, diplomacy, and international relations today.

The People's Republic of China provides a good example. As I
penned these words in 2023, fentanyl manufactured (against Chinese law) in China, an opioid drug that has tragically wreaked
havoc in US society and shows little sign of slowing down, was
a big news item. While I doubt few English language readers
will ever make a connection between this horrific modern-day
drug crisis and the Opium Wars of the nineteenth century, a
billion Chinese people will.

Defeat in those wars heralded what is known in China as the
"Century of Humiliation," during which one of the world's
richest and most powerful nations became one of its poorest and
weakest. This bitter memory powers China's rise today.

Few British people remember the tens of millions of Indians
who died during famines while tax collection to fatten London wallets continued without let or hindrance. But a billion
Indians do. These memories inform modern India's foreign relations, strict control of foreign capital, and nationalist political
movements to this day.

There are many other such histories which are unforgotten
by local peoples on every continent but generally washed from
school history curriculums and the collective memories of the
former imperialists' descendants.

Of course, it is not wise to apply modern thought patterns

and ethical standards to historical times and places, and it is presumptuous for us to judge the actions of those who came before us. They lived in worlds we cannot imagine and would not survive long in.

But that is not the point; we now profess to know better, and to act in more humane and ethical ways.

Yet, current diplomacy of what is normally termed the "West," seems to take little heed of the deeper trends in history. Most international relations models are built on very short-term assumptions, ignoring the histories that founded our modern world, and the long-term perspectives and experiences of global "partners" and "rivals."

Empathy, understanding, and a degree of contrition, rather than an iron fist and selective amnesia, would seem wiser and more honorable ways of approaching this postcolonial, but often still imperial-feeling world.

Christopher was there at the beginning of the world's transformation; we are here in the present.

At a time when the drums of war, and chest-beating of posturing leaders seem to get louder and louder, just as we need to work together to combat humankind's toughest existential challenge yet, only one thing is certain; if a future of ecological disaster, conflict, and extreme strife is to be avoided, the rebalancing of East and West, North and South, must be built on secure historical understanding to achieve a peaceful future.

The past is here to stay; it cannot simply be airbrushed away.

★ ★ ★ ★ ★

Author Note

Christopher lived approximately between the years of 1567 and 1592.

However unreal some of the escapades and episodes may appear, his life as told within these pages is as close to fact as eight years of research, contemplation, and a dozen rewrites could achieve. Ultimately, I have tried to re-create the astonishing story so as to transport the reader into the past to experience that world, in the words of the historian David Gilmour, as "walked, observed, smelt, drunk."

I was helped in this by the fact that the late Elizabethan England which Christopher discovered was experiencing a publishing boom, very much at the same time as it was finding a new confidence and vigor that, due to the eternal-seeming civil wars, constant loss of continental territory, and religious and social rupture, had been absent before.

In particular, Richard Hakluyt's wonderful collection of firsthand testimony and translated secondhand reports from all around the globe gave me the intimate details I needed to reconstruct the voyages recounted in these pages.

Following Hakluyt's death, Samuel Purchas took up the

baton, publishing a series of books which eventually included an account of the 1613 English voyage to Japan, and Anthony Knyvett's adventures among many others.

John Davis, Robert Hues, Thomas Lodge, William Barlowe, and many others left fascinating treatises and books. Men like William Adams, Richard Cocks, and James Garet Jr. wrote letters and diaries, rich in detail. Examples of Emery Molyneux's innovative globes, and Luo Hongxian's cutting-edge printed maps have thankfully survived to the modern age.

Furthermore, the groundbreaking work of people like the Sinologist Joseph Needham in the twentieth century opened up the rich world of original sources pertaining to historical Chinese and Asian technological know-how, in many cases helpfully comparing them to European endeavors. My details on Chinese compasses, knowledge of the cosmos, and other details are taken directly from Needham's awesome works of history and anthropology.

Finally, the untiring work of so many modern scholars, interpreters of history, and writers was invaluable, and I have recorded as many of their works as possible in the bibliography below.

Before his meeting with Thomas Cavendish, much of Christopher's youth is unclear. The things we do know about both him and his colleague Cosmus as reported in European sources, is that they were born in Kyoto (although I suspect that was a fabrication to boost their status), that they both had a high level of education for the time and were literate in Japanese, and probably Chinese (most literate Japanese people wrote in a form of Chinese at this time), that they were experienced in marine matters, and that Cosmus was a beloved enslaved boy of the Spanish canon of Manila.

Of the three Filipino lads who were also abducted, the eldest, Alphonso, did get a little attention from the London naturalists, but the others virtually none, probably because they were too young to be specialized in any particular skill.

The original sources for Christopher's life, some of which are quoted directly in the text, and all of which are listed in the bibliography at the end of the book, are regrettably patchy at times. For example, while we do know that it was Christopher who was friends with Knyvett because he is specifically named, we do not know which of the Japanese lads managed to escape during the disastrous raid on São Vicente in June 1592 in which only three of *Leicester*'s shore party made it back alive, the survivor is simply referred to as a "Japan boye."

There are also gaps in the narrative. After Christopher's meeting with Cavendish, the sources for his life are rich, but then suddenly the trail goes cold. For example, we have ample information about how amazing the English literati thought it was that he and his "gentlemen" or "naturalist" colleagues were in England, and of the scholarly exchanges that took place. However, while several sources indicate that events took place in or near London, for example Lime Street, most give no location at all.

Drawing on the experience of other visitors to London from far-flung corners of the earth at this time, I concluded that Cavendish would have wanted them away from the disease and corruption of the city (1589 was a plague year), and sent them, at least temporarily, to his ancestral fiefdom in Suffolk. There is no document to confirm this, but neither is there any evidence that they stayed in London all the time they remained in England. Cities were dangerous places, and it would have made little sense to keep Christopher and his comrades under that threat.

The speed with which nomenclature changed from "gentlemen," i.e., noble, to "naturalist," i.e., scholar, is fascinating. It was clear that the English wanted to maintain a certain status for Christopher and his colleagues, who are always referred to in respectful terms, a highly significant point in this highly class-conscious and relatively xenophobic age.

Status of course also conferred weight to their experience and expertise in botany, foreign languages, and navigation and of course, it sounds much better to say "I was told this by a naturalist of the East Indies" than "a Japanese slave told me."

The parts for which I have only fragmentary evidence, the origin stories of Christopher and Cosmus, are most likely scenarios based on real historical episodes.

After the Cagayan battle, survivors would have been taken to Manila where enslaved and free Japanese people were becoming common. All the other possible scenarios of how Christopher got to Manila are problematic due to there being little recorded contact between the Japanese and Spanish at this time.

The raid I describe Cosmus as having been captured in also happened. The Satsuma clan from what is now Kagoshima Prefecture in the south of Japan, did enslave a large number of victims. Furthermore, a large human cargo, comprising mostly of children, embarked from Kuchinotsu in the year 1579.

The giant African warrior who observed Cosmus is Yasuke, the subject of a book that I co-authored with Geoffrey Girard, *African Samurai*. He was newly arrived in Japan and lodging in or near the port at the same time so could hardly have missed it.

I have referred to the factual records of other lives, excellently researched by Lúcio de Sousa, when describing Christopher's time in Manila and on board *Santa Ana*.

Mistress Tei, consort of the historical pirate Tay Fusa, while not named directly in sources, is also based upon real women, as females were often purchased as "wives" and some rose to be respected in society as such. Her name also conveniently matches that of the legendary Chinese pirate, Madam Zheng (Rendered *Tei* in Japanese) who rose from sex slavery to rule the South China Sea with a fleet of over three hundred ships in the early nineteenth century.

Because of the documentary confusion, there is of course the possibility that some of the events and deeds that I ascribe to Christopher could in fact have been Cosmus, and in one or two cases one of the young Filipino men. In the majority of cases though, I am sure that this is not the case.

Christopher is our man.

Records show that he was the oldest, most knowledgeable, and quite clearly the leader of the five young Asians abducted by Cavendish in California.

Given all this, a question that has occurred to me again and again during the writing of this book is: Why was Christopher forgotten about for so long?

There is no easy answer, but Cavendish's attempted deception of the Queen, subsequent failure, and probable suicide, contributed greatly to the glossing over of his and therefore Christopher's story in England. The lack of a newspaper or large-scale pamphlet-publishing industry at the time also contributed. Later in history, London's journalists would have, as many later examples of "very foreign foreigners" show, covered the story extensively, and we would have a lot more information to go on.

The fact that similar and equally celebrated contemporary Native American visits have been researched extensively and are now remembered is due to the fact that American academics have been keen to research their own nation's past. Christopher has never been known in Japan, and therefore interest in researching his life has been nonexistent.

African visitors to England at the time have also, until recently, been forgotten, but knowledge of the Black British people of the wider early modern era has increased greatly in the past few years with the excellent work of people like Onyeka Nubia and Cliff Pereira.

So much of the world of four hundred plus years ago remains opaque, but that is one of its fascinations. History is only uncovered if somebody is motivated to research it.

History rarely has a Disney ending; Christopher's story certainly doesn't.

Acknowledgements

There are an awful lot of people who helped make this book happen and I would like to extend my heartfelt gratitude to all of them.

Peter Joseph and his team at Hanover Square Press who commissioned and edited the book beautifully.

Peter McGuigan and his team at Ultra Literary in the USA. Manami Tamaoki, and her colleagues, particularly Ken Mori, and Alex Korenori, at Tuttle-Mori Agency in Tokyo. Alex has since retired, and I wish him all the best in his future projects.

Timon Screech, Susan Maxwell, and Lúcio de Sousa for long-term interest, support with their amazing expertise, and encouragement for the project.

Rafael Cardenas Lizarraga, José Manuel Renteria Cobos, and Marcos Roldan whose expert eyes spared my blushes as to the landscape and resources available in Baja California.

Christopher and Raquel Angela Balita, for sharing knowledge of the Philippines that I could never have found elsewhere, and correcting some innocent blunders.

For support, advice, and knowledge, President Emeritus Robin James Maynard, President Paul Christie, Vice President and Treasurer Tokugawa Yasuhisa, Chairman Tim Minton, and Secretary Chris Wells of the William Adams Club (WAC) in 2023.

WAC is an organization dedicated to commemorating the vast achievements of William Adams, the first English mariner to reach Japan, and promote wider Anglo-Japanese relations. It has been my deep honor to have been involved with the club over the years.

Anyone wishing to find out more can contact WAC at the website https://williamadamsclub.org/.

Robert Batchelor, Tonio Andrade, Cliff Pereira, Jerry Brotton, Peter Kornicki, Onyeka Nubia, Marika Sherwood, Iain Gately, Kawane Tomo, Alden Vaughan, Chris and Tom Wells, Ryan Hartley, Geoffrey Girard, Gary Hayden, Simon Cooke, Joe Geluso, and so many others. Without their willingness to volunteer information, expertise, insights, and friendly support, many loose ends could not have been tied and a thousand further questions not answered.

Renae Satterley at Middle Temple library in London for allowing me to examine one of the only remaining Molyneux globes and the original versions of Hakluyt's and Barlowe's great tomes. I was so excited to study the globes that she had to hush me! In a good-natured way of course.

John's College Library in Oxford for allowing me to consult an original copy of Robert Parke's *The Historie of the Great and Mightie Kingdome of China*.

William Chatterton for being my companion and guide around Tudor London on a cold winter's day in January 2019. It was great fun, and Julius Caesar's tomb was a particular highlight.

All the people in museums, castles, temples, churches, archives, and on boats in Kuchinotsu, Shimabara, Nagasaki, Amakusa, London, Plymouth, and Trimley, and elsewhere who shared their local knowledge and gave advice while I was visiting for on-the-ground research.

My employer, Nihon University, for providing me with a sabbatical to do the research in the UK and Helen Macnaughtan at SOAS University of London for granting me a visiting scholar position.

Philip Lockley and Naomi Martins Lockley, my siblings, for their comments on the story. Andrew and Caryl Lockley (to whom the book is dedicated). Masae and Yusaburo Kinoshita, my parents-in-law, for all their hard work supporting my family.

And finally, as always, my wife, Junko, for everything she does. She was a much later Japanese sojourner in a very different England, but her take was nonetheless a fascinating and enlightening source of information for Christopher's story too.

Thomas Lockley, Tokyo, 2023

The Primary Sources
for Christopher

Barlowe, William. *The Nauigators Supply Conteining Many Things of Principall Importance Belonging to Nauigation, with the Description and VSE of Diuerse Instruments Framed Chiefly for That Purpose.* London: R. Newbury, and R. Barker, 1597. (The Epistle, b.1, and A.4).

Cavendish, Thomas, cited in *"Advertissement certain contenant les pertes aduenues en l'armee d'Espagne… Auec deux lettres, l'vne d'vn Flamen…demeurant a Londres…et l'autre de Monsieur Candiche, qui a passe le destroit de Magellan, pour aller aux Indes, & est retourne par le Cap de Bonne Esperance,"* Paris, 1588.

Garet, James Jr. to Clusius, Carolus, July 28, 1589, *Leiden University Library Digital Collection*, accessed March 4, 2023, https://socrates.leidenuniv.nl/view/item/1588022?solr_nav%5Bid%5D=0eb54b9926218cf930ce&solr_nav%5Bpage%5D=0&solr_nav%5Boffset%5D=2#page/4/mode/1up.

Hakluyt, Richard. *The Principal Navigations Voyages Traffiques and Discoveries of the English Nation*, 1589. (The Epistle Dedicatori, p.XXI.)

Knivet, Antonie. *The admirable adventures and strange fortunes of Master Antonie Knivet, which went with Master Thomas Candish in his second voyage to the South Sea*. In *The admirable adventures and strange fortunes of Master Antonie Knivet, which went with Master Thomas Candish in his second voyage to the South Sea An English Pirate in 16th Century Brazil* (Vivien Kogut Lessa de Sa). Cambridge: Cambridge University Press, 2015, p.46 and p.50–51.

Parke, Robert. *The Historie of the Great and Mightie Kingdome of China, and the Situation Thereof: Togither with the Great Riches, Huge Citties, Politike Governement, and Rare Inventions in the Same*. London: Edward White, 1589, p.2–3.

Pretty, Francis. *The admirable and prosperous voyage of the Worshipfull Master Thomas Candish of Trimley in the Countie of Suffolke Esquire, into the South sea, and from thence round about the circumference of the whole earth, begun in the yeere of our Lord 1586, and finished 1588. Written by Master Francis Pretty lately of Ey in Suffolke, a Gentleman employed in the same action*. In Hakluyt's *The Principal Navigations Voyages Traffiques and Discoveries of the English Nation*, 1598.

Mangabay, Francisco. Testimony given in the city of Manila to Gabriel de Ribera, High Sheriff, April 16, 1588. Archivo General De Indias (Seville), FILIPINAS, 34.

Mocenigo, Giovanni (Venetian Ambassador to France), to the Doge and Senate, "Venice: October 17, 1588," in *Calendar of State Papers Relating To English Affairs in the Archives of Venice, Volume 8, 1581–1591*, ed. Horatio F. Brown (London: Her Majesty's Stationery Office, 1894), 396–409. *British History Online*, accessed March 4, 2023, http://www.british-history.ac.uk/cal-state-papers/venice/vol8/pp396-409.

Yates, John, SJ (aka John Vincent) c. June 1593. Letter to Francis Englefield. Cited in Quinn, D. *The Last Voyage of Thomas Cavendish 1591–1592*, Chicago: The University of Chicago Press, 1975.

Selected Bibliography

Alden, Dauril. *The Making of an Enterprise: The Society of Jesus in Portugal, Its Empire, and beyond; 1540–1750*. Stanford, CA: Stanford University Press, 1999.

Andrews, Kenneth Raymond. *Elizabethan Privateering*, 1964.

Antony, Robert. *Elusive Pirates, Pervasive Smugglers Violence and Clandestine Trade in the Greater China Seas*. Hong Kong: Hong Kong University Press, 2010.

Appleton, William. *A Cycle of Cathay*. Columbia University Press, 1951.

Backwood, B. G. *Tudor and Stuart Suffolk*. Lancaster: Carnegie Publishing, 2001.

Barlow, William. *The Navigators Supply*. London: R. Newbury, and R. Barker, 1597.

Batchelor, Robert K. *London: The Selden Map and the Making of a Global City, 1549–1689*. Chicago: The University of Chicago Press, 2014.

Bawlf, Samuel. *The Secret Voyage of Sir Francis Drake*. London: Penguin, 2004.

Berry, Mary Elizabeth. *Hideyoshi*. Cambridge, MA: Harvard University Press, 1990.

Bicheno, Hugh. *Elizabeth's Sea Dogs: How the English Became the Scourge of the Seas*. London: Adlard Coles Nautical, 2018.

Brooke-Hitching, Edward. *The Phantom Atlas: The Greatest Myths, Lies and Blunders on Maps*. San Francisco: Chronicle Books, 2018.

Brooke-Hitching, Edward. *The Sky Atlas: The Greatest Maps, Myths and Discoveries of the Universe*. San Francisco: Chronicle Books, 2020.

Brook, Timothy. *Mr Selden's Map of China: The Spice Trade, a Lost Chart and the South China Sea*. London: Profile Books, 2015.

Brotton, Jerry. *This Orient Isle: Elizabethan England and the Islamic World*. London: Penguin Books, 2017.

Burton Paradise, Nathaniel. *Thomas Lodge: The History of an Elizabethan*. New Haven, CT: Yale University Press, 1931.

Carey, Daniel, and Claire Jowitt. *Richard Hakluyt and Travel Writing in Early Modern Europe.* Farnham, Surrey, England: Ashgate, 2012.

Cooper, Michael. *They Came to Japan: An Anthology of European Reports on Japan, 1543–1640. Edited by Michael Cooper.* Berkeley and Los Angeles: University of California Press, 1965.

Crampton, Caroline. *Way to the Sea: The Forgotten Histories of the Thames Estuary.* London: Granta Books, 2020.

Dalrymple, William. *The Anarchy. The Relentless Rise of the East India Company.* London: Bloomsbury, 2019.

De Sousa, Lúcio. *The Portuguese Slave Trade in Early Modern Japan: Merchants, Jesuits and Japanese, Chinese, and Korean Slaves.* Leiden: Brill, 2019.

Egmond, Florike. *The World of Carolus Clusius: Natural History in the Making, 1550–1610.* London: Routledge, 2016.

Fernandez-Armesto, Felipe. *Straits: Beyond the Myth of Magellan.* London: Bloomsbury Publishing, 2023.

Fish, Shirley. *The Manila-Acapulco Galleons: The Treasure Ships of the Pacific: With an Annotated List of the Transpacific Galleons 1565–1815.* Central Milton Keynes, UK: AuthorHouse, 2012.

Foley, Henry. *Records of the English Province of the Society of Jesus.* Roehampton: The Manresa Press, 1875, accessed July 1, 2023, http://www.fondazioneintorcetta.info/pdf/biblioteca-virtuale/documento912/RecordsII.pdf.

Frois, Luis. *The First European Description of Japan, 1585: A Criti-*

cal English-Language Edition of Striking Contrasts in the Customs of Europe and Japan by Luis Frois, S.J. Routledge, 2016.

Fujita, Kayoko, Momoki, Shiro, and Reid Anthony. *Offshore Asia: Maritime Interactions in Eastern Asia before Steamships.* Institute of Southeast Asian Studies, 2013.

Fury, Cheryl A. *Tides in the Affairs of Men the Social History of Elizabethan Seamen, 1580–1603.* Westport, CT: Greenwood Press, 2002.

Gill, Crispin. *Plymouth: A New History.* Tiverton: Devon Books, 2003.

Giráldez, Arturo. *The Age of Trade: The Manila Galleons and the Dawn of the Global Economy.* Lanham, MD: Rowman & Littlefield, 2015.

Goodman, Ruth. *How to Be a Tudor: A Dawn-to-Dusk Guide to Everyday Life.* Penguin Books Ltd, 2016.

Gurney, Alan. *Compass: A Story of Exploration and Innovation.* New York: W.W. Norton, 2005.

Harkness, Deborah E. *The Jewel House: Elizabethan London and the Scientific Revolution.* New Haven, CT: Yale University Press, 2008.

Hesselink, Reiner H. *The Dream of Christian Nagasaki World Trade and the Clash of Cultures, 1560–1640.* Jefferson, NC: McFarland & Company, Inc., Publishers, 2016.

Hues, Robert. *Tractatus De Globis Et Eorum Usu.* London: The Hakluyt Society, 1889.

Hutchinson, Robert. *Elizabeth's Spy Master: Francis Walsingham and the Secret War That Saved England.* London: Phoenix, 2007.

Jerram, Sibyl. *Old Plymouth.* Plymouth: Western Morning News Co., 1920.

Jowitt, Claire. *Culture of Piracy 1580–1630: English Literature and Seaborne Crime.* Routledge, 2016.

Kang, David C. *East Asia before the West: Five Centuries of Trade and Tribute.* New York: Columbia University Press, 2012.

Kaufmann, Miranda. *Black Tudors: The Untold Story.* London: Oneworld Publications, 2020.

Keen, Maurice. *The Origins of the English Gentleman: Heraldy, Chivalry and Gentility in Medival England, c. 1300–c. 1500.* Brimscombe Port: Tempus, 2002.

Kimura, Jun. *Archaeology of East Asian Shipbuilding.* University of Florida, Board of Trustees, 2016.

Knivet, Anthony, and Vivien Kogut. *The Admirable Adventures and Strange Fortunes of Master Anthony Knivet: An English Pirate in Sixteenth-Century Brazil.* New York, NY: Cambridge University Press, 2015.

Konstam, Angus. *The Armada Campaign, 1588: The Great Enterprise against England.* Westport, CT: Praeger, 2005.

Lee, Adele. *English Renaissance and the Far East: Cross-Cultural Encounters.* Fairleigh Dickinson University Press, 2019.

Lodge, Thomas. *A Margarite of America.* Edited with introduction and annotations by Donald Beecher and Henry D. Janzen. Toronto: Barnabe Richie Society, 2005.

Markley, Robert. *The Far East and the English Imagination: 1600–1730*. Cambridge: Cambridge University Press, 2007.

Massarella, Derek. *A World Elsewhere: Europe's Encounter with Japan in the Sixteenth and Seventeenth Centuries*. New Haven, London: Yale University Press, 1990.

Massarella, Derek. *Japanese Travellers in Sixteenth-Century Europe: A Dialogue Concerning the Mission of the Japanese Ambassadors to the Roman Curia (1590)*. London: Routledge, 2022.

Mathes, W. Michael. *Vizcaíno And Spanish Expansion in the Pacific Ocean: 1580–1630*. San Francisco: California Historical Society, 1968.

Mathes, W. Michael. *The Capture of the Santa Ana: Cabo San Lucas, November, 1587*. Los Angeles: Dawson's Book Shop, 1969.

Miller, Lee. *Roanoke: Solving the Mystery of England's Lost Colony*. London: Penguin, 2002.

Mortimer, Ian. *The Time Traveller's Guide to Elizabethan England*. London: Vintage, 2013.

Muir, Kenneth. *Shakespeare Survey: An Annual Survey of Shakespearian Study and Production, 32. The Middle Comedies*. Cambridge: Cambridge University Press, 1979.

Murrin, Michael Joseph. *Trade and Romance*. Chicago: The University of Chicago Press, 2014.

Needham, Joseph. *Science and Civilisation in China. Volume 3: Mathematics and the Sciences of the Heavens and Earth.* Cambridge: Cambridge University Press, 1959.

Needham, Joseph. *Science and Civilisation in China. Volume 4: Physics and Physical Technology.* Cambridge: Cambridge University Press, 1962.

Onyeka. *Blackamoores: Africans in Tudor England, Their Presence, Status and Origins.* London?: Narrative Eye, 2014.

Paul, Joanne. *House of Dudley: A New History of Tudor England.* London: Penguin Books, 2023.

Peat, Rachael. (ed.) *Japan, Courts and Culture.* London: Royal Collection Trust, 2020.

Picard, Liza. *Elizabeth's London: Everyday Life in Elizabethan London.* New York: St. Martin's Griffin, 2005.

Riesenberg, Felix. *Cape Horn.* London: Readers Union, 1950.

Rubinger, Richard. *Popular Literacy in Early Modern Japan.* Honolulu: University of Hawai'i Press, 2007.

Russell-Wood, A J. *Society and Government in Colonial Brazil, 1500–1822.* Hampshire, Great Britain: Variorum, 1992.

Sanghera, Sathnam. *Empireland: How Imperialism has Shaped Modern Britain.* London: Penguin, 2021.

Screech, Timon. *The Shogun's Silver Telescope: God, Art, and Money in the English Quest for Japan, 1600–1625.* Oxford: Oxford University Press, 2020.

Stone, Peter. *The History of the Port of London*. Barnsley: Pen & Sword History, 2021.

Swope, Kenneth, Tonio Andrade, and John E. Wills. *Early Modern East Asia: War, Commerce, and Cultural Exchange: Essays in Honor of John E. Wills, Jr.* London: Routledge, 2019.

Thomson, Arline K. *Discovering Elizabethan London*. Orono: University of Maine Press, 1994.

Tremml-Werner, Birgit. *Spain, China and Japan in Manila, 1571–1644: Local Comparisons and Global Connections*. Amsterdam: Amsterdam University Press, 2015.

Vaughan, Alden T. *Transatlantic Encounters: American Indians in Britain, 1500–1776*. New York, NY: Cambridge University Press, 2009.

Vigne, Randolph, and Charles Littleton. *From Strangers to Citizens: The Integration of Immigrant Communities in Britain, Ireland, and Colonial America, 1550–1750*. London: The Huguenot Society of Great Britain and Ireland, 2001.

Wilson, Derek. *Elizabethan Society: High and Low Life, 1558–1603*. Little, Brown Book Group Limited, 2019.

Chapter Notes

Note on Currency

To establish what sums are worth in modern terms, for English currency I have used the National Archives Currency Convertor which can be found at https://www.nationalarchives.gov.uk/currency-converter/.

For other currencies, due to fluctuations in value by time and place, I have simply used the amount stated in the source without trying to convert it.

Prologue

Tun

In Christopher's time a tun was a measure of liquid equal to 252 gallons (US) or around 954 liters. A ship's size was measured by tun capacity, i.e., how many tun size barrels could in theory be stored within.

Virginia

Virginia was a name given by Arthur Barlowe, probably on the orders of Walter Raleigh, to lands on the East Coast of North

America from what is now South Carolina to parts of today's Canada. It also included the Atlantic island of Bermuda.

Although it is commonly thought that the name refers to the Virgin Queen, Elizabeth, it could also have been a corruption of "Wyngandacoia," the word that the English thought was the Indigenous name for the lands, or conceivably be derived from both. The modern US state of Virginia derives its nomenclature from this historical territory name.

Walter Raleigh (c. 1552–1618)

Walter Raleigh was a key player in English efforts to improve maritime skills and endeavors. He led through both captaining voyages, predominantly to South America, and also enabled the sharing of skills such as mapmaking and navigation in London among those who he mentored. Thomas Cavendish is believed to have been one of the young men in his circle during the early 1580s.

The Royal Patent he was granted for exploration in the lands that came to be called "Virginia" formed the basis of English claims to legitimate settlement. It was under his auspices that Roanoke was founded, and hence Thomas Cavendish, and through him Christopher, became connected to Raleigh's story.

He was famously one of Elizabeth's favorites, but when he married one of the Queen's ladies in waiting Elizabeth Throckmorton without permission in 1591, they were both imprisoned in the Tower of London.

He was never a favorite of King James I, and was eventually executed for treason in 1618.

The Cavendish Family

The Cavendish family is thought to date back to the Norman Conquest of England in 1066, and eventually became one of the richest and most powerful families in England. Thomas

Cavendish was a member of a cadet line of the family, and due to his death without offspring, his Trimley branch died out.

The yellow banana which we commonly eat today has the distinction of being known as the Cavendish banana, because the first place they were cultivated in England was at the home of William George Spencer Cavendish, 6th Duke of Devonshire, in his home at Chatsworth House, Derbyshire.

Japan, Disambiguation

"Japan" is the name of a modern nation-state in East Asia, which interestingly enough has the distinction of having the shortest name of any country on the planet. Japanese speakers know the country as *Nihon*, which in Chinese characters means the origin of the sun, hence it is often called "Land of the Rising Sun."

Japan as a nation-state did not exist until the mid-nineteenth century, when like many places such as Germany and Italy, a host of small state-like entities joined together to form larger countries based upon a belief in ethnic and linguistic fraternity.

In Japan's case the small states, *kuni*, or in English "domains," had been forged together into a realm of sorts by Tokugawa Ieyasu after the Battle of Sekigahara in 1600, and forced to make peace with each other under the Tokugawa thumb. Foreign and "national" defense policy were directed by the shogunate, but individual domains had their own laws and even minted their own money.

While the Japanese did not call themselves "Japanese" until modern times, still primarily identifying as members of specific clans, people outside Japan have referred to the main islands collectively as "Japan" for a long time.

The "Empire of Japan" was formally declared in 1868, the clan domains were abolished shortly afterward, and the people became "Japanese."

The territory of what we now call Japan comprises the three

main islands, Honshu, Kyushu, and Shikoku, as well as the Ryukyu Archipelago (modern-day Okinawa Prefecture) and the northern islands whose borders are still disputed with Russia, but mainly comprise Hokkaido Prefecture. The former and latter were both independent territories until enforced incorporation within the new empire as the first two colonies in the mid- to late nineteenth century. Other parts of the region were formally and forcibly incorporated into the Empire of Japan in the late nineteenth and early twentieth century, most notably Taiwan and the Korean Peninsula. The people of these territories became Japanese citizens until forced to choose to remain Japanese or affiliate with North or South Korea, or the Republic of China after Japan's 1945 defeat in World War II.

Japan has had other names in history, most notably *Wa*, an ancient group name for the diverse peoples and clans of the archipelago, and the poetic *Fuso*, both of which derive from Chinese terminology. "Wa" is still commonly used to denote specifically Japanese things like *Washoku* (traditional Japanese cuisine).

For ease of understanding, I use the English term "Japan" throughout the book.

China, Disambiguation

What has long been known as "China" in English is not necessarily called that by "Chinese" people who today are mostly made up of the Han ethnicity.

Since ancient times, various states have occupied the territory now known loosely as China. The first time that the diverse and competing states of the classic Chinese lands were unified under one rule was in 221 BCE, under the Qin dynasty (where the word China comes from), followed shortly afterward by the Han dynasty, which waxed and waned until 220 CE.

Solidified recentralized rule seemed a dream until the short-lived Sui dynasty in 581, which was replaced by the long-lasting

Tang dynasty in 618. The Tang expanded their territory and dependencies to something which was visibly similar to modern "China" on a map.

Upon the final Tang collapse in 907, there followed a long period of disunity which ended with the Mongol conquest of the whole region, including what we now know as independent nations like the Koreas, in the thirteenth century. The Mongols were traditionally ruled by a Khan, which is the name by which the English knew their Great Asian Hope, the "Great Khan" who they wanted to petition for military support and alliance.

In 1368, the Mongols were thrown out and a new "Great Ming" Empire proclaimed. Nearby peoples such as the Koreans and Japanese knew China at this time by the Imperial name "Great Ming," not "China," although Europeans continued with the ancient terminology they knew, "China," and sometimes, ambiguously, "Cathay."

In 1636, after long and protracted invasion, a new Qing Empire was proclaimed by conquerors from Manchuria. The "Great Qing" state lasted until 1911, and was initially the most powerful of the "Chinese" Empires, but in the end succumbed to European, American, and Japanese aggression in the nineteenth century, and finally internal revolution.

In 1911, China at last became China.

The "Republic of China" was proclaimed by the great statesman Sun Yat-sen, and a troubled half century of civil and international war ensued before the Chinese Communist Party expelled the Republican "Nationalists" to Taiwan. Mainland China then became the "People's Republic of China," and remains so to this day, as the island of Taiwan remains under the control of the "Republic."

Other Chinese countries, i.e., states or territories which largely speak languages historically included in the Chinese language family, include Singapore, and the Special Administrative Regions of Hong Kong and Macao.

For ease of understanding in English, I use the term "China" throughout the book.

Chapter 1

Mount Fuji as Viewed from the Sea

The men and women on the Manila Galleon often saw the peak of Mount Fuji from far out to sea as the Kuroshio current swept them past Japan and across the Pacific. As such for Japanese travelers, it was often the last sight of their homeland before starting a new life overseas.

Mazu

Mazu, also known by several other names in different parts of the world, including Tianhou, Empress of Heaven, and Tianfei, Princess of Heaven, is a Chinese goddess of the sea, who can also help female believers find life partners.

She is thought to be the deified form of Lin Mo (or Moniang), a shaman whose life is traditionally dated from 960 to 987. Believers hold that she protects the peoples of the sea, and can sometimes be observed as a flame at the head of ships' masts. Temples to her are predominantly found in the Chinese world, but also in countries as far afield as Australia, the United Sates, Thailand, and Japan, which have seen significant migration from southern China.

As a sea goddess, she is predominantly known in the coastal and island communities of the south, and far less known, if at all, in the interior of Mainland China.

Lutheran/Heretic Pirates

The English would not have described themselves as Lutherans, and the nascent Church of England was a broad church which attempted to find a path between anti-Reformation Catholicism and Puritanism, as the more aggressive protestants were called. Some Puritans referred to themselves as evangelicals.

However, the Spanish of the time referred to all of the post-Reformation non-Catholic Europeans as heretics, and most as Lutheran. In the sources used for this book, Lutheran and heretic are used virtually interchangeably.

Non-European non-Catholics were generally referred to as heathens.

California as an Island

In the earlier part of the sixteenth century, California appeared on European maps as an island. By Christopher's time, it was generally known to be a peninsula, but due to slow dissemination of knowledge, and widespread copying of earlier maps, the island kept on cropping up in seventeenth-century maps before the idea was finally debunked in the eighteenth century.

Multicultural Crews on European Ships

While ships leaving from Europe normally comprised overwhelmingly Indigenous crews, in far-flung corners of the world they were rarely entirely manned by Europeans.

The reasons for this are several. Firstly, that ships like *Santa Ana*, while flying under a Spanish flag, would never actually go anywhere near Spain. The crews therefore were made up of anyone in the locality who wanted to, or who was forced to, sign on.

Secondly, the sheer hardship and terror of the journeys out of the Atlantic were often enough to ensure that men never wanted to set foot on a ship again. For example, many Portuguese sailors, if they survived the passage, staggered off their ships and stayed put on the Indian subcontinent. They were replaced by local, or African sailors, who made the journey back to Europe.

Some would settle there, and others signed on again for the return journey. Japanese sailors were often recruited, as is shown by those who arrived in London in 1614.

Chapter 2

Silk Road/Roads/Routes

Silk Road/Roads/Routes are terms which became popular in the nineteenth century to describe the network of transport and trade routes which have extended between China and the territories and regions to its west, as far as Africa and Europe, throughout history. It is named for the most lucrative product historically manufactured in China, silk.

In reality it is not one road, or even a continuous route, but a vast network which covered most of Eurasia and parts of Africa, and included maritime passages to islands and archipelagos such as Java and Japan. No one person would have normally traveled its lengths, as products were traded by intermediaries, and new traders took up where previous ones had terminated their travels.

Mansa Muhammad ibn Qu of Mali

Mali was a powerful African Empire in the approximate area of the modern-day West African states of Senegal, the Gambia, Mauritania, and Mali. Muhammad ibn Qu who is believed to have lived in the late thirteenth–early fourteenth century, was the predecessor of Mali's most famous ruler, Mansa Musa, who is said to have been the richest man in the world in his time (some say the wealthiest in history, although the accuracy of this is impossible to quantify accurately). The exact dates of Muhammad ibn Qu's reign are not known with certainty, but it would have been at the beginning of the fourteenth century.

Antilla (fabled island of)

When the Muslim Moors conquered the Iberian Peninsula in the eighth century, seven refugee bishops are said to have taken to the seas and headed westward into the Atlantic Ocean where they found an island called Antillia and built seven great cities. At least that is the legend which gave rise to the idea of Antilla, an island that fifteenth-century Europeans believed could be an easy stop-off point on the way to Japan.

India/Indians, Disambiguation

The largest state on the Indian subcontinent is the Republic of India, which came into being in 1947 upon gaining independence from the British Empire. At the same time, other states on the Indian subcontinent were partitioned from the former Imperial territories and also became independent, most notably the Islamic Republic of Pakistan (which later separated into two, with East Pakistan becoming the People's Republic of Bangladesh after a further war of independence from West Pakistan in 1972). Other modern-day nation-states in this region are Nepal, Bhutan, Sri Lanka, and the Maldives. Writing in 2023, there is a movement to rename "India" as "Bharat" due to the non-Indigenous (European) roots of the word "India."

India as referred to by Europeans in Christopher's time could refer to several concepts.

1. In very fuzzy terms, anywhere east of Mozambique Island, but south of the Himalayas, not generally including Arab, Persian, Mongol, or Turkic lands. This could include Japan and China as well as other East Asian space as well, hence Christopher sometimes being referred to as an Indian.
2. The Indian subcontinent, which throughout history has been a highly diverse patchwork of cultures and states, sometimes partially unified, at other times comparable to Europe (prior to the EU) in its political disunity.
3. Confusingly, and because Columbus initially thought he had arrived in Asia (the Indies), the Indigenous peoples of the Americas were referred to as Indians. The name stuck, hence the coining of wild generalizing names such as "American

Indian" to cover cultures and peoples that had nothing to do with actual "India," never mind that these peoples were as culturally dispersed and diverse as those of the Indian subcontinent itself, and of course other parts of the world such as Africa and Europe.

Isabella I of Castile (1451–1504)

Queen Isabella (Isabella is the Spanish rendering of Elizabeth) was the first person to be called Queen of Spain, although Spain as we know it did not fully come into being until after her death.

Her reign, mostly jointly with her husband King Ferdinand II, was eventful to say the least. The two monarchs joined their respective kingdoms, Castile and Aragon, to form a rump which later unified with the other states in the Iberian Peninsula (except Portugal) to form Spain. The two "Catholic Monarchs" started the process of expelling all Jews and Muslims who refused to convert to Christianity, resulting in a mass exodus of people, primarily to North Africa.

Isabella funded Columbus' voyages, thereby establishing the financial roots on which the Spanish Empire was based.

Himiko (believed to have lived in the second/third century CE)

Himiko was a shaman and queen of the peoples of "Wa," in what is now the Japanese archipelago. Her capital, which is traditionally referred to as Yamatai, is believed to have been in either northern Kyushu or near modern-day Kyoto.

Her existence is known of because she sent envoys to the Cao Wei Kingdom which was in what is now northern Mainland China.

She is said to have lived in a heavily fortified palace, and been served by one thousand female servants, but only one man, who acted as her mouthpiece to the world outside.

As she lived in an era before Indigenous written records exist, no Japanese source mentions her.

Marco Polo (1254–1324)

Marco Polo was a Venetian merchant, traveler, and courtier to the Mongol emperor of China, Kublai Khan. His travels were written up as *The Travels of Marco Polo*, which he co-wrote with Rustichello da Pisa while a prisoner of war in Genoa.

His published observations of the Asian world were mind-blowing to Europeans; the story was spread far and wide, and translated into many languages. While some of his tales do not stand the test of time, and have led to skepticism about whether he really did serve Kublai Khan and travel in Asia, even if merely compiled from other travelers' tales, his book is still more accurate than any other account that was available at the time.

The first English-language edition of *Polo* by John Frampton was translated from a Spanish edition and published in 1579.

Nova/New Albion

Having passed through the Strait of Magellan, and raided the western coast of Spain's American territory (as Cavendish would also later do), Francis Drake needed to find a place to refit, revictual, and rest before attempting the return voyage to England through unknown seas. Far to the north of Spanish settlements he found a well-situated bay, probably just north of what is now San Francisco.

The ship was careened, necessary repairs carried out, and they peacefully received supplies of venison from the local people.

Before departing, Drake claimed the land in perpetuity for his monarch, and those who succeeded her, calling it Nova Albion, or New Albion.

Chapter 3

Otomo Sorin, Omura Sumitada, and Arima Harunobu

The three Japanese warlords who were represented by the Tensho legates in Europe were all first-generation Catholic converts, and all probably converted for questionable reasons. Otomo wanted to divorce his powerful wife, and the Jesuits were happy to legitimize it if he converted. Omura and Arima were hard-pressed by enemies from all sides, and needed the weaponry that the Jesuits supplied to friendly lords. They put it to good effect, and their clans managed to survive until Tokugawa Ieyasu imposed peace on the land.

Yasuke

Yasuke was a man of African origin who arrived in Japan as the bodyguard of the Jesuit Alessandro Valignano. He was taken into the service of the warlord Nobunaga, and rose to become a confidant and valued advisor, as well as a soldier. He was present when Nobunaga was assassinated in 1582, and is traditionally considered to have been ordered to save the warlord's severed head from falling into enemy hands.

What became of Yasuke afterward is unknown, but research suggests that he may have stayed in Japan.

Japanese Slaves in Europe

No one knows exactly when the first enslaved Japanese person arrived in Europe, but it was likely in the 1550s via Portuguese trading networks. Human trafficking continued until the Tokugawa shogunate outlawed overseas travel by Japanese people in the 1630s.

Chapter 5

The Japanese Age of the Country at War

During this age, which is traditionally dated from 1467 until 1615 (though Japan was not exactly a realm of serenity and peace before this either), what had once been a loosely unified realm governed from Kyoto became splintered into many domains and spheres of influence.

As a consequence, samurai lords, warrior monks, bandits, special operations mercenaries (ninja), pirates, and armed peasants engaged in interminable conflict. In the second half of this era, several samurai warlords established their hegemony over vast areas and snuffed out the threat from warrior monks and ninja. The pirates were for the most part co-opted, and peasants conscripted into samurai armies to form forces tens of thousands strong.

The last two major battles were at Sekigahara in 1600, and Osaka in 1614–1615, victory in which left the Tokugawa family on top to rule until 1867 as shoguns, although everyday governing was left to the regional lords as long as they toed the line.

Ningbo Incident, 1523 (leading to trade with Japan being banned by China)

During the time of the early Ming Empire, Japan was granted tributary trade with China. This meant accepting an inferior position in the Sinocentric world order, but being allowed access to the trade and manufacturers of China's great industrial workshops (it was not only Europeans who dreamed of the wonders of China). This was done on the basis of allotted tallies which indicated permission from the Ming emperor to engage in trade.

As the *Age of the Country at War* dragged on, once-powerful clans like the Ouchi, who had traditionally been allowed to use those tallies as representatives of the shogun, found themselves challenged by other powerful (and green-eyed) clans. One such was the Hosokawa, who traditionally had their powerbase in Kyoto far from the international trading centers of western Japan.

In 1523, both clans sent missions to the allotted Chinese port, Ningbo. The Ouchi had a correct tally, and the Hosokawa had an old one, but thanks to a large bribe, the Hosokawa were permitted to trade, while the legitimate Ouchi tally was refused.

The enraged Ouchi ran riot, plundering, laying waste, and taking officials prisoner before sailing away. One of their ships was wrecked in Korea. The crew were put to death as pirates apart from two who were sent back to China to face justice.

The long-term result was that China closed Ningbo to trade, effectively forbidding Japanese ships from docking legally. This led to a massive resurgence of piracy, and Christopher was probably one of these pirates.

African pirates

There are a number of African pirates recorded in East Asia at this time; many had originally been hired as mercenaries or enslaved warriors in the Indian subcontinent, and sailed east with Portuguese mariners such as Bartolomeu Vaz Landeiro, while others, like those in service to the Chinese Zheng family, are believed to have been originally enslaved in Macao, but when manumitted, joined the pirate bands.

Catholic Missions to Japan

The first Jesuit missionary, Francis Xavier, arrived in Japan in 1549, and although he only stayed a short time, he was able to establish a foundation for the future mission by befriending certain local lords and Buddhist priests. Missionaries from Europe, India, and China formed the next cohorts, arriving in the next decades, later added to by Japanese converts and second-generation believers.

The Jesuits decided they had to adapt to local mores if they were to win over a skeptical population, and so they began to eat and dress in Japanese fashion, and many became highly proficient in the language. Jesuits were the first Europeans to write bilingual dictionaries of the Japanese language, write treatises on local cultures, translate Japanese classics into European languages, and even record Japanese history. They also of course mass-produced Christian goods, especially devotional pictures, with which to demonstrate the rightness of their religion.

Later came Franciscans and Dominicans, but they were not so sensitive in obeying local temporal powers, nor amenable to adopting Japanese ways, and eventually provoked a severe reaction from Imperial Regent Toyotomi Hideyoshi. In 1597, twenty-six Christians, mainly Franciscans, were marched from Kyoto to Nagasaki and crucified.

Propagation continued, quietly at first but more confidently following Hideyoshi's death. Tokugawa Ieyasu, the new shogun, and his son were far more tolerant of missionary work as they believed that the increased trade via Macao, Manila, and Acapulco would disappear without Jesuits to organize it. However, a lingering suspicion of missionary motives remained, and when Dutch and English companies established trading outposts without any religious conditions attached, the days of Catholic proselytizing were numbered.

The English in particular engaged in a game of whispers, ensuring that the Catholics were seen in the worst possible light, and when in 1614 the second Tokugawa shogun, Hidetada, heard that the Jesuits were implicated in European regicide, an immediate expulsion order was promulgated. A few years later, a program of enforced renunciation of the Catholic faith, by torture where necessary, ensued, mixed-heritage children and their Catholic fathers were expelled, and slowly but surely Christianity went underground.

Many high-ranking Japanese Christians chose exile rather than apostasy, and many less high-profile believers followed them, swelling the populations of Japanese trading enclaves all over Asia.

Over time, the persecutions did their job, and only a handful of "hidden Christians" remained in remote islands to keep a kind of Christian faith which astonished the world when they emerged from hiding more than two centuries later. Those who took refuge overseas assimilated into the local populations.

Miyako (Kyoto)

"Miyako" simple means "capital city" in archaic Japanese, and in Christopher's time referred to the ancient capital city, which we now know as Kyoto.

Chapter 6

Cabo San Lucas

Referred to by Cavendish and his men as Cabo S. Lucar, Cabo
San Lucas is at the southern tip of California, in the modern-day
Mexican state of Baja California Sur. At Christopher's time, it
had yet to be conquered by the Spanish, and was the abode of
the Indigenous Pericú people.

Chapter 7

Sebastián Vizcaíno (c. 1548–1624)

Vizcaíno put his horrific experience on *Santa Ana* behind
him, and was commissioned to explore the Californian coast,
hoping to find a suitable place for the Manila Galleon to stop en
route to Acapulco. During his work, he gave European names
to many prominent places in the current US state of California, including Monterey, the Carmel River, and the Santa Lucia
Mountains. Monterey later became the much sought-after stopping point for the galleon.

The dreams of Japan, which he had written of in the letter
confiscated by Cavendish, not in fact an eyewitness account, but
second-hand report, continued to fester, and when he got the
chance, he returned to Asia with the first Japanese diplomat to
the Americas, Tanaka Shosuke, in 1611.

He was received at court, but refused to remove his shoes, and
sword, and would not bow to the floor as etiquette required. This
along with his demands which included free access for missionaries, a request to survey the Japanese coastline, and the construction of a ship to make this easier, did not endear him to his hosts.

In the end he achieved little, but succeeded in lessening the
standing of Catholicism, partly due to the fact that William
Adams was being consulted by the court, and while defending
Japanese interests, was also able to put an English spin on how
Vizcaíno was viewed.

Chapter 8

Toyotomi Hideyoshi (1537–1598)

The man who would later become Toyotomi Hideyoshi was born into obscurity in Owari Province (where Nagoya is now situated). His first official name was Kinoshita Tokichiro, under which name he entered the service of Oda Nobunaga in one of the lowest ranks, *ashigaru*. He appears to have distinguished himself as Nobunaga's sandal bearer, by keeping the footwear warm under his clothing, for which he was promoted. And so begun his meteoric rise.

By the time of Nobunaga's death in 1582, Hideyoshi was one of his most important generals, commanding an army of thirty thousand in the field. In the chaos which followed Nobunaga's assassination, Hideyoshi managed to come out on top, and have himself appointed imperial regent in 1585. The new clan name Toyotomi was bestowed upon him by the emperor's court.

Whereas Nobunaga's strategy had been to conquer by absolute force, Hideyoshi approached his foe with great armies to intimidate, and then often came to terms with the enemy. The opposition fell before him like dominoes. Within five years of becoming imperial regent, he had subjugated the whole country and was the undisputed ruler of Japan.

The last decade of his life was dominated by his attempt to conquer China via Korea. His troops became bogged down, and in the face of a highly effective Chinese counterattack (one of the very few moments in history before modern times that Chinese and Japanese troops have actually met on formal battlefields), and a Korean naval resistance that rendered him unable to effectively resupply his samurai in the field, the campaigns dwindled into stalemate. After Hideyoshi's death, Tokugawa Ieyasu made it his first priority to bring the surviving samurai home, and to make peace.

Chapter 9

Cagayan

The Spanish did not make major moves to establish their power in the northeast of Luzon island until around 1581. They found that Japanese/Chinese pirates had beaten them to it, and were well established.

As with all other external threats to the lands they had begun to dominate, the Spanish sent an expeditionary force with as much strength as they could muster.

Following their victory, the settlement of Nueva Segovia was founded, and this part of Luzon was absorbed within the empire as the Province of Cagayan.

Lord Tei (Tay Fusa), (believed to have died in 1582)

Tay Fusa is the name of a pirate who is recorded in Spanish sources regarding the Japanese settlement in Cagayan, and sea battles preceding the attack on his base.

The Spanish transliteration of his name suggests he could actually have been called *Tei*, which is the Japanese pronunciation of the Chinese name (common among the seafarers of southern China), *Zheng*. I suspect he was actually Chinese, although many of his followers appear to have been Japanese.

There is no other record of him, but it is possible that he had aliases, and was known by other names in different parts of the region.

The pirate Limahon and Chinese attempts at colony planting in the Philippines

In the first decades of Spain claiming Manila and some other areas of the modern Philippines as colonies, their hold on the territory was tenuous and contested. Not necessarily by other governments external to the islands, but by pirates who wished to create their own kingdoms far from Imperial Chinese interference.

While Cagayan was a predominantly Japanese affair, most colonies were settled by Chinese seafarers. The biggest and most threatening (to the Spanish) of these was that of Limahon.

Limahon attacked Manila twice in 1574, narrowly failing to take the settlement. He then attempted to found his own city at Pangasinan. As with Cagayan, the Spanish sent as large a force as they could to destroy it. Chinese government forces also seem to have observed the attack, but did not engage, happy to leave the battle to the Spanish and their local allies.

Raquel Angela Balita, who is mentioned in the acknowledgements for having graciously helped with the chapters concerning the Philippines, is believed to be related via marriage to Limahon.

Chapter 10

The Manila Galleon

The Manila Galleon, or Galleon of China, ran virtually without pause between 1565 and 1815 when the Mexican War of Independence severed this link between Spain and its Asian colonies.

As the taking of *Santa Ana* showed, the volume of trade facilitated by this route was huge and highly lucrative for those involved. Furthermore, the transfer of American precious metals to Asia, predominantly China, kept economies monetized, and enabled living standards to remain high throughout the period.

Its establishment marks the true birth of a global economy, as it was the first direct trade route between the Americas and Asia.

Chapter 11

Satsuma clan (under the white cross within a black circle)

The Satsuma clan dominated the very tip of the Japanese isles, both from their home province of Satsuma (modern-day Kagoshima) but also through conquest of the southern Amami and Ryuku Kingdom (modern-day Okinawa Prefecture).

Under the Tokugawa shogunate, they were permitted a degree of independence that few other clans enjoyed, including being the only clan allowed to clandestinely trade with China.

In Christopher and Cosmus' time, they were attempting to control the island of Kyushu, something that they nearly achieved before Hideyoshi defeated and subjugated them in 1587.

Chapter 12

Pocahontas/Lady Rebecca Rolfe (ca 1596–1617)

Lady Rebecca was the first recorded American female to arrive in London; already familiar with English ways, she spoke excellent English, and unusually, she was already quite well-known before she arrived. Therefore, her nine-month stay was feted.

In 1613, she had been taken hostage to try to force her father, the local king Powhatan, to release some English hostages. When his council refused to allow him to fully comply with English demands, the Europeans raided and destroyed settlements until Powhatan and his council capitulated.

During her captivity, an Englishman called John Rolfe had proposed to her, and she had accepted. Their marriage became something of a peacemaking event, and tensions were calmed. It was the reports of this, and her baptism, that reached London ahead of her and formed the basis of her celebrity.

Sadly, she died on the return journey in 1617.

Samurai

The samurai class of warriors grew from a lower class of hired muscle, tasked with defending farmland and collecting taxes, to the ruling class of Japan in the several centuries leading up to 1185.

As the power of the nonmilitary traditional aristocracy declined, samurai increasingly became seen at court in Kyoto, until two powerful clans, the Taira and the Minamoto, came to dominate the political scene. War between them ended with the latter's victory, and the severing of political power from Kyoto in 1185. The Minamoto capital was established at Kamkura, the first time eastern Japan had been chosen as a seat of power.

The most powerful samurai was the shogun (short for *Sei-i Taishogun*), an ancient rank given to generals who led expeditionary forces against the unpacified peoples of the archipelago. The shogun became titular head of the samurai government, although real power over the next few centuries lay with advisors and powerful relatives.

Samurai government in one form or another survived various threats from invading Mongols, vengeful Kyoto aristocrats, fanatic warrior monks, and peasant revolutionaries, for seven hundred years, until 1868. While the "non-samurai governments" after 1868 professed to be imperial governments, with an emperor at the nation's helm, it took the American occupation after World War II to finally end the national political domination of the samurai class.

Chapter 15

Golden Hinde

Golden Hinde was the ship on which Francis Drake completed his circumnavigation of the globe. It was originally called *Pelican*, but was renamed partway through the voyage. A replica of the ship can be seen at Saint Mary Overie Dock near the southern end of London Bridge.

Desire is believed to have been of a very similar design to *Golden Hinde*, so to get an idea of just how small Christopher's shipborne world was, a tour is highly recommended.

Harquebus

The harquebus, or arquebus, was originally a defensive weapon to be mounted on city walls. Its origins are unclear, but it is believed to have first been used in the Ottoman Empire before spreading swiftly around Europe. It spread around the world, under different names, and experienced extensive localization. For example, bores were standardized in Japan, and in other places harquebuses sprouted longer muzzles to reduce recoil, such as jezails in the South Asian world.

Larger-bore harquebuses developed into muskets, and from there over the centuries to rifles.

History of potatoes

Potatoes originated in South America, specifically in the area now covered by Peru and Bolivia.

The sweet potato, *ipomoea batatas*, was introduced to southern Europe, but probably not England, early in the sixteenth century, but the now-common *solanum tuberosum* type seems to have reached England around 1588, exactly the same time as Christopher arrived from the western coast of the Americas where they originated. Sadly, no one on *Desire* thought to record the plant life that reached England, although potatoes of myriad varieties are recorded as being eaten at various stages of the voyage. Thank you to Chris and Tom Wells for expounding on this early history of potatoes in Europe, which allowed me to make this tenuous connection.

Interestingly, although Knyvett describes eating potatoes in Brazil, it must have been some other root, because the *solanum tuberosum*, known locally as *batata inglesa* (English potato), does not seem to have been cultivated there until the nineteenth century.

Chapter 16

Islas de los Ladrones, the "Islands of Thieves" (modern-day Mariana Islands)

When Magellan's tired and hungry crew became the first Europeans to arrive in the Marianas, their ship was almost immediately boarded and, unable to fight back, they watched as the Indigenous people walked away with anything that wasn't nailed down. Eventually the shocked Europeans got it together, and managed to chase the assault parties overboard.

Magellan then launched a punitive raid, killing, burning, and laying waste. He christened the archipelago the "Islands of Thieves."

Luo Hongxian (1504–1564)

As a response to piratical raids on the southern coasts, the accomplished scholar was assigned to improve cartographical knowledge in the region and the Ming Empire in general. His beautiful maps were published in the years following 1561, and not only came to form the basis of Chinese mapmaking for the next century but were copied to inform European maps, as well.

Michael Alphonsus Shen Fuzong (c. 1658–1691)

Shen was the educated son of a doctor from Nanjing who converted to Catholicism and traveled to Europe with the Jesuit Philippe Couplet.

They traveled to Antwerp, Rome, France, and England, and while Shen provoked similarly astonished reactions to Christopher and the Tensho legates nearly a century before, as a scholar of renown in his own right, he was consulted among other things for the cataloging of the Chinese manuscripts held in the Bodleian Library at Oxford for which he was paid £6. Thomas Hyde, the librarian, became the first-ever English-speaking student of Chinese over the six weeks that Shen stayed in Oxford.

Chapter 17

Emery Molyneux (died 1598)

Little is known of Molyneux's early life, or indeed his life in general apart from his globes, but the fact that Hakluyt describes him as a gentleman probably means that he was of that rank.

His globes, both terrestrial and celestial, were truly revolutionary, not least in that they were mass-produced, and portable versions were small and cheap enough to actually be carried on board ship rather than remain as mere curiosities and decoration in a land-bound noble's library.

Following the globe project, he tried to patent a new form of cannon, but when support for this project could not be secured in England, he took it to Amsterdam to try to find Dutch patronage. He was initially successful, but died only shortly afterward and the project seems to have died with him.

Chapter 18

1572 Parisian Bloodbath

The Saint Bartholomew's Day massacre was a butchering of French Protestants on an occasion when they had gathered in Paris to celebrate the wedding of King Henri III of Navarre (later Henri IV of France), also a Protestant, to Margaret of Valois, sister to the king of France, Charles IX.

The killing spread to the provinces and many of France's major cities. Estimates of how many people died are contested, and range from two thousand to seventy thousand, but the figure of around ten thousand seems to be most accurate.

It was seen as a major setback for the Protestant cause in one of Europe's most powerful countries, and observers such as Francis Walsingham used it as a cause célèbre for decades to come.

Society of Jesus (Jesuits)

The Society of Jesus was founded by Ignatius of Loyola, a former soldier, and six companions, one of whom was Francis Xavier, later the first Catholic missionary in Japan. It received papal approval in 1540.

Their mission was thus:

to strive especially for the defence and propagation of the faith and for the progress of souls in Christian life and doctrine, by means of public preaching, lectures and any other ministration whatsoever of the Word of God, and further by means of retreats, the education of children and unlettered persons in Christianity, and the spiritual consolation of Christ's faithful through hearing confessions and administering the other sacraments. Moreover, [the missionary] should show himself ready to reconcile the estranged, compassionately assist and serve those who are in prisons or hospitals, and indeed, to perform any other works of charity, according to what will seem expedient for the glory of God and the common good.

The Jesuits recognized the need for education, and therefore their members were often from the elites of the countries where they recruited, including Japan and China.

Over time, the military and political connections of members came to mean that many paths to the fulfilment of their mission were not always within the strict teachings of Jesus. Often their political maneuverings were violently destabilizing to host states.

Their reputation, especially in non-Catholic countries, including places like Japan, England, and Abyssinia (modern-day Ethiopia) became so tarnished in the late sixteenth and early seventeenth centuries, that they were expelled and the Catholic Church's long-term interests harmed in ways which would never recover.

However, by the late eighteenth century, most countries in Europe, even Catholic ones, had expelled the Jesuits, and it was not until the modern age that they resurfaced.

Chapter 19

The metal penis pin with spear-like points

This unique custom was also reported in records of Magellan's voyage to these Pacific islands. Pigafetta, one of the survivors, recorded that "in the middle of the bolt is a hole through which they urinate. They say that their women wish it so, and that if they did otherwise they would not have intercourse with them."

Chapter 21

Mal de Luanda, Malaria

Luanda is the name of the capital of the modern nation-state of Angola. In Christopher's time, the settlement had only recently been founded and settled as a remote Portuguese outpost where enslaved people could be trafficked to Brazil. The diseases that afflicted the inhabitants were unknown, and hence simple became called "Luanda disease." This is what we would know as malaria, and the description of *Desire*'s sailors' malady matches the symptoms of that sickness.

Spice trade wars, the Amboyna Massacre

Of all the conflicts that Japanese mercenaries were involved in outside Japan, the Amboyna Massacre is the best-recorded in English. It took place in the Spice Islands (modern-day Maluku Islands, Indonesia), an area of intense competition for Europeans who wished to control the highly lucrative trade in products such as pepper. Tensions and rivalries spiked in 1623 on the island of Ambon when the Dutch believed they had caught a samurai in English employ spying on their defenses.

Under torture, the mercenary confessed to a plan to take over the Dutch fortress and kill the governor. As the Japanese were working for the English, they were also implicated in the alleged plot. Ten Englishmen, nine Japanese men (of whom at least one was actually Korean), and one Portuguese man were condemned to death.

Sidney Miguel, Pedro Congie, and Thome Corea of Nagasaki; Zanchoe from Hisen; Quiondayo from Karatsu;, Sabinda of Chikuzen; and Hitieso, Tsiosa, Sinsa from Hirado lost their heads. Four Englishmen and two Japanese men, Soysimo and Sacoube, were pardoned.

The incident became a huge scandal in Europe. An international war of pamphlets (contemporary propaganda tools) as to whether the executions had been legal, ensued, and it eventually even became a casus belli, in the first, second, *and* third Anglo-Dutch Wars later in the century.

The Japanese government was appalled. Japanese freelance warriors, smugglers, and pirates were heavily involved not only in Ambon but in other Asian conflicts and political intrigue, especially in Taiwan and Siam (modern-day Thailand). A ban on Japanese subjects traveling outside Japan was instituted in 1634.

Iberian Union

The other states of the Iberian Peninsula had already been unified to form Spain, and it would have seemed inevitable at the time that Portugal would also fall at some point. So when Portugal's King Sebastian died at the Battle of Alcácer Quibir in Morocco and a succession crisis ensued, King Philip II saw an opportunity. He took his troops into Portugal, defeated the forces of Dom António, Prior of Crato, who had been acclaimed king by many Portuguese power makers, sacked and plundered Lisbon and forced the Portuguese to recognize him as their rightful monarch in 1581.

Dom António took refuge in France and England, dying in Paris in 1595.

The Iberian Union officially lasted until 1668, when after a long war of independence, and de facto self-rule since 1640, Portugal was once more recognized by Spain as a sovereign state.

Chapter 22

Cape of Good Hope

The Cape of Good Hope is not actually the landmark that signifies entrance into the Atlantic Ocean, but mariners of the time believed it was.

The International Hydrographic Organization marks Cape Agulhas "Cape of the Needles," named for the sharp rocks mentioned in the text, as the place where the Atlantic and Indian Oceans collide. It is approximately half a degree of latitude further south than the Cape of Good Hope.

Chapter 23

Battle of Gravelines and the Defeat of the Armada (August 8, 1588)

The small port of Gravelines was the closest sliver of Spanish-held territory to England, and hence held great strategic significance as it was where Spanish troops were supposed to be embarked and escorted across the Channel to England.

Having survived the flying English attacks along the Channel and the chaos caused by fire ships the day before, the ships at Gravelines were attempting to regain their crescent formation and prepare to escort the troop ships.

The English had kept the last of their powder and shot for this anticipated engagement, and seeing how weak a position the Armada was in, closed in at dawn on August 8 with all guns blazing. The bombardment lasted most of the day, and was highly effective.

The Spanish suffered heavy losses, and could not get back into formation. The English continued to pressure them, and when the wind changed, the disorganized and demoralized Spanish and Portuguese crews took their ships north to avoid running aground on the Dutch or English coasts. This meant that the invasion army could not proceed, and was effectively the end of the "Enterprise of England," as the Spanish termed their invasion plans.

Chinese remains in London in ancient times

Astonishingly, two sets of human remains from the time when much of the island of Britain was part of the Roman Empire appear to be Chinese. The skeletons were unearthed in Southwark, and dated between the second and fourth centuries CE. Nothing more is known about who these people were or how they got there.

Chapter 24

Saint Andrew's Church, Plymouth

The first church on what is now the site of Saint Andrew's is thought to have been built in the mid-eighth century, and has been in something like its current form since the fifteenth century, more than one hundred years before Christopher likely graced its floors.

As the principal church of what was one of England's principal towns, it is huge, at 185 feet (56 meters) long, 96 feet (29 meters) wide, and the tower has a height of 136 feet (41 meters).

Sir Francis Walsingham (c. 1532–1590)

Sir Francis Walsingham was principal secretary to Queen Elizabeth I for sixteen years, and as such one of the key players in Tudor England.

Among other things, he directed the intelligence network which kept Elizabeth in power, and as a committed Protestant, did much to promote the furtherance of anti-Catholic policies.

Chapter 26

Greenwich Palace/Palace of Placentia

The Palace of Placentia was a country retreat, but in effect the principle residence for the Tudors, away from the foul air and stifling politics of London and Westminster. King Henry VIII, his eldest daughter, Mary (later married to Philip II of Spain), and Elizabeth were born there, and Edward VI, Henry's only son, died there.

It was from Placentia that many pioneering voyages were bid farewell, and of course where triumphant homecomings like Cavendish's were cheered on their return.

After Elizabeth's death, James I, and his successor Charles I, continued its use, but after Charles was executed, it was used as a military site. After the monarchy's restitution, Charles II thought to build a new palace there, and had the old one torn down. However, it was never built, and the site went out of court use for good, entering into Royal Navy service.

Chapter 27

Manchet bread

Manchet bread was the highest quality of bread available in the late sixteenth century, and would have looked something like a white bread roll today. At a time when most people commonly ate pottage, a kind of soup thickened with grains, and bread of even the roughest kind was a treat for common people, manchet was a luxury for the rich only.

Chapter 28

"Sir" Thomas Cavendish (mistaken appellation)

Thomas Cavendish is often misleadingly referred to as a knight, a practice which probably originates with the fact that his feats were far greater that many others who were honored with that rank. As we see in this book, the reasons why he was not knighted are a mystery.

Chapter 29

Moroccan Sultan Ahmad al-Mansur (c. 1549–1603)

Ahmad al-Mansur was the son of Mohammed al-Shaykh, the ruler who is largely credited with asserting Moroccan power against the Portuguese and Ottomans. After his father's assassination, al-Mansur fled the country and lived among the Ottomans for seventeen years before returning as sultan after his brother died fighting the Portuguese in 1574.

Al-Mansur was said to be a wise and learned ruler, but he was also a warrior statesman who played the European diplomatic game with panache. He made an alliance with Elizabeth and also played other powers such as the Spanish and Ottomans off each other. His military conquests to the south effectively ended the powerful Songhai Empire in 1591, though Morocco could not hold on to such a far-flung desert territory for long.

Jews in England

William I, the Conqueror, brought the first major Jewish communities to England with him to help in modernizing the country with new tax and cash-based economic systems. Jews were given the special status of direct subjects, and were not tied to feudal lords, which also meant that they were subject to burdensome taxation themselves when a monarch decided he needed money.

The population at large was not welcoming, largely due to the Jewish connection with the taxation system, and also due to Church teachings against "Christ killers." This resulted in occasional pogroms where hundreds of people were massacred.

In 1290, Edward I, who had previously expelled Jews from his territories in Gascony, issued an Edict of Expulsion from England. Jews had to leave with immediate effect, taking only portable possessions with them. As in Gascony, the rest of their estate was forfeited too.

Jewish people were only formally allowed to return in 1655, although they had been informally allowed residence for a decade or so beforehand.

Chapter 31

River Orwell (Ipswich Water)

The River Orwell would have probably been known to Christopher and Cavendish as Ipswich Water, for the large town and ancient shipbuilding center of Ipswich that lies a few miles from Trimley.

Today, at the mouth of the river and at the very edge of Cavendish's former estate, is the Port of Felixstowe, the UK's largest container port.

Martinmas

Martinmas marked the end of the harvest season and beginning of winter, and was hence when animals were slaughtered and their meat preserved to keep it edible through the cold and hungry months that followed.

Minced pies/Mince pies

Mince pies are, to this day, a British Christmas delicacy, but are not made with actual minced meat. Instead preserved fruits such as raisins and sweet winter-season vegetables and fruit such as carrots and apples are used.

In Tudor times, minced pies were very different, and imbued with religious significance. There were exactly thirteen ingredients including dried fruit such as raisins, prunes, and figs to represent Jesus and his disciples, and minced mutton to represent the shepherds. The Three Kings from the East were, naturally, represented by Asian spices such as cinnamon, cloves, and nutmeg.

Chapter 32

Scientist

The word "scientist" was coined in 1834 by the Cambridge University professor William Whewell. It replaced a host of other terms such as "natural philosopher," "man of science," "savant," and of course "naturalist," which had gone out of use by then anyway.

The word "science" in the sense of "knowledge" has been used since at least the fourteenth century.

Republic of Letters

The Republic of Letters was a community of scholars, literary figures, and knowledgeable amateurs that crossed national and cultural boundaries to exchange knowledge, discoveries, and curiosities in the early modern period of Europe. Participants exchanged letters and parcels, and often continued deep friendships for years or decades without ever meeting in person.

These letter-writing networks led to salons, academic societies, and academic journals over the following centuries.

Carolus Clusius/Charles de l'écluse (1526–1609)

Charles de l'écluse was born in Arras in the Spanish Netherlands, and in 1573 was appointed director of the Imperial medical garden in Vienna by Emperor Maximilian II. He became known in particular for collecting Ottoman and New World botany, and is credited with pioneering the cultivation of a number of plants in Europe, including the tulip, potato, and horse chestnut.

After leaving Vienna in the late 1580s he established himself in Frankfurt (where he heard about Christopher), before being appointed to the University of Leiden in October 1593. Throughout his life, he wrote letters to a wide network of correspondents, mainly in Latin, and published many works on botany.

Chapter 33

True North and Magnetic North

Magnetic north is the direction that a compass detects as it aligns with the Earth's ever-changing magnetic field. True north is a fixed point on the globe.

Chapter 34

The Two Spanish Armadas in the 1590s

The two Armadas of 1596 and 1597 were in retaliation for continued English piracy, and a joint Dutch raid on Cadiz in 1596 when the city, one of Spain's most important ports, was sacked. Both Armadas failed due to storms, very much as the first one had.

Chapter 35

Portuguese Colonization of Brazil

The Portuguese first claimed territory in what is now Brazil, on April 22, 1500, after a fleet heading for the Indian subcontinent was blown off course. As other European mariners began to arrive in the region for trade, and to load cargoes of valuable Brazil wood, the Portuguese decided to establish settlements in the 1530s.

Initial hopes of easy discovery of precious metals, as Spain had done further north, proved overoptimistic. Instead, plantations growing valuable crops such as sugar were established, and enslaved Indigenous peoples put to work.

As native populations dwindled, people were increasingly trafficked from Africa, and today Brazil has the second largest population of people of African heritage in the world after Nigeria.

Musicians on Ships

Voyages were long and boring affairs for the most part, with large amounts of time spent idle with nowhere to go. Sailors had to devise their own entertainments, both to relieve the tedium, and also to take their minds off the danger that could erupt at any second. Music was one of the ways of doing this, and many common sailors as well as gentlemen adventurers played instruments, or sang along with gusto.

Cavendish, as a wealthy aristocrat, evidently decided it was worth it to hire a team of professional musicians to entertain him, and probably the crew as well. Little more is known about this particular group of men.

Chapter 40

John Yates (Alias John Vincent) (c. 1550–)

John Yates joined the Jesuits in 1574, and was sent to Brazil in 1577. After spending three years in an Indigenous village learning one of the local languages, he spent nearly a decade traveling in the interior, both converting and administering to spiritual needs such as through confession. As befitted a man who had to live in the shadows and exile to escape persecution at home, little more is known of John Yates.

He was "sent away" from the Jesuits for fornication in 1601.

Epilogue

Catherine of Braganza (1638–1705)

Catherine of Braganza was Queen of England, Scotland, and Ireland during her marriage to King Charles II between 1662 and his death in 1685. She was unpopular in England due to her Catholic faith, but is credited with introducing the habit of tea drinking. The tea she drank is believed to have come from Japan, as China was in the middle of dynastic change at the time, and trade came to a virtual standstill.

Rangaku (Western Science in Japan)

Rangaku literally means "Dutch learning" and was so called because much new information and technology came through the Dutch trading post in Nagasaki.

Starting in the fifteenth and sixteenth centuries, European technology started to branch off in wildly innovative directions. By the mid-seventeenth century, European backwardness (compared with East Asia) in most spheres of technology, the reason why Christopher's knowledge was so prized, was beginning to reverse and Japanese scholars started to look toward Europe for new ideas.

Starting with geographical and medical knowledge, the Japanese studied this Dutch learning extensively. There was pretty much no limit to what the Dutch could provide, so Japanese scholars, aristocrats, and wealthy merchants ordered items such as books, eyeglasses, exotic glass tableware, guns, medical equipment, architectural blueprints, and eventually industrial equipment from Europe. Experiments with electricity, hot air balloons, chemicals, steam, and medical drugs ensued, and even led to pioneering global firsts such as the first operation under general anesthetic being carried out in 1804 by Hanaoka Seishu.

First Opium War

The First Opium War was a conflict fought between Britain and Qing China from 1839 to 1842.

Opium addiction was causing havoc in Chinese society, and despite pleas to European and American traders to stop importing it, Chinese requests were ignored. In 1839, Emperor Daoguang acted decisively, sending Lin Zexu to Guangzhou (Canton), a southern port where overseas trade was permitted, to put an end to it.

Lin seized the opium he found by force, and had it destroyed in public. He threatened to impose the death penalty on repeat offenders, and sent a letter to Queen Victoria appealing for her to intervene in her subjects' crimes. It is thought that Victoria was not aware of the letter, but regardless, her government was not willing to give up on the profitable trade which was the lifeblood of the colonies in India and reduced the balance of payment deficit. The British Empire in India would not survive without dealing opium to China.

The Royal Navy was sent to teach the Chinese people a lesson, which due to an extreme difference in maritime firepower, it did very effectively, killing thousands for the loss of only a few dozen British personnel.

The war was concluded by the Treaty of Nanking, in which China agreed to compensate the drug-running British merchants, was granted the right to pay handsomely for its humiliation, and the continued right to enjoy smoking itself into oblivion. Britain also secured the opening of several ports to international trade, including Shanghai, and was ceded the island of Hong Kong as a colonial possession, which served nicely to bring in more opium.

The United States Consulate in Shimoda

After the signing of the Treaty of Kanagawa in 1854, the first US consulate was established at Gyokusen Temple in Shimoda on the Izu Peninsula, just south of Mount Fuji. Five years later, after having negotiated the Treaty of Amity and Commerce, the consul general, Townsend Harris, moved it to Zenpuku Temple in what is now the upmarket quarter of Azabu in Tokyo, but was then considered a sleepy suburb of lordly mansions.

The current US Embassy is not far away in the Akasaka neighborhood of Tokyo.

Unequal Treaties

The Unequal Treaties were a series of highly penalizing treaties imposed upon Asian countries by the European and American imperial powers, and later the Empire of Japan in the nineteenth and early twentieth century. The first of these was the 1842 Treaty of Nanking, which ended the First Opium War.

While there was local variance in the Unequal Treaties, the characteristics they had in common were that they were often signed after military defeat, or with the threat of imminent conflict if the victim refused to sign.

The Shogun's Silver Telescope

The design of the now-lost silver gilt telescope gifted to Ieyasu is sadly unknown, but as part of the celebrations of four hundred years of Japan-British relations in 2013, an eighteenth-century-style brass telescope and tripod was expertly crafted to stand in its stead. Funding was provided by Robin James Maynard, MBE, founder and president of The William Adams Club (an organization dedicated to "remember and commemorate the life and achievements" of the great mariner). It was donated to the people of Japan and is now displayed at the new Shizuoka Museum of History in the shadow of Mount Fuji, the last sliver of Japan that Christopher would have seen on his long voyage across the Pacific to meet Thomas Cavendish.

The telescope is the subject of an excellent book by Timon Screech called *The Shogun's Silver Telescope, God, Art, and Money in the English Quest for Japan 1600–1625.*

The Gifted Japanese Armor

The two sets of armor sent to King James I by Shogun Tokugawa Hidetada were crafted by Iwai Yozaemon, an armorer whose productions reached numerous European royals as gifts from the Tokugawa clan.

Their full career in England is hard to trace, but after Charles I's execution, at least one was sold to a Major Bas for £10 in 1651. Upon the restoration of the monarchy, it was returned, but wrongly labeled as Indian armor.

Today, both can be seen by the public, one in the Tower of London, and the other in the Royal Armouries Museum in Leeds, West Yorkshire.

Pax Tokugawa

The legacy and horror of the more than century-long *Age of the Country at War*—the era that determined Christopher's destiny—was such that by the time peace broke out in the early seventeenth century, the new stable and secure nation was so allergic to the terrors of war that it was willing to put up with almost anything to preserve peace. Any perceived threats were stamped down upon hard. Among the threats were the lords who had fought against the victorious Tokugawa clan, banditry, Catholicism, social mobility, and the risk of antagonizing nearby foreign states through piracy—Japan, no less than England, truly desired to reopen the lucrative trade with China, and the bitter legacy of pirates was something that the government wished to erase.

Therefore, as countermeasures to all the above ills, the Pax Tokugawa eventually came to comprise an absolute ban on foreign travel, an uncompromising attitude to foreign trade (aside from China, Ryukyu, Korea, and the Dutch East India Company) where most countries were banned from commerce and those that were permitted were restricted to certain areas, a strict caste system, heavy criminal codes, and a hereditary military dictatorship headed by the Tokugawa clan and their close allies. For the sake of peace and security, this was all by and large accepted and supported by a previously semi-anarchic, rebellious, globe-traveling, freedom-loving people.

Peace allowed the arts to flourish, the population to multiply, and the foundation of modern-day commercial success to be built. It permitted a different kind of liberty where people with full bellies, raucous entertainments, refined high culture, and well-policed cities did not have to watch their backs for knives and guns in the night. It essentially lasted until the 1850s. Two whole centuries. One of the longest sustained periods of peace in human history.

The First British Embassy to China
The first time that Britain was permitted to send an embassy to Beijing in 1793 provided a perfect example of two world views colliding. The Chinese expected an embassy to be a polite exchange of greetings with the aim of establishing harmonious relations; the British were all business and rudely refused to follow local diplomatic protocol. They demanded results speedily, but that was not the way things were done in East Asia where business was dealt with by merchants, not Imperial courts.

In the end, exasperated by the British Embassy's perceived rudeness, Emperor Qianlong informed the ambassador, Lord Macartney, that "the productions of our Empire are manifold, and in great Abundance; nor do we stand in the least Need of the Produce of other Countries."

One wonders whether an envoy from China who refused to recognize European norms and habits would have gotten further? The differing success of Japanese visitors to Europe probably gives us our answer—those that were clearly "nativized" to European mores as regards clothes and manners were far more warmly received. Those who insisted on their own dignity and cultural ways, as they saw it, were often not.

Interestingly, the Dutch, who were more sensitive in their respect of local diplomatic protocol, were generally able to succeed in their Chinese and Japanese aims without the use of violence. They only used force against people who were militarily weaker, like those of what is now Indonesia.

Porcelain in Europe

Porcelain was the most significant product to arrive in the Far West from Asia, so important that it simply became known as "china," although much of it actually came from Japan.

It's hard for us to conceive of just how mysterious an item like porcelain was for Europeans and Americans of the time. They simply had no idea of how to make it. Japanese porcelain, actually copied from Chinese styles, often manufactured specifically for the Western market by the descendants of enslaved Korean potters based in Japan, was exported by the Dutch, reaching a huge volume—181,930 pieces in 1711 alone.

The English and other Europeans tried to copy these beautiful works of art; some thought it was made from powered eggshells, others from mysterious liquids, some were correct in that it was a kind of clay, but no one could reproduce the Chinese imports. Because of the value of porcelain, the person who discovered its secrets was bound to be instantly rich, so there was no lack of people willing to try.

It took until 1708 to solve the porcelain manufacture mystery. The eventual discoverers of these Asian secrets, the combination of china clay (kaolin) and other minerals, were probably Walter von Tschirnhausen and Johann Boettger of Dresden, although the point is sometimes disputed.

Porcelain technology quickly spread in Europe, due to the lucrative potential of undercutting exports from the other side of the globe, and workshops competed to perfect the most exquisite examples of this cutting-edge product. Perhaps the most famous copier, and further developer of this new technology, though by no means the first, was an English artisan called Josiah Wedgwood, who experimented extensively with new methods, and produced both his own patterns and copies of Chinese and Japanese originals.

Chinese and Japanese patterns and styles like the blue willow pattern grace European and American tables to this day, and few diners have any idea of the rich history to be found beneath their food.

Elizabeth's Japanese Desk

Porcelain-making was only one of the technologies passed from Asia to Europe, and America at this time. Among other innovations, it is even thought that drawers were introduced though Japanese import furniture, particularly desks of the type which Thomas Cavendish took from *Santa Ana*'s captain and presented to Queen Elizabeth.

What happened to Elizabeth's desk is unknown, although there is a Japanese chest, now held at Chirk Castle in Wales, that dates from approximately the correct era. It is not quite a desk though, so is probably not the same item.

China as Dinnerware

So precious was porcelain, that it was rarely used for its intended purpose, dining, but instead hoarded as a status symbol.

The first time in English history that china was used as dinnerware was at a banquet to celebrate the launch of two East India Company ships in 1609. It was such a revolutionary event that all the guests were allowed to take their dishes home as a souvenir.

Index

Page numbers in italics refer to illustrations.

THOMAS LOCKLEY

Black Pinnace (ship), 258, 259, 280, 293, 305, 325
Boleyn, Anne, 146
Boston Tea Party (1773), 335
Bragança family, 49–50
Brandão, Guilherme, 77
Brazil
   Christopher in, 273–288, 307–320
   Desire in, 280, 324
   Jesuit missionaries in, 410–411
   Leicester in, 273–288, 307–322
   Portuguese colonization of, 264, 410
   Santos settlement, 264, 279–285, 308–313
   São Vicente settlement, 264, 285, 326
   slavery in, 264–265, 402, 410
   Vitória settlement, 314–320, 326
Bruneur, Caspar, 147

C
Cabo San Lucas, 21, 69–73, 107–110, 196, 392
Cabot, John and Sebastian, 35
California, 17, 18, 349, 383, 392
Cape of Good Hope, 45, 176–177, 302, 403–404
Carrión, Juan Pablo de, 84–85, 89–90
Cathay Company, 42
Catherine of Braganza, 342, 411
Catholicism. See also Jesuits
   baptism of enslaved persons, 76, 91
   Japan and, 49, 54–55, 64, 387–388, 390–391, 392
   Spain and, 12, 65, 156

Cavendish, Thomas. See also Desire (ship); Leicester (ship)
   Armendariz and, 108–110
   Brazil settlement raids by, 279–285
   on Christopher as gentleman, 102–104
   circumnavigation voyage, 12–15, 58–59, 141–142, 228
   death of, 323
   diplomacy of, 160–162, 170
   Elizabeth I and, 10, 14, 212–214
   fall from royal favor, 217–218
   family background, 14, 378–379
   home in Saint Katherine's parish, 221–222
   Raleigh and, 14, 116, 117
   Roanoke colony and, 9–10, 12, 14, 117, 378
   Santa Ana attack and seizure, 22–29, 67–74
   Trimley estate of, 231–236, 257
   will written by, 323
Cecil, William, 104, 148, 227
Charles I (England), 405, 414
Charles II (England), 342, 405–406, 411
Chidley, John, 241–243, 245
Chijiwa Miguel, 49–55
China
   astronomy in, 270, 271
   British Embassy in, 415–416
   compasses in, 247–252, 248, 250
   economic and cultural power of, 32, 350
   Elizabeth I's letter to emperor of, 333–334